Harry B. Overstreet
Bonaro W. Overstreet

THE MIND GOES FORTH

Books by H. A. Overstreet

ABOUT OURSELVES
INFLUENCING HUMAN BEHAVIOR
THE MATURE MIND
THE GREAT ENTERPRISE

Books by The Overstreets

THE MIND ALIVE
THE MIND GOES FORTH

Books by Bonaro W. Overstreet

UNDERSTANDING FEAR (Harpers)
HANDS LAID UPON THE WIND

THE
MIND
GOES FORTH

The Drama of Understanding

HARRY AND BONARO OVERSTREET

W · W · NORTON & COMPANY · INC ·
NEW YORK

TO
L. B. N.

CONTENTS

PART ONE

THE DRAMA OF UNDERSTANDING

ONE	THE PRACTICE OF UNDERSTANDING	13
TWO	THE DIRECTION OF ENERGY	31
THREE	MAKING PSYCHIC SPACE FOR ONE ANOTHER	49
FOUR	SPACE FOR OURSELVES ALSO	66
FIVE	THE DIMENSION OF KNOWLEDGE	86
SIX	TO ERR IS HUMAN	103
SEVEN	GRATITUDE: THE MATURE EMOTION	124
EIGHT	THE SPACE-MAKING PERSONALITY	139

PART TWO

OUR STRUCTURED RELATIONSHIPS

NINE	FUNCTION OF A LIFE ROLE	161
TEN	ROLES CHOSEN AND UNCHOSEN	185

8 THE MIND GOES FORTH

ELEVEN LIFE LINE TO CHILDHOOD 205
TWELVE BRIDGES BETWEEN MINDS 221
THIRTEEN OUR BASIC HUMAN ROLE 240

PART THREE

IN THE PUBLIC DOMAIN

FOURTEEN CLEAR AND PRESENT DANGER 265
FIFTEEN VARIETIES OF VIGILANCE 291
SIXTEEN WHEN PERSONAL PROBLEMS BECOME SO-
CIAL PROBLEMS 315
SEVENTEEN SPACE-MAKING INSTITUTIONS 337
EIGHTEEN THE LIBERATING MIND 364
INDEX 375

FOREWORD

IN THIS book we try to come to grips with what we feel to
be the central problem of our time: the growth among us
of extremisms and hostilities. Curtains of anger and suspicion
have everywhere been lowered, not only between nations,
but between individuals and generations under the same
roof; and between groups and races that must work constructively together if our kind of society is to have a future.
Today, all too often, we look upon one another with guarded
eyes.

How can the will to make room for one another's minds
replace the almost automatic readiness to shut others out?
Through what wider ventures of knowing and more seasoned action can we restore creative confidence among ourselves?

We believe that the most appropriate drama in which we
humans can engage is that of understanding. This is the
drama of the mind's going forth to meet life more than half
way. It is the drama of trying to see the other person's point
of view; of trying to look at problems through other people's

9

concerns and life conditions. Wherever this drama is enacted, the qualities that make us *human* have a chance to find
expression and endow life with meaning.

This book is about the ways in which the will to understand can create conditions that make life a spacious and
rewarding experience.

Our debt to the experts in our field is, of course, a constant one; and we again give our thanks. In this book, however, we want also to express a wider gratitude. We remember the many persons in many callings with whom, during
the past few years, we have had the privilege of talking
things out. They have given us the chance, in many ways, to
start over again; to break up our too rigid assumptions, and
to think with a new freshness about human perplexities.

"To be old," wrote Martin Buber in his *Eclipse of God*, "is
a glorious thing when one has not unlearned what it means
to begin." It is a glorious thing, we would add, to have
friends who can invite us into new beginnings.

H.A.O. AND B.W.O.

Falls Church, Virginia
February, 1956

PART ONE

THE DRAMA OF UNDERSTANDING

ONE

THE PRACTICE OF
UNDERSTANDING

THERE ARE many directions the human mind can take; but the most exacting—and rewarding—is toward another human being. There is hazard in taking this direction, as there is hazard, for that matter, in all use of our human powers. Living itself has to be counted as an act of faith; and there is a faith appropriate to every venture life offers.

The faith appropriate to the drama of approach to one another is that where mind meets mind, the rewards of mutual discovery and the satisfactions of mutual confidence are worth all the risks.

However, while the willingness to venture and to run the risks that go with venturing is necessary, there is no reason why the manner of the mind's going forth to meet other minds—even those that widely disagree—should not be as expert as any other well-learned skill. In this greatest of our undertakings, there is no virtue in being clumsy.

To be skilled in our approach to other minds does justice to them and to ourselves. It lets us pay respect to what is subtle and unique in each human being. Man must live with man. He does well to make generous room for his fellow man; and he may rightly hope that generous room will be made for him.

The voice of anger is louder than the voice of love; that of fear more strident than that of understanding. Mental and emotional values, however, are not measured in decibels of sound. Life is not more dramatic in noise than in silence, in conflict than in peace.

Most of us know this—though we often seem to forget it. We know it from experience. The moments when we have most keenly felt the astonishment of life have not been those when someone was calling someone else a fool, or outshouting him in argument, or knocking him down. They have been those in which we have met understanding in some unexpected place. It is in such moments that we have felt within ourselves the sudden upsurge of life's possibilities; and it is where understanding and shared purpose have been built into a going relationship that life feels good at each day's return.

Unless we are deeply disturbed in our emotional make-up, we know that destructive conflict is a poor substitute for the adventures of searching things out together. There may be a crescendo of noise and action when two men get going in argument and pass from angry words to angry blows. Yet far more is actually happening—more human powers are at work —when two men, finding themselves on the edge of angry argument, veer away from that edge and sit down to talk things over—until, finally, one of them gets up, takes a few turns back and forth, stops and looks down at the other, and says quietly, "Yes . . . I think I understand."

We recall here a cartoon. It shows two duelists standing back to back, poised for the signal that will make them pace off the fatal distance from which they must shoot to kill. All is in order for one of the traditional, formalized dramas of conflict. Their seconds, standing in the background now, have seen to the proper preliminaries. All is in order . . . except that one duelist has turned his head enough to say wistfully to the other, over his shoulder, "I don't feel very insulted this morning, do you?" [1]

He does not feel very insulted. Yet in a few moments he may be dead. For the drama of conflict does not easily set free even those who start it, once it has taken over and cast them as its victims.

It would be impossible to estimate the number of human lives and relationships that have ended in ruin because individuals, groups, and nations that no longer feel "very insulted," but only tired and trapped, still see nothing to do except pace off, as it were, the final irrevocable steps to disaster.

However useful and stimulating, in brief, conflict may be as an emergency measure, it can never serve as the sustaining drama of life. It too easily brings all parties involved to a point where pride, fear, and an inability to see any choice except to "liquidate" or "be liquidated" make broad the way that leads to destruction.

In this day when we have new psychological insights to work with, we can perhaps take a fresh look at this oldest of problems. We can ask why we so frequently get ourselves into hostile situations from which we cannot then extricate ourselves.

[1] Burr Shafer, "Through History with J. Wesley Smith," *Saturday Review*, January 29, 1955.

One answer seems to lie in the way we set up our alternatives. Whenever our will is pitted against that of another person, we tend to move into the rigid pattern of *winning or losing:* of overcoming or submitting; of saving our pride or being humiliated; of proving ourselves right or being proved wrong. What this means, in effect, is that our sense of personal integrity is staked on how much fighting strength of one kind or another we can marshal, rather than on how close we can keep ourselves to the realities of a situation.

The importance of changing our mental image from that of *winning or losing* to that of *understanding or misunderstanding* can scarcely be overestimated. It may well be the very thing on which the survival of the race depends. Certainly it is that upon which a multitude of human relationships depend; for if we began to feel as embarrassed about misunderstanding another person as we now feel about having him prove us weak or mistaken, the whole focus of our pride would change. We could then no longer preen ourselves on our simple capacity to argue him down or knock him down: recourse to such methods would mean that we had gone off half-cocked or had somehow fallen short of a proper engagement with the allover facts and values that are at stake.

When people talk about man as a combative creature, much of what they say is beside the point. The real question is not whether conflict—self-defensive, oppositional, competitive—is ever "natural" and necessary, but *how much* of it is necessary and under what conditions. Our common trouble is that we tend to think of it as a *first* resort where there is disagreement or antagonism, instead of as a *last* resort. Thus, to a quite needless extent we let it take over our personalities and our practices.

The reason why conflict in any of its destructive forms should be regarded as a last resort is that it has at most a limited utility. If it gets out of hand, it loses even that. It then becomes not life-preserving but life-inhibiting, and even life-destroying. On the other hand, the utility of understanding is unlimited. It opens up further and yet further vistas of aliveness.

When a personality or group is strongly slanted toward understanding and good will—as in a sound family—it can accommodate its share of conflicts without letting them get out of bounds in either their intensity or their spread. Such conflicts rarely do the sort of harm that cannot be undone. They do not get wholly out of hand; nor do thay spill over to permeate with open or latent ferocity all relationships and undertakings. They remain *conflicts limited*.

Where, on the other hand, a personality or group is strongly slanted toward conflict—so that attention and energy are more often focused by fear and hostility than by confidence and good will; and where the maintenance of pride and security is made to depend upon winning and dominating— disaster lies ahead. Such a personality or group will more and more insistently start what it cannot finish, and will tear down what it cannot rebuild; and as the tensions of conflict become the very condition of its being, it will progressively deny itself the types of growth by which it might save itself.

What do we mean, in psychological terms, when we say that conflict has only a limited utility and, if not kept well within bounds, loses even that?

Take a family quarrel, for example. This particular quarrel began, perhaps, as many do, in a disagreement too small to matter—or so it would seem. It has taken on size, however, from the hurt pride of each party and the growing determination of each to prove his point and have his own way. Now husband and wife, tense with rage, spit out bitter reproaches; call each other names; drag up past mistakes; generalize each other's faults: "You never . . ." and "You always . . ."

With tempers and prides thus at fever pitch, what can happen? Or, to start with, what cannot happen? The latter question is easily answered: the quarrel cannot continue for long at its present level of intensity. It has to stop being what it is and become something else.

It may become a thing of the past—with anger swallowed up in affection, mutual respect, and a shared sense of the stupidity of the whole thing. That is to say, the drama of conflict may be superseded by the drama of understanding.

Or it may become a thing of the future, developing through stages of bickering, nagging, stiff silence, and recurrent rage to the point where the home becomes a perpetual battlefield or is broken up by divorce.

We may well agree that differences of opinion—even occasional angers—are a normal part of family life. Within the close confines of the home, someone is sure, at times, to get on someone else's nerves. Prides are sure to be ruffled. Desires bred of mood and preoccupation are certain, many times, to pull individuals in opposite directions: no one will always want to lay down his book or his tools at the precise moment when someone else says it is time to be up and going somewhere. Things that seem important to one person— who has been privately thinking about them for days—may be brushed aside as unimportant by another person who is told about them for the first time. Some things that are said are sure to sound sharp and unperceptive.

The utility of such disagreements, however, is certainly limited. They may seem, now and then, to clear the air. But they do so only if they are infrequent, and if they end when they end—with no destructive aftermath of sulks, broodings, hurts, and resentful daydreams about getting even. They invite disaster when they become either chronic or extreme in violence: whether because no one knows how to put an end to them, or because one party or the other is neurotically incapable of feeling stimulated by the drama of peace and wants quarrels and reconciliations to punctuate what he would otherwise experience as a boring dead level of life.

Or we can turn from private conflict to public. Politically, we believe in a two-party system. We believe that there are always enough legitimate differences of viewpoint and enough truth on both sides of most issues to make a one-party system a coercive monstrosity. We believe that periodic campaigns conducted along party lines, and the steady division of legislative bodies into majority and minority groups, make for soundness. They keep those in power and those out of power on their mental toes, and prevent any one group from having exclusive command of the public ear and mind. Here, *within limits,* the drama of conflict appears normal and healthy. This is organized conflict, with rules of order.

But again if conflict limited becomes conflict unlimited, disaster is the outcome. We say that one man's freedom leaves off at another man's nose. There is a similar point at which partisanship must leave off—if it is not to destroy the frame of its own existence. It has to leave off where the common welfare begins. Also, it has to stop short of those extremes of partisan self-eulogy and denunciation of opponents that move outside the frame of reality: excesses that treat politics as exempt from ethical standards; that make rancor and distrust the order of the day; that call black white and white black if party loyalty dictates; that exploit national problems for partisan ends; that cynically revise history for the sake of making campaign capital; and that foster in a weary public the readiness to say, "A plague on both your houses." It has been remarked that every political party dies in the end of swallowing its own lies. We can be fairly sure that where such suicide occurs, healthy partisanship has already been replaced by *conflict unlimited.*

If conflict must be kept within limits, so also must our reliance upon it. There are things it can usefully do for us. As a drama of defense and of competitive choice in a world of many possibilities, it plays its role. Within rules that set bounds to its destructiveness, it stimulates ingenuity, channels effort, and provides a legitimate test of strength and skill.

But equally important are the things it cannot do. Because the drama of conflict is primarily that of gaining our own ends—of self-defense and self-advantage—it does not make for broad perspective. It does not make for a searching appraisal of either our own faults or our opponent's virtues and rights. It tends to make us see both our opponent and ourselves *as we are not;* to act on what we thus see; to justify our own actions; to intensify them more and more as the conflict continues; and thus to arrive at a point where even to consider reconciliation except wholly on our own terms seems dangerous, soft-headed, and even morally reprehensible. This way madness lies: the madness of a progressive retreat from the shared realities of our living together into a private world where *our* truth is *the* truth.

All this brings us to certain practical considerations. If we cannot rely upon "againstness" as a first or sufficient method of self-defense and self-proving, what can we do instead? Shakespeare, we recall, pointed out that

> "There is a tide in the affairs of men,
> Which, taken at the flood, leads on to fortune;
> Omitted, all the voyage of their life
> Is bound in shallows and in miseries."

We might paraphrase Shakespeare: there is a point in the conflicts of men where good-willed initiative has a chance to take over; omitted . . . all the voyage of individual lives, or the lives of nations and cultures, may well be bound in shallows and miseries.

One of the most dramatic and creative arts that we human

beings are privileged to practice is that of learning how and when to take the initiative in good will; and one of the most stringent tests by which personality can be measured is its courage and skill in trying to resolve conflicts that threaten to assume the proportions of *conflict unlimited*.

We cannot take such creative initiative if we are obsessively concerned with saving face. Neither can we take it if our only definition of success is getting our own way. Sometimes, to be sure, we may find ourselves in predicaments where the disaster of being overcome would be so ultimate a disaster—to our own lives, the lives of those who depend upon us, and the deepest values we cherish—that there may seem nothing to do except resist and, if possible, overcome. Here the law of survival must prevail. In most of the conflicts that mark our personal and group lives, however, this is by no means the case; and even where we can see no immediate thing to do except defend ourselves, there is still the obligation to welcome any reasonable alternative to mutual liquidation that may appear. There is still the obligation, also, to look beyond the intense immediacies of conflict and take some thought of tomorrow—and of the many tomorrows in which the results of conflict will have to be lived with. Carl Sandburg has written,

"Pity us when we shackle and kill each other
And believe at first we understand
And later say we wonder why." [1]

One of the basic arts of civility is that of "wondering why" at an earlier stage of the conflict: before damage has been done that cannot be undone.

In any event, the harm we would suffer from offering good will and having it rejected is, in most cases, greatly ex-

[1] Carl Sandburg, "The Windy City," in *Collected Poems*, p. 277. New York: Harcourt, Brace and Company, 1950.

aggerated. We tend to see this harm as overwhelming—as something we dare not risk—less because we have made a realistic appraisal of the threat than because we are unable to experience rebuff without also experiencing deep humiliation and self-distrust.

The likelihood of having good will rejected if it is rightly offered is also, in most cases, exaggerated. Too many of us define this likelihood in terms of a few painful incidents we have not known how to handle, rather than in terms of what most commonly and naturally happens between human beings.

There is, in plain fact, nothing wholly predictable—nothing cut and dried—about what takes place in situations of actual or impending conflict. Both responses and outcomes are various.

We might illustrate with three experiences reported to us by a man of our acquaintance: a man who has worked for many years in the field of adult education and has spoken from many platforms across the country. In three different communities, during a single recent season, he found that there were being circulated about him certain derogatory "facts" that were either plain falsehoods or misinterpretations. On all three occasions, in short, he felt himself undeservedly put into a position to suffer harm.

In one case, he told us, he gave a prize demonstration of the "self-defensive reflex." His not to reason why—nor ask why. His but to bristle; argue; and denounce. Had he lived in the age of the duel, he might have found himself, by the next morning, irrevocably committed to killing or being killed. Having at his command, however, more time to cool off than had the hasty duelist, he was able, in the end, to get into touch with his accusers and to work his way through with them to a tardy, makeshift sort of understanding. But the experience, he felt sure, had left at least minor scars on both himself and his erstwhile opponents. It might have left fewer scars, he suspected, if he had made in the beginning the same approach that, with far greater difficulty, he made in the end.

In the second case, his effort to clear things up with the individuals "on the other side" was promptly and, he thought, reasonably made. Yet it came to nothing. Those who had labeled him as dangerous simply refused to meet or talk with him. Having described him in certain derogatory terms, they were unwilling, it would appear, to run the risk of having to modify their description or to admit an error. They found it easier to keep him outside the pale.

In the third place, he was able—after taking a long walk by himself and thinking the thing through—to go to the individual who seemed responsible for what was being said about him and simply ask about it. He learned that this person had been honestly misled by "evidence" that he had accepted in good faith; but that he was more than ready to put his mind at the disposal of contrary evidence. In this instance, the effort to move out of self-defensiveness into understanding brought results that our acquaintance felt to be greatly worth while: new insights for himself; a relaxing of stereotypes that had almost kept him from venturing the approach; a warm new friendship; and a certain confirming of his faith that it makes better sense to try to resolve misunderstandings than simply to take them as final.

These three examples may seem to prove nothing—except, perhaps, that the rewards of effort are unpredictable. They may seem to cancel one another out. We believe, however—as did the man who told us about them—that, added together, they carry a subtle charge of meaning. They constitute, in fact, a kind of imperative. They suggest that the rewards of understanding are so valuable that they far outweigh the risks involved in seeking them. They also suggest that while there is no guarantee that an effort to replace mis-understanding by understanding will succeed, the batting average is about as good as in most other human endeavors.

After all, we live by batting averages, not by perfect scores. The research scientist does not expect that every hypothesis he sets up will prove out. The teacher does not expect every day's lesson to set aflame the minds of youth. We live by making plans and by making efforts that are, so far as we can see, in line with the results we want; by improving our plans and efforts as experience dictates; and by believing that a fair batting average constitutes enough success to justify our staying on the job.

The curious thing, however, is that when it comes to human relationships our ego-preserving mechanism [1] is often so rigidly geared to the win-or-lose pattern that we take a single setback as a sufficient reason for giving up the effort. We even take the possibility of setback as a sufficient reason for not making the effort. All too often, therefore, we let a small conflict grow into a large one. Instead of conflict limited we get conflict unlimited—and final disaster.

What is the essence of the drama of understanding? Most of us experience it most vividly, perhaps, in personal love. Here, we say, the barriers go down. Why is such love an experience, at once, of astonishment and "homecoming"— of heightened awareness and deep peace? What makes it roomy enough to hold, at one and the same time, a new sense of personal worth, a new readiness to give one's self into another's keeping, and a new sense of the unique worth of this other person?

[1] James Plant, in *The Envelope,* pp. 46 ff. (Cambridge: Harvard University Press, 1950), uses the term "status-preserving mechanism" to cover much the same thing we mean here by "ego-preserving mechanism"; and he analyzes in clarifying detail the way it often develops in children and the effect it has upon their growth.

The answer seems literally to be that love casts out fear. Extended from one human being to another, it is an emotion that says, in effect, "I single you out as valuable. You don't need to be on guard with me. I won't think any of your thoughts are queer. You aren't alone any longer. Your plans are my plans, your security my security, and your hopes my hopes."

Thus it is through love that we come closest to harmonizing our sense of separate identity and our deep need to belong. Love tells us that we do not have to choose between maintaining the inviolability of the self and enjoying that sense of togetherness for which all members of our social species are fated to hunger. In love, we can have our identity and also give it away.

Writing of the physical joy that is much more than physical where love is genuine, E. E. Cummings says,

> "i like my body when it is with your
> body. It is so quite new a thing." [1]

He might equally well have said, "I like my mind when it is with your mind; my words when they mingle with yours; and my laughter when it is you I am laughing with. I like even my sorrow when you share it, and my shortcomings when you redeem them by your understanding. When I am with you, these are all such quite new things."

This is the sort of experience we hunger for. As it releases us from fear, it releases us into an enriched contact with the world around us and into an enriched use of our own inner powers. Through such experience we come our closest, perhaps, to a type of fulfillment that is not static but growing: that holds both security and surprise; that operates through both giving and receiving. This is what we seek in the most

[1] *Collected Poems of E. E. Cummings,* #96. New York: Harcourt, Brace and Company, 1938.

intimate of relationships; and it tells us, if we have the wit and courage to face the implications of our own experience, that the practice of understanding has far more to contribute to the drama of daily life than has the practice of conflict.

To appraise what we most want in our relationships with one another, we need not, however, hold to instances of intimate personal love or even of close friendship. We can take an example from the workaday world. For business reasons, let us say, we have to approach a stranger who has the power to help us if we can get our project across to him, or the power to turn us down. We dread the interview: approach it warily. To our surprise, however, he makes us welcome; listens; puts friendly questions; and finally restates our project in such a way that we realize he not only understands it but dignifies it with his understanding.

What happens? We feel lifted up. Where we expected to dash our foot against the stone of obtuse power, we find ourselves buoyantly supported by his insight. Responsively, we ourselves—with wariness put aside—become more clear and interesting and more able to enter with him into a back and forth weighing of possibilities.

Even if he cannot, in the end, grant what we ask, he has nonetheless bestowed upon us a subtle gift. He has made us more ready to meet with courage and resourcefulness whatever may come next. We trust ourselves more, somehow, than when we approached his office. Also, we trust our project more for having heard him treat it with respect. It is, suddenly, "so quite new a thing": this project that is no longer confined within our own anxious mind, but that has come back to us, clarified and appreciated, from the mind of a stranger whom we no longer think of as a stranger.

A business interview of this sort may seem far removed

from the intimate astonishment of love. Yet it partakes of the nature of love; and we thrive on it accordingly. It promotes the kind of peace that is *unguardedness,* and the sense of being at home in a situation and equal to its demands, instead of being a clumsy outsider. Thus it grants the gift of freedom: freedom to move out toward reality and explore and appreciate what it holds, and run risks appropriate to the insights we earn, instead of peering cautiously out at reality from behind barriers of self-defense.

Where go-getter stereotypes prevail, we may hear it said of someone who has subverted all other values to those of his own advancement, "He knows what he wants and goes after it." But suppose we conclude that such an individual has never, except in the most narrow sense, known what he wants. Suppose he has never faced the true meaning of his own "best and happiest moments," but has, instead, dismissed these as sentimental and unrealistic. Suppose he has adopted aggression and a philosophy of "the devil take the hindmost" as the basic imperative of life, not because they are what he wants, but because they are the only way he sees to get something he does actually want and that we all want: a sense of security and of personal significance.

Then we must reappraise his overbearing approach to life and see it, not as a mark of his realism and success, but as a mark of his confusion and failure. Then we must say, "This is what tragically happens to those who do not notice or do not trust the message of their own experiences of affection and understanding—or who have known too few of these to risk the belief that they can be made the basis for a way of life."

If, in spite of all the pressures that tempt us to define success and security in terms of power over others, we listen to the voice of our own most fulfilling experiences—our own "best and happiest moments"—that voice is likely to tell us that we are most ourselves when we are least on guard. We are, quite simply, most ourselves when we are most free to explore our world, work productively with its materials, bring our ingenuity to bear upon its problems, and build relationships of mutual trust and appreciation with the people around us.

If we realize this, we may very well "know what we want and go after it." We may want, and know that we want, to participate as often and as deeply as possible in the drama of understanding. If we want this, and know that we want it, we will accept the risks that go with our venturing—just as the "man on the make" accepts the risks of his self-assertive enterprises.

We will, moreover, as in any other project we really care about, set ourselves to learn how to do what we want to do. It will be the thesis of this book that there are experiments, self-disciplines, and adventures of the mind and spirit that properly belong to the project of self-understanding and of interpersonal and intergroup understanding; and, further, that "human nature being what it is," we can scarcely do better than to practice these.

We have used the phrase "human nature being what it is" with deliberate intent. We have used it to challenge its customary use. We cannot count the times we have heard it employed in derogation of mankind: as though everyone automatically knows "human nature" is pretty poor stuff and that since it is what it is, not much can be expected of it.

One of the privileges, we believe, of living in this time when the psychological sciences are no longer infant sciences, but have begun to take on the lineaments of their maturity, is that of getting from them a new estimate of human nature.

There is something paradoxical about the fact that in the very period when, looking at the disordered affairs of men and nations, we are most tempted to belittle our human nature, the psychological scientists are showing a strong new inclination to dignify and trust it. They can afford to do so; for, having studied its needs, they have been witness to the strength and tenacity of its urge to grow; and having offered it the proper conditions for the release of good will, they have been witness to the emergence of good will.

We might say that Gordon Allport speaks a conviction born not alone of his own psychological researches but of most of the researches and clinical practices on the present pioneering front of psychology and psychiatry when he writes of "the simple fact that human nature seems, on the whole, to prefer the sight of kindness and friendliness to the sight of cruelty. Normal men everywhere reject, in principle and by preference, the path of war and destruction. They like to live in peace and friendship with their neighbors; they prefer to love and be loved rather than to hate and be hated. . . . While wars rage, yet our desire is for peace, and while animosity prevails, the weight of mankind's approval is on the side of affiliation." [1]

To indicate his bases for these assertions—which seem to fly in the face of every day's headline "evidence"—he points to an accumulating body of scientific knowledge about the causes of destructive conflict and adds, "Within the past decade or two there has been more solid and enlightening study in this area than in all previous centuries combined." That such studies have proved, by and large, to be not only solid and enlightening but also reassuring in their estimate of human nature may well be the top-level news of our day:

[1] Gordon W. Allport, *The Nature of Prejudice,* pp. xiii-xiv. Boston: The Beacon Press, 1954.

the news that we most need to hear, trust, and act upon.

It is with this testimony of psychological science added to the testimony of our personal experience that we venture to believe that the practice of understanding is that for which the anxious, but still creatively tenacious, spirit of man is now, under the surface clamor of antagonisms, making ready.

TWO

THE DIRECTION OF ENERGY

T HE PERSON who feels cornered, physically or psychologically, has a right and natural job to do. He has to
protect himself. He may concentrate on simply holding his
own. Or he may try to edge his way out of the corner into
which he has been driven; or to plead his way out; or, by
counter-attack, to force his way out.

With consciousness and energy pin-pointed for such defensive effort, he will not simultaneously let his interest range
over broad fields of experience. Neither will he focus upon
some creative enterprise that takes him out of himself and
puts him, as it were, *out there*—in the problem to be solved,
the material to be shaped, the relationships to be established
and enjoyed.

A small boy, playing alone at the edge of a pool, has in his
own way been seeing a world—or the makings of a world—
"in a grain of sand." He has scooped out a "harbor." On its
surface, now, he carefully places a boat made out of a scrap

of bark with an upright mast and a paper sail. The boat tips over: the mast is too far to one side. He corrects the fault; sets the boat on the water again. It is all right this time. He moves it gently across the still surface of the harbor to the point where an eddy catches it and swirls it out, still triumphantly upright, into the broad ocean of the pool. The child looks at his handiwork, and sees that it is good; and sitting back on his heels, he looks around for another suitable piece of bark. He will make a whole fleet. . . .

Suddenly, however, doom is upon him. Absorbed, he has not even heard the approach of an older boy, the neighborhood bully. But now a cruel, deliberate boot comes down an inch from his hand, reducing the harbor to a wallow. . . .

There is no longer a world to be made. There is only a shrinking, inadequate self to be preserved—against hopeless odds.

Or so it seems until, as abruptly as the bully himself, a yet older boy appears. With the ease of strength, he sends the bully packing and then turns his attention to the ruined harbor. "It's all right," he says. "We can fix it up. . . ."

The "we" is pure magic. Again the child has room to move. His world has been given back to him—and given back larger than before. All the original possibilities are there, and to them has been added the spacious gift of comradeship. In almost a frenzy of relief, he goes down on his knees again and starts scooping at the harbor. "Sure we can," he says, his voice shrill with too much feeling. "We can fix it."

The wet sand is good in his hands. It is the sort of thing out of which a world can be made and into which life can be breathed. He will make the harbor bigger than ever. The two of them together will make a great big harbor. As he works, the tensions of fear, and even those of his initial relief and uncontainable love, gradually relax. He becomes again the human being *who has gone out of himself into a project.* Soon he will be ready, once more, for the intentness of fitting a mast into a piece of bark and getting it just right, so that the boat does not tip over.

We can see what the child does in such a case. If we could also see the inner responses of his body—chemical, vascular, and muscular—we would know much that it would be good for us to know about the child, our adult selves, and what we do to one another.

Even the unaided eye can give us clues. We can see the child's face turn pale and, later, regain its normal color. We can recognize the difference between a body rigid with fear and one that is relaxedly "open" to experience or delicately tensed for the business of getting a mast just right. We can see that the child's eyes, staring up in terror at the bully, are likewise rigid in their focus; they have a fixed look, and even when they are withdrawn from the bully's face, it is to dart about, seeking an avenue of escape, rather than to survey the situation. His frightened eyes, moreover, are larger and darker than they were when he was simply looking around for pieces of bark that would be proper material for a fleet.

We can see these things. But there is much we cannot see except with the inner eye of knowledge. Here the physiologist comes to our aid. He tells us that the human body, under the compulsion of fear and anger, behaves exactly after the manner of the animal body under similar compulsion: it "arms" itself to protect itself. By a process at once intricate and abrupt, it makes ready to run away, ward off, or hit back.

The glandular system takes care of part of this "armaments program." Adrenalin is released into the blood stream, raising the sugar content and therefore the energy level. When an angry or frightened human being does not "know his own strength," it is because that strength is greater than it regularly is: it has been chemically jacked up to meet an emergency.

The vascular system takes on part of the responsibility.

Blood that is normally circulated throughout the body for the balanced business of living is now no longer thus evenly distributed. The muscles are given more than their customary share. By the same token, various parts of the body not so immediately involved in the behaviors of crisis are obliged to make do with less than their usual share of blood—and therefore of nourishment. The "higher" brain, the digestive system, the sexual area: all these are temporarily underprivileged. This, we might say, is the "guns or butter" program of the physical organism. When it arms for combat, it makes itself less ready than usual for the accuracies of thought, the assimilation of food, and the relationships of affection.

We read something of this inner drama of the body when we see a face go pale with fear. We read another part of it in eyes that go wide and dark: the pupils are enlarged, for the creature readied for self-defense cannot afford to miss any danger signal in the environment. We read yet a further part in the language of muscular tension. Most of us, moreover, have experienced it in the halting of the digestive processes at a time of intense fear or anger; and we have experienced the aftermath as a "postwar" letdown that makes us feel tired all over.

We introduce this matter of the body's response to danger because it tells in fairly precise terms what we do to a fellow human being when we "corner" him: thus putting him so under threat that we almost guarantee his energies being focused for self-defense. What we do, in such a case, is to make him ready for fight or flight, and unready for loving and learning. *We make him ready, we might say, for animal behavior, and unready for distinctively human behavior.*

The words and actions by which we put him on the defensive may be those of sheer ignorance—as when a teacher believes that she can make a backward child improve his reading ability by threatening and humiliating him every time he makes a mistake. Actually, she makes him more backward.

Or we may be acting out our exasperation—as when the parent of a "clumsy" child makes him more clumsy by keeping him edgy with the expectation that he will be scolded or belittled; or that, if he does not act in haste, things will be taken impatiently out of his hands before he can finish them.

Or we may be reacting to our own past defeats: working off some deep, unconscious rage at life or hiding from ourselves our own fears. Thus, we think of the type of executive who likes to make a subordinate stand waiting, unrecognized and awkward, before his big desk. We can be fairly sure that the executive, in so doing, is revealing his own earlier frustrations.

Or we may move the other person to self-defensiveness by going on the defensive ourselves. It is by such mutual and mounting self-defensiveness, we know, that quarrels and arguments often take on an intensity out of all proportion to their cause. The process is rather like that of the old children's game of fist-upon-fist. As each individual tops the other's irate words with words at a higher pitch of irateness, trivial differences are raised to the level of major differences, and each party to the argument feels that the hazard of "giving in" becomes greater and greater.

In other cases we may be simply obtuse: temporarily too preoccupied or chronically too self-centered to feel the psychic reality of anyone but ourselves; and therefore as unconcerned about crowding another individual into a corner, out of our way, as we would be about shoving aside a chair that blocked our path.

Or, finally, we may know what we are doing to the other person and do it deliberately, for our own calculated reasons.

The speaker, for example, who needles a platform adversary into making a fool of himself, or the investigator or trial lawyer who similarly needles a witness, acts with open-eyed deliberation. So does the wife who knows that if she can needle her husband into a quarrel, she will eventually get her own way. His tactics, for a while, may be those of "fight"; but she has learned that they will, sooner or later, change to those of "flight." He will give in to her for the sake of ending the quarrel.

No matter what our motive is, however, what we do when we force another individual into an intensity of self-defense is, in effect, to reverse the process of evolution. We subtract from him, temporarily, those cubits of distinctive humanity —of thoughtfulness, perspective, humor, creativity, and affection—that have been hard won by the species. We return him to the status of a fighting animal.

There are occasions, of course, when the only suitable response to threat is that of fight or flight. When the danger is akin to the dangers encountered at the animal level of life, it can be handled by the body's "war economy" of mobilized muscle and demobilized head and heart. Thus, the best response for a pedestrian to make when a car that has gone out of control comes bearing down upon him is to get out of the way *fast*. He will do well, temporarily, to forego the human subtleties of thought and affection. If the force that has gone out of control happens to be human, a reaction of "flight"— or it may be, of "fight"—may similarly be called for.

In the world of interpersonal and intergroup relations, however, most of the "cornerings" that induce fear and anger are not of this simple type. They are far more complex. They involve a threat, not to the body alone, but to self-respect, reputation, long-range plans, and cherished values. Where these are at stake, the body's "preparedness program" may be worse than none at all: it may go directly counter to the head's "preparedness program." It may move the individual merely to hit out at someone or something at the very time when thoughtful behavior is most urgently called for; or move him to shortsighted actions where long-range consequences must be taken into account. Thus, it may make him say and do what must later be unsaid and undone if vital human relationships are to be salvaged.

A sound person is one who, by and large, makes distinctively human (i.e., thoughtful) responses to complex problems, and refrains from elbowing or badgering other people into corners where they are forced to meet such problems with the weapons of fight or flight.

It would appear self-evident, today, that our disturbed world needs to be ministered to by head and heart and not by muscle alone—whether it be the muscle of an individual's arm or that of a nation's armaments. It needs to be ministered to by men as creatures of clear thought and warm emotion and not merely—or chiefly—by men as creatures of hard fist and cold steel.

For better or worse, we are fated to live out our lives in a convulsive period of history: a period when the incitements to fear and anger seem more numerous, obvious, and imperative than the incitements to love and understanding. Yet love and understanding, however mild they may *seem* as a counterforce to fear and anger, appear to be what the world must have. They are our human resource for building workable patterns for our living together—not merely patterns for our fighting one another.

We know this. Yet all too often we are tempted to ask, "What can *I* do?"—and to ask it in a tone that implies that the answer is, "Nothing." To that question, however, there is at least one practical answer: the "I" who is the individual human being can learn and practice the art of making mental and emotional space—*psychic space,* we might call it—in any situation in which he finds himself. Wherever he does this, he gives some other person room to grow; and because he makes growth possible, he sets going in society this other person's quota of distinctively human traits. Thus, in some small measure at least, he increases the likelihood that problems will be brought to some considered and generous solution.

One reason, perhaps, why we do not more clearly see that this is what we can do is that we tend to look at our human situation today with what might be called "night vision." Anyone who has walked far on country roads at night knows how large and strange the ordinary—and even the familiar—can appear when small, intimate details are no longer visible and the landscape is made up wholly of dark shapes within darkness. In the social and political "night" that we are repeatedly told we are in, we see looming shapes—of hostile nations and peoples, delinquent youth, public corruption, abandoned value systems, civil liberties toppling toward collapse, broken homes, alcoholism, rampant criminality, mental illness, depleted natural resources, swarming populations that press hard upon the world's food supply, and atomic warfare.

These are dark bulks in the enveloping "night" described to us by commentator, scientist, platform speaker, politician, and minister in the pulpit. Staring at these bulks with "night vision," we do not see the individual human beings and countless separate situations that "day vision" would reveal. Failing to see them, we fail to respond to them. We let our behaviors fall into the pattern of fear and hostility; or, as though paralyzed by the presence of the "night shapes" that loom around us, we ask helplessly, "What can *I* do?"

To map out what we can do—and what man as a creative moral entity has always done—we need to take account of two facts. The first is that *we human beings are so inescapably social in our make-up that whenever we are conscious of one another's presence, we are also, in some measure, responsive to it.* This means that every person is a sort of walking, talking reason why the people around him act as they do and not otherwise. He is, to be sure, only one reason. But he *is* one reason. He is a stimulus at large in their environment. His words and actions are, in effect, invitations to them to speak and act in certain ways.

The second fact is that *each of us has some area of influence peculiarly his own.* He lives and moves within some kind of daily environment that he shares with other people. Some of these people—his children, friends, neighbors, fellow workers, fellow members of various groups, and even fellow commuters and fellow shoppers in local stores—come repeatedly within his sphere of psychic influence: within the range of his words, tones of voice, moods, attitudes, and actions. His total personality structure thus operates as a sustained force in their lives. Beyond these individuals, moreover, there are always others: those who come occasionally within his sphere and who, for however brief a time, take the impact of what he is and does and are moved to some response. No one of us can rightly say, then, "It doesn't matter what *I* do."

To check up on this we have only to remind ourselves of certain experiences so common that we have all known some version of them at first hand.

Each of us, no doubt, knows someone with whom everything he says sounds stupid. He tries, perhaps, in the presence of this individual, to express some idea he really cares about and that has seemed, within his own mind, well worth saying. He starts putting it into words. Nothing happens: nothing to make him feel that the other person knows or cares what he is talking about. He meets only a "fish stare." He wishes he had not started; but it is too late, now, for that wish to do any good. He has landed himself in the middle of things and can only stammer his way to a lame and clumsy ending.

Subtly, during this process, his attitude changes from that of *outreach* to that of *self-defense*. This means, as we have seen, that his actual distribution of energy changes. Whereas he was ready, at the beginning, to explore an idea and enter into constructive give-and-take with regard to it, his awareness has been narrowed now to *self*-awareness. His energies are marshaled for "flight": for getting out of what he has got himself into.

Each of us has experienced in some form this "tightening up" of the self at the touch of psychic coldness. But each of us, also, in all likelihood, has had the happily contrasted experience of feeling the self relax and expand in response to psychic warmth.

The word "expand" has real meaning here. The self *feels larger* when it is engaged in loving and learning than when it is tensed for fight and flight. It feels larger because it is reaching out with more of its human powers to more aspects of its environment; is exposing itself more broadly to impressions from that environment; and is therefore taking in more as raw material for understanding.

Each of us, no doubt, knows someone with whom he is surprised, again and again, at how interesting he is. Not how interesting the other person is; but how interesting he himself is. He has started, let us say, to try out an idea: has started tentatively, not too sure of himself. The person to whom he is talking shows warm and appreciative interest that says, in effect, "That's *good!*" Before long, the speaker finds himself—quickened and released by this response—thinking better thoughts than he knew he possessed, and expressing them with unwonted clarity and vividness.

There are yet other familiar experiences worth noting. Each of us, for example, has probably known someone with whom, time and again, he ends up in an argument. He has not been feeling particularly belligerent. The day has been going all right. Then he comes within a certain individual's "psychic atmosphere"; and before he knows what has happened, or how it has happened, he finds himself virtually defending to the death something that he does not actually care a hoot about. He finds himself defending it as though the survival of his own ego were at stake.

Or the opposite sort of thing may take place. He may have been going about all day with a chip on his shoulder. He knows his own mood does not make sense. Yet there it is; and it has left in its wake a whole train of irritations and hurt feelings that will have to be patched up another time. Then he comes within the "psychic atmosphere" of someone who does not rise to the bait he offers; who does not take offense; who is neither smug nor superior about it, but who simply does not respond in kind, and whose warmth and humor are large enough *to include him*—not put him on the spot or on the defensive.

What happens to him—and in him? He might well say, in the words of Edwin Arlington Robinson,

> "I felt a comfortable sudden change
> All over and inside. Partly it seemed
> As if the strings of me had all at once
> Gone down a tone or two. . . ." [1]

This is about as explicit a way as any of reporting that abnormal tensions have relaxed and that the blood is coursing evenly through the body again, readying that body for normally interested and good-willed relationship to its environment.

---

[1] Edwin Arlington Robinson, "Captain Craig," in *Collected Poems*, p. 123. New York: The Macmillan Company, 1937.

The important fact is that no matter how strong and independent we may like to think we are, our feelings and actions are largely *responsive* feelings and actions. We acknowledge this whenever we use such phrasings as "He makes me mad" and "It makes me feel good just to see him coming." The word *makes*, in such context, tells how far all our moods and behaviors are from being self-made.

To know this much, however, is to know something else also: namely, that we ourselves are inescapably *makers* of other people's moods and behaviors; and if these others live within our daily area of influence—as our children do, for example—we may well be in on the making of their personality structures.

When we acknowledge this, we define, in effect, the privilege, responsibility, and strange authority that are ours simply by virtue of our being alive and at large in the human scene. It means that the most telling description of ourselves is the one that is given, every day of our lives, in the responsive behaviors of other people: in what they say and do, or refrain from saying and doing, because we are around. It means also that we can never, so long as we are alive, escape from our role as member of the human race by any act of abdication. We cannot escape by pleading our helplessness: by saying that nothing we do will make any difference. Neither can we escape by protesting that we are not our brother's keeper; for in countless small and large ways we are our brother's *maker*.

Throughout this book we shall be exploring the ways in which we all play in upon one another's thoughts and feelings and, through these, upon our wider society. Whether by deliberate intent or simple contagion, all of us are continually making and remaking certain portions of the human world in our own psychological image. Only as we accept the responsibility implicit in this fact are we likely to be, in any genuine sense, safe to have around—or good to have around.

Here, for the time being, we must be satisfied with a sketchy map of our areas of influence: areas that are, in some measure, common to all our normal selves and that yet are different in detail for each of us.

There are, first of all, those places where we exert an influence upon individuals who have to be around us a good part of their waking lives whether they like it or not. They live with us; or work where we work; or sit in classrooms where we teach; or are otherwise kept so constantly within our "psychic atmosphere" that they have no choice except to breathe it in—and to feel, as a result, vitalized or suffocated.

What begins in these constant associates of ours as a *reaction to us* will tend, in greater or lesser degree, to consolidate itself as *their way of reacting to life.* The type of behavior we manifest in our daily environment is, quite simply, the type that there is likely to be more and more of in that environment as time goes on—and beyond this, in other environments where those who live and work with us make themselves felt.

Far wider than the areas of our constant influence are those in which we come and go among casual acquaintances and strangers. Here, as in more intimate relationships, our best equipment for building a sound psychic atmosphere are those consolidated aspects of character we call civility, fairness, perspective, thoughtfulness, consideration, humor, hospitality, friendliness, integrity.

Where these are readily on tap, the spontaneities of life can be trusted; for things done on the spur of the moment are then likely to be done in such a way that they will confirm the fact that we are all in on the predicament and privilege of being human.

One of the signs of emotional immaturity in a person of any

age is a tendency to dismiss as of no importance the multitude of touch-and-go relationships that are part of our daily life. The immature individual is "good" only to please or placate some authority—or to avoid being caught. He tends to think, therefore, that it does not matter how he acts toward a stranger he will never see again. The emotionally mature person, in contrast, knows and voluntarily bows to the fact that *people are responsive to people*. This, we might say, is the clue fact of our human existence. People are responsive to one another not only in their sustained relationships but even in their momentary meetings; and what is done to the stranger is likely to become what that stranger carries with him as he moves into a next situation.

Driving through a New England town, one day, we had to make a right turn from one street to another. It was in the sort of quiet neighborhood where people easily become absentminded about traffic; and a man who had driven up the street into which we were turning, and who was slightly over the middle line, glanced in the other direction but not in ours before starting to cut left across our bow. We gave a warning honk: a honk that came out louder and sharper than we had intended. It served its purpose: brought him alive to the situation. But also it startled and irritated him—and his expression said so. As he looked at us, however, we smiled. He smiled back. In this exchange, fleeting as it was, we both said, in effect, "Sorry": we for the blare of our horn; he for his absentmindedness. We went our way, and he his, warmed by friendliness rather than chilled by animosity.

This is the sort of passing situation in which we all find ourselves more times than we can number: a situation that simply happens; that has no significant ties to past or future; in which nothing of moment seems to be at stake; and yet in which the emotions generated are precisely the same *in kind* as those that add up to happiness or tragedy in our larger affairs. There is no encounter between human beings too trivial or too brief to stimulate a response that is characteristically that of outreach or, in contrast, that of self-defense.

The foregoing analysis may help us to define what must be called wrong in human behavior and what can be called right. It shows up demagoguery and hate-mongering as unmistakably wrong. They are wrong because they make the human being less human: they deliberately effect in him a marshaling of aggressive or self-defensive energies that prevent his calling into use his distinctively human capacity for affection and for getting on to the hang of things. They are wrong because they set out to make some people "corner" others—and to feel virtuous in the act of cornering them. They incite the "elect" to trap and badger the "damned."

For similar reasons, excesses of partisanship show up as wrong. Such excesses encourage human beings to maneuver others into positions of disadvantage regardless of what they individually deserve; and encourage them also to hold themselves within such rigid, constricted loyalties that they can never see any problem whole, nor appreciate the genuine worth of any person who wears the wrong label.

By this type of measurement, again, the wrongs of Communism—as of Fascism—are made to stand clear. Communism is not wrong because its competitive presence on the world stage happens to inconvenience us. It is not, as "neutralists" would have us think, wrong merely as all human systems are wrong: because it makes its quota of mistakes while we are making our quota, and is tolerating its share of injustices while we are tolerating our share. It is wrong in relation to the way that human energies are distributed— how they are marshaled for creative outreach or for self-defensive hostility.

Communism is wrong, we would say, because it establishes on a gigantic scale *a way of life in which the calculated denial of "growing space" is rationalized, idealized, and entrenched as permanent policy.* It does this by declaring that it has *the truth;* that this truth is so absolute and so particularized that it overspans every public action and every private relationship; and that all who "deviate" from this truth are truth's enemies and must be silenced.

What makes Communism wrong, in brief, is not that it has faults, but that it cannot correct these within the frame of "reality" it sets up as its own. This, basically, is what distinguishes it from the western societies. The wrongs that the latter perpetrate and tolerate are those of falling short of the spirit and letter of their own law and their own philosophy; for the spirit and letter of that law and philosophy are dedicated to the making of room for human growth. Thus, they allow room for differences and for the correction of error as insight matures. Also, they are designed to prevent people's being trapped by false accusations and constrictive prejudices. The proper undertaking of the western democracies, in short, is to become more and more genuinely and consistently themselves. The more they become themselves, the more encouragement they give to the creative and self-corrective powers of man. It is not so with totalitarian Communism. The more Communism becomes itself, the more it denies room for growth—not only to its foes, but to its own people. Its pretenses to the contrary are what give to its use of words—such as "peace," "freedom," "liberation," "democracy," and "free elections"—such baffling unreality.

Our role as citizens comprises far more, of course, than defining and opposing wrong ways of life. Once we get the feel of our human energy patterns and recognize how they are influenced by the "psychic atmospheres" we create for one another, we begin to discover hitherto unnoticed areas in which our creative ingenuity can go to work: to prevent "psychic cornering" before it occurs and to encourage a meeting of minds.

The relationships of parents to children, teachers to students, communities to their young people and their old people, management to labor and labor to management, religious groups to one another: all of these are relationships in which it is possible, in some measure at least, to anticipate destructive "cornerings" and take steps to prevent them.

We know, for example, that the prolongation of life, on the one hand, and a fixed age for retirement, on the other, have added up to a "psychic trap" for countless elderly men and women. Therefore, we as a society are beginning to explore the ways in which these men and women can have more spacious opportunities for usefulness and self-respect as long as they live.

We have learned, also, that a worker who is afraid to voice a grievance for fear of losing his job is a trapped worker. Therefore, as an industrial society, we have learned to make arrangements in advance of grievances, before anyone has been put on the spot, for prompt and fair hearings of grievances *as they occur.*

We have learned, to take another example from our educational system, that exceptional children at both ends of the scale are given less than a fair chance to develop their powers within classrooms designed to minister to the growth-needs of children of average ability. Therefore, we have set ourselves, with an increasing clarity of intent, to provide right classroom conditions both for those who can only suffer continuous defeat within the ordinary educational set-up, and for those who, within those same classrooms, can only suffer continuous boredom.

Whether we are thinking merely in terms of preventive measures or, more creatively, in terms of measures that expand and enrich life, each of us has some area of influence to call his own: as citizen; as member of voluntary groups; as one who knows his own field of work; and as member of a family and a neighborhood. Once this fact takes hold of our imagination, we are less likely to ask despairingly or self-excusingly, "What can *I* do?" Rather, we ask, "Where so much can be done, what do I do first, and next?"

THREE

MAKING PSYCHIC SPACE
FOR ONE ANOTHER

WHERE IT is known in advance that crowds will compete for standing room, signs are often posted: PLEASE DON'T PUSH. These are to remind each individual that he is not the only one present and that his own share of the space will remain comfortably his only so long as pushing and shoving, elbowing and stepping on toes are kept to a minimum.

As soon as pushing and shoving begin, tempers are frayed, irritation takes over, and attention is diverted from the purpose that has brought people together. The man whose toe has been trampled, whose ribs have been jabbed, or who finds himself pinned against a wall, becomes quite simply a man on the defensive: angry or scared or both; not a man whose powers are focused for consideration or appreciation.

We know this in physical terms—as we observed in the preceding chapter. Also, we know it in psychological terms. If physical elbow-jabbing makes us want to jab back, so

49

does psychological. If we can feel physically cornered, so we can feel mentally and emotionally cornered. We testify to this fact when we say, "I felt trapped"; or "He backed me up against a wall."

What this points to is clear: namely, that if we wish other people to think broadly and feel deeply in our presence, we must give them room to do so. We must provide space enough to hold the sort of thoughts and feelings we ask them to have. If, for example, we want them to consider all sides of a subject, we must give them the mental chance to walk around it and look at it from all sides. It makes no sense for us to argue them into a corner where they can think only of how to hold their own against us or how to escape. If we want them to be people of vision, it makes no sense for us to suspend over them, like the sword of Damocles, our own particular viewpoint—letting them know that they had better see things as we see them, or else.

Energies marshaled for self-defense, attack, or escape are not simultaneously marshaled for quiet thought, warm affection, deep appreciation, long-range planning, or compassion. Before we yield, then, to the impulse to put another person on the spot, bludgeon him into compliance, or trap him into making a fool of himself, we must decide what kind of person we want him to become: what marshaling of his energies we hope to encourage.

In *The Little World of Don Camillo*, Giovanni Guareschi shows what happens when a normal town becomes a frightened one. No one planned the coming of the fear to that little town in the Po Valley. But the situation was ripe for it. Political partisanship between Communists and anti-Communists had been running high. Then an unplanned incident occurred. Smilzo, a leading Communist, was accidentally injured. His fellow Communists, finding him unconscious, jumped to the conclusion for which they had been emotionally set: a bomb had been thrown by the opposition. Who could have done it? They were ready with their answer: a certain man was said to have voiced a threat. As a mob they surged off to this man's house, primed for violence.

The supposed murderer was at home with his wife and child: had been there all evening. But the mob was in no mood to see him as innocent. He was accused; threatened. Then, even while the argument continued in the farmhouse kitchen, someone in the mob outside shot at him through the window. He died next morning.

From that moment, fear stalked the town. Every man looked at every other with suspicion in his eyes. Before, people had been friends, neighbors, or openly acknowledged opponents; they were strangers now. Walled about by mutual fear, they were unable any longer to think the frank thoughts or make the frank movements of free men. Although physically the town lay unaltered—as large as ever—psychologically it had become too small for people to live in.

One evening shortly before Christmas, Don Camillo was at work in the rectory, touching up the figures of the crèche. There, Peppone, mayor and leader of the Communist Party, found him. Peppone was his political enemy. Yet because they had been comrades in the resistance movement against the Fascists, they were united by bonds that came closer to being those of affection than either wanted to acknowledge.

Peppone was in a black mood. In the miasma of fear, he trusted no one, not even himself. He had relied, always, on his big fists. Now these were of no use to him. The enemy was a faceless emotion, not localized in a specific body that could be knocked down. Worst of all, he had, in his depression, begun to doubt the cause to which he had devoted his prowess.

" 'I'd like to give it all up,' said Peppone, 'but it can't be done.'

" 'What stops you?'

" 'Stops me? With an iron bar in my hand I could stand up against a regiment!'

" 'Are you afraid?'

" 'I've never been afraid in my life!'

" 'I have, Peppone. Sometimes I am frightened.' "

"Peppone's next remark was one that he could not possibly have given a few moments earlier:

" 'Well; so am I, sometimes,' he said, and his voice was almost inaudible." [1]

What made possible this final admission of Peppone's, so out of character with his burly strength and Communistic belligerence? To answer this question, we might take the liberty of revising the conversation. Suppose it had gone this way:

"Are you afraid?"

"I've never been afraid in my life!"

"That's what *you* say! I'll bet you're scared stiff right now!"

Would Peppone then have acknowledged his fear? Obviously, he would not and could not have done so. There was nothing in his way of life to make him meek in the face of such a challenge. He could answer as he did only because Don Camillo *made room for that answer by admitting his own fear.* When Don Camillo said, "I have, Peppone. Sometimes I am frightened," the rectory became, in psychological terms, a roomier place than all the rest of the town put together. It was the only place in town large enough to let fear in, let it be recognized and named, and yet not crowd out self-respect and mutual respect.

What Don Camillo did for Peppone—and thereby for himself and for the whole town—was the sort of thing we are

---

[1] Giovanni Guareschi, *The Little World of Don Camillo*, pp. 202–203. New York: Pellegrini and Cudahy, 1950.

repeatedly called upon to do for one another, and that we all
too repeatedly fail to do. Instead, more often than it is
pleasant to realize, we say something that guarantees the
other person's remaining on the defensive: something equivalent to, "That's what *you* say! I'll bet you're scared stiff right
now!" It takes a generously structured self to make for another person the kind of psychic space in which he can find
room for both his self-respect and the acknowledgement of
his emotional problems and limitations.

Making psychic space for one another, in short, means,
among other things, making room for thoughts and feelings
that may not be pretty or brave or noble, but that are human
—and that are harmful chiefly when "bottling up" and self-
deception have made them explosive, surreptitious, or per-
verted.

One more question is here in order. Suppose Don Camillo
had, by skepticism or contempt, forced Peppone into a corner
where he had to keep up his boast that he had never been
afraid. Would this have made him safer to have around?
Would it have made him less likely to do the destructive
things that scared men do? Obviously not. Only when Peppone admitted his fear did he stage a return from the world
of fiction to the world of reality—where he could take his
fears in hand. He was far less likely thereafter to indulge in
the extravagant fictions of self-proving. When he said—
though almost inaudibly—"Well; so am I, sometimes," he
was speaking truth to himself no less than to Don Camillo;
and he became more able, not less able, to help restore himself and his frightened community to sane and normal life.

People need room to recognize and acknowledge their less
praiseworthy thoughts and emotions so that they can manage them while they are still manageable; but even more,
perhaps, people need room to turn around when they find

themselves going in the wrong direction. They need psychic space in which to correct errors—and move beyond them.

Man is a mistake-maker. This fact is at once his embarrassment and his glory. It is his embarrassment because his mistakes so often make him look stupid, in his own eyes and those of the people around him, and because they repeatedly get him into situations from which he does not know how to extricate himself. But it is his glory, also; for his power to make more mistakes, and more varied mistakes, than can be made by any lower animal is the badge of his having escaped from the tight prison of instinct and become an explorer of life's wider possibilities.

Likewise, however, *man is an ego-defending creature.* If his ego is put under threat every time he makes a mistake; if he is taunted, punished, or cast in the role of fool, he will almost certainly develop tactics of self-defense that are also tactics of self-deception and self-distortion. He will learn to disown his errors, or excuse them. Or, by way of compensation, he will become hypercritical of others. Or he will avoid situations that put him to the test. He may even convert his way of error into his "style of life"—as do those delinquents and criminals who take perverse pride in their antisocial skills. As a matter of self-defense, in brief, he will refuse to see himself as a mistake-maker—and so will both stunt his own growth and become a problem to other people.

This fact points up our obligation to let one another make a normal quota of mistakes, acknowledge them, learn from them, and move beyond them—keeping intact, all the while, a reasonable self-respect and self-confidence.

Most of us do not admire either people who never admit a mistake or those who never let anyone else forget a mistake: who time and time again drag up old errors as a basis for new reproaches. Furthermore, most of us hold to a religious philosophy that recognizes our human fallibility and our consequent need to forgive and be forgiven. Yet for all this, it seems, we try every dodge where our own mistakes are concerned, except the simple one of admitting them; and we often make it as hard as possible for other people to admit theirs. Instead of giving them room to turn around, and supportive companionship while they make the turn, we edge them into a corner—where they, after the manner of all trapped creatures, defend themselves as best they can.

This, we believe, is the tragic story back of many of the personality disorders, stubbornly maintained injustices, and rampant hostilities that so beset our private lives and public practices. It is the story of errors defended or disowned because those who have made them have seen no way, and have not been helped to find any way, in which to harmonize self-defense with the admission and correction of error.

We might consider, for example, one sort of case that has become familiar in our time. Here, we will say, is a man who, during the 30's and the years of the Second World War, gave support of one kind or another to various groups that have since been classified as Communist "fronts." He made a donation here; signed a petition there; let his name be listed among the sponsors of a meeting; was briefly a member, though never a policy-making member, in one or more such organizations.

His "affiliations" expressed no commitment to Communism and certainly no intention of undermining our government. He donated, signed, sponsored, or joined because the groups, as portrayed in the materials made available to him, seemed wholly legitimate and humanitarian in purpose. He gave his support, in brief, in exactly the same spirit and for exactly the same reasons that he gave it, and has continued to give it, to other groups that have never been viewed with suspicion.

Because of a handful of such past "affiliations," however, he may now find himself officially or unofficially "listed," with his reputation and even his livelihood put under threat. It is a matter of vital importance not only to himself but also to his family, friends, and employer that his equivocal position be clarified. More than this, however, it is a matter of vital importance to our democracy itself, in a time when real dangers need to be distinguished from pseudo dangers, and when those who have deliberately infiltrated an organization must be distinguished from those who joined in good faith, that confusions of this sort be cleared up.

It is important, in this kind of a case, that no needless ambiguities remain; for each such ambiguity gives aid and comfort to destructive forces in our midst and provides a "cause" for those disturbed personalities that make their own importance out of pointing condemnatory fingers at their neighbors. It can be readily exploited by demagogues and by those new profiteers among us who have found that fear and suspicion are marketable commodities. It can, likewise, be turned to good account by the Communists themselves, who most of all benefit by our mutual recriminations.

What is needed in such a case, in brief, is a quietly resolute determination to replace confusion with clarity. This determination, moreover, should characterize both the individual himself and those whose minds frame questions about his past. All too often, we know, it characterizes neither—and after enough condemnatory things have been said, on the one hand, and enough self-defensive things, on the other, and after enough people have rallied in support of each side, and enough publicity has been given to the denunciations and denials, there seems little room left for any movement toward understanding. The victory, then, belongs to those who thrive on confusion.

What commonly happens in such a case? And how does it comport with either the broad realities of the situation or the common integrities and decencies of our living together?

The challenged individual feels himself to be innocent—and feels that the open record of his life, taken in its entirety, testifies to that innocence. Also, he suspects that the chief reason why some of his most vociferous accusers never got caught themselves by any similarly ambiguous groups is that they have never supported *any* moment on the risky pioneering edge of society. Their "virtue," as he sees it, is not the keen discrimination they now charge him with having lacked, but simply a habit of social unconcern. This habit, now, by a turn of the wheel of history, is paying them peculiar dividends: enabling them to set themselves up as "experts in patriotism." The more he ponders this, the more deeply he feels the unfairness of his situation; and the more he feels, also, that to take any steps to set the record straight would be humiliating and unprincipled. Thus, *not* acknowledging past ignorances and errors becomes in itself a "cause."

If the individual in question does try to approach his most determined accusers with clarifying evidence, he may have the shocking experience, moreover, of discovering that even though they loudly demand that he clear up his record, they do not want it cleared up. Moved by a sort of psychological "blood lust," they want him to be guilty. They want him to be guilty because they have called him so. Or they want him to be guilty because he is the sort of "liberal intellectual" or "scientist" whom they have long feared and distrusted, but whom they have never before had such a good chance to put on the spot. Therefore, they may—and frequently do—refuse even to talk with him. Or with a wholly complacent sense of their own virtue, they settle for calling him, not a Communist indeed, but a gullible "dupe" of the Communists.

Focusing with more and more anxiety and anger upon those who thus seem determined to misjudge or deliberately to injure him, the challenged individual is likely to lose sight of the fact that, in spite of the noise they make and the claims they make for themselves as experts, his accusers are not typical. They are not a majority—either among his neighbors or within his local or national government. Staring at them, however, until he sees their afterimage everywhere, he makes them a majority in his own consciousness. He assumes that as they act, so people in general would act if he ventured toward them with his problem.

From that point on, he is in grim reality trapped by those who will not grant him psychic space. Feeling himself hemmed in, he cannot do quietly and simply what is called for: he cannot walk around the self-deluded few, and beyond them, toward those who may be variously confused by what they have heard about him, and confused also about what does and does not promote national security, but who still prefer facts to unfounded charges: who do not want to hate or to be unjust. He does not approach those, in or out of government, who want sanity to prevail—and who will give him all the room he needs for stretching his mind and clarifying his position—because he has persuaded himself that, outside his own particular group of supporters, such people are almost nonexistent.

If by good luck, however, or on good advice, he finds himself in the presence of someone who simply relaxes and says, "Tell me about it," he may abruptly discover what psychic space means. It is the kind of space in which broad realities can be looked at; in which thoughts can range widely; in which truths can be sorted out from among half-truths and falsehoods; and in which a human being can stand tall in self-respect even while he acknowledges that he has not always acted wisely and does not know all the answers.

When an individual is called a gullible dupe of the Communists, he has room only for the emotions and gestures of self-defense. But it is different where the person to whom he is talking says, "That was a different period of history, back there. It's hard to see how you could have detected Communist influence at that time in some of those groups. You probably didn't even have reason to look for it." Within the spacious generosity and realism of such a judgment, the individual can afford to wonder about his own attitudes and decisions—and to think aloud, perhaps, about the fact that more than once, in earlier years, he dismissed evidence of Communist infiltration as the trumped-up stock in trade of reactionaries and Fascists. Not being called blind, in short, he does not have to prove that he has always seen clearly. Not being called wrong, he does not have to prove himself right. Not being called guilty, he does not have to protest his innocence.

Given room, he can explore his own judgments, as well as those of his opponents and supporters. He can see fanaticism, demagoguery, and stereotyped thinking for what they are, without seeing himself as above reproach, or seeing as a fanatic or demagogue everyone who takes seriously the problem of Communist infiltration. Having received psychic space, he can move around in it; and far more than when he was rigidly on the defensive, he can grant such space to others—thereby helping to restore the sanity of our common life.

We need to give one another room, however, for far more than the correction of error. We need to give room for what is individually unique and constructively human in one another: curiosity about the make-up of things, zest in experimentation, pride in accomplishment, creative imagination, appreciation of the beautiful, admiration, gratitude, and love. For all of these we must provide psychic space; for they make up the spaciousness of life.

Yet often, for reasons that lie deep within our own personalities, we do not make room for them. We drive them into hiding with our flippancies and pseudosophistications. We cut across them with our impatience. We hedge them about with our dogmatisms, our narrow definitions of the "practical," and our nervous definitions of the "proper."

More than thirty years ago, in her novel *So Big*, Edna Ferber gave us a sentence that summed up the contempt of the "practical" man for the "impractical" lover of beauty: "Cabbages is beautiful!"

Many readers will remember the story of Selina who, left alone while still almost a child, fed her hungry spirit on poetry and on every beautiful thing that met her eyes. Out of these she made her courage; and this courage took her out of Chicago, as a teen-age girl, to teach in the Dutch school of High Prairie. She was driven there seated beside Klaas Pool, farmer and school director, in the wagon in which he brought his garden produce to the Chicago market.

"So they jolted up the long Halstead road through the late October sunset. . . . Mile after mile of cabbage fields, jade-green against the earth. Mile after mile of red cabbage, a rich plummy Burgundy veined with black. Between these, heaps of corn were piled up sunshine. Against the horizon an occasional patch of woods showed the late russet and bronze of oak and maple. These things Selina saw with her beauty-loving eyes. . . ."

She saw them, and she responded as a human being is equipped to respond: with the joy of appreciation.

" 'Oh, Mr. Pool!' she cried. 'Mr. Pool! How beautiful it is here!' "

Klaas Pool had been driving with his eyes straight ahead. It took time for his mind to receive her words even enough to be surprised by them. When they did work in, he turned toward Selina a slow head and pale, uncomprehending eyes:

" 'Beautiful?' he echoed, in puzzled interrogation. 'What is beautiful?' "

Then Selina made the mistake—if we count it a mistake—
that was to establish her, at the very start of her teaching
career in High Prairie, as a proper object of heavy, obtuse
humor. She answered his question: "This! The—the cabbages."

Klaas Pool "knew cabbages from seed to sauerkraut; he
knew and grew varieties from the sturdy Flat Dutch to the
early Wakefield." But for Selina to see them as she did was
incomprehensible absurdity.

" 'Cabbages is beautiful!' his round pop eyes staring at her
in a fixity of glee. 'Cabbages is beautiful!' " [1]

The humor of Klaas Pool was not malicious. He had no wish
to make the young girl at his side retreat from spontaneity
into a prim correctness: to retreat, as it were, from being
freely herself to being stiltedly the new teacher. But because his own experience had given him no room in which to
hold together the two concepts of *beauty* and *cash crop,* he
could not grant to Selina her right to see cabbages as beautiful.

We may not have the physical or mental heaviness of a
Klaas Pool. Yet all too many of us have definitions of the
practical, the important, the efficient, the smart, the respectable, and the interesting that we impose like strait jackets
upon other people's thoughts and feelings. We have our own
ways of declaring that "everyone knows this"; or "anyone in
his right mind can see"; or "no one but a sentimental fool
would believe"—when what we actually mean is that some
people of our own kind (who confirm us in our particular
pattern of life, as we confirm them in theirs) thus "know,"
"see," and "refuse to believe."

There is one further type of space we must grant to one
another if we are to do what is called for not only in behalf
of individual growth but for the sake of democracy's fulfill-

[1] Edna Ferber, *So Big,* pp. 23–25. New York: Grosset and Dunlap, 1924.

ment: we must make room for the *outsider* to move in and become an *insider*.

The word *outsider* is one of the lonely words of our language. It calls up the image of the human being isolated from his kind: not able to move into their fellowship; not able to interpret what is going on, and therefore anxious and awkward in any approach he tries to make; not able to contribute his knowledge and skill, and to be valued accordingly.

We think of the displaced person, for example, doomed to physical life in a cultural vacuum. Around him, people put in their days after the common manner of human beings. They talk to one another—in a language not his. They have work to do that is their work. They have accustomed ways: ways that are not intrinsically right or wrong, but which constitute the easy "second nature" of their communal life. They are free to express opinions about how things should be done; free, when they feel like it, to judge and criticize. It is *their* society. It is not his.

Or we think of the child of migrant parents, dragged from school to school, from one area of ripening crops to another: a child who never stays long enough in any one classroom to feel easy with what is expected of him, nor long enough on any playground to make friends—so that he can feel confident that where two or three of these are gathered together, they will spontaneously widen their circle to include him if he runs to join them. He is the outsider against whom, intentionally or thoughtlessly, the other children keep their circle closed.

Not in such drastic cases only, however, can we recognize the outsider. We think of the teen-ager who never knows why his words and actions are not right by the standards of the group: why he is marked as "different" and "queer." Or we think of the individual who is an outsider in his own family: quiet among the boisterous; frail among those who are proud of muscle; slow among the quick of mind—and therefore one to be taunted or handled with a too obvious patience or looked at with eyes that are puzzled even when they mean to be kind. Or we think of the old person—an outsider under the roof of the vigorous young—who knows that those who help him, with brisk conscience, to find small ways to occupy his hours, hold the unacknowledged belief that his proper occupation is to die.

However we may have come by the experience of "outsideness"—however any person comes by it—the important thing is for us to know what it does to a human being. It excludes him. With reference to some part of his world—some group, activity, field of knowledge, scheme of values, even topic of conversation—it leaves him in the dark: unsure of both his footing and his direction. He cannot see—and therefore cannot do—what would make him an insider.

If the situation from which he feels excluded is emotionally important to him; if, try as he will, he cannot get on to the hang of it; and if, further, the experience ties in with many previous experiences of exclusion, it may exert a deeply disruptive influence on his personality. The individual's awareness, in such a case, may become an in-turning awareness—so that he cannot give to the objective world the sort of interest and attention that would make him, gradually, an insider. His estimate of that world, moreover, may become progressively based on one fact: that it has, or seems to have, shut him out.

Here, for example, is a man who long ago got off to a bad start in school. His home gave him no friendliness with books. Neither was it hospitable to "impractical" questions nor to the sort of "idle" staring by which a small boy becomes an insider to the world of bugs, plants, clouds, and stars. From almost his first day in school, being ignorant of much that the other children knew, and inhibited where they seemed emotionally free, he was rated as "backward" by his teacher. His classmates, catching him time and again in some ignorance that seemed to them incredible, decided he didn't know anything.

He was an outsider—among the students, among books, among the gadgets and natural objects the teacher brought in for illustration. Whether in the classroom or on the play-ground, he experienced chiefly the sense that the human circle was closed against him. No one, not even the teacher, widened that circle to welcome him. He hated school. Or, in more precise psychological terms, *he hated being what school made him be; hated feeling about himself what school made him feel.*

This individual, now, is a man in his late forties. He has no use for "intellectuals." "If anyone blows up the world, it will be those guys." In his community, he is first to suspect the educated person—almost any educated person—of being disloyal. In his home, he is first to make sure that no kid of his will sit around with his nose in a book. The type of psychic space that was denied to him during his formative years, he now denies to others.

The concept of such space, however, does not need for its illumination merely one example after another. It is the core concept of our maturing psychological sciences. Where-ever these sciences begin to have a genuine impact upon us, their primary effect is that of persuading people to give other people room to breathe, to move freely with their minds, to turn around if need be—and therefore to grow.

This development has had conspicuous triumphs in the field of parent-child relationships. Here, the essential insight is that growth will take place only where there is mental and emotional room for growth. Neither child nor adult will mani-fest an increasing good will and creativeness if he is kept so on the defensive that his energies are chiefly focused for fight and flight. The infant who screams in fear and rage when it is held so tightly that it cannot move when it wants to, is, we might say, our whole humanity writ small.

The principle of space-making is operating, also, in the emerging programs of human relations in industry. What these programs chiefly provide is more psychic space in situations of daily work than was there before.

In a certain New England mill town, factory buildings that have stood for generations were recently taken over by a new enterprise. The cubic footage of the buildings has not materially changed since the 1880's. The psychic "footage," however, has increased almost unbelievably. This particular mill was once a place where workers—men, women, and children —were treated as expendable; and where, if they wished to stay on the job, they kept their mouths shut and their minds empty of questions. Today, workers who go in through the same old doors to their allocated desks or machines move in an atmosphere of astonishing new spaciousness. If they see ways to improve production or human relationships, they can talk these out; and if they can make them seem even fairly practical, try them out. The enterprise still has, to be sure, its points of friction. Yet the contrast with what the same walls once contained dramatically illustrates the fact that where the psychological sciences move into industry, they become makers of a highly valuable product: breathing space for the minds of men.

When the priest, Don Camillo, said to Peppone, the Communist mayor, "Sometimes I am afraid," he gave Peppone room in which to say, in effect, "Me too." Wherever human beings are permitted to move from a strictly defensive position to one of free and honest association with their kind— and with their own thoughts—they begin to discover the common bases of their living together, and, no less, the unique and stimulating diversity of their many minds.

FOUR

SPACE FOR OURSELVES ALSO

PSYCHIC space is not something we can make for others if we cannot make it for ourselves. The power to treat life as "roomy" rather than cramped will show forth in all our attitudes—or in none. It will reveal, in short, something quite basic about ourselves.

One triumphant aspect of our nature is expressed in the familiar lines:

> "Stone walls do not a prison make,
> Nor iron bars a cage."

One tragic aspect of our nature, however, lies in the fact that it does not take stone walls to make a prison nor iron bars to make a cage. It takes only a distorted notion of what will happen to us if we undertake any new venture.

This is what neurosis stems from: the fact that the human being has a capacity to make invisible fetters for himself. How he does this is one central insight of modern psychology. *The neurotic translates experience that he has not been able to negotiate into derogatory generalizations about life.* He then acts upon these derogatory generalizations and not upon objective evidence. Whatever happens around him or to him, in fact, becomes for him "evidence" to support his unhappy "truths."

Conrad Aiken, in "The House of Dust," observes that

". . . one, with death in his eyes, comes walking slowly
And sees the shadow of death in many faces. . . ." [1]

A neurotic, we might say, bears in his own eyes that which makes him see all persons and situations as threatening. He has, therefore, no room to move. He can only huddle within whatever psychic enclosure he has devised for himself as being less awful than the world outside.

The victim of neurotic self-pity is a case in point. The world he sees holds chiefly people who, to his mind, do not understand or appreciate him and circumstances that are against him. He hates that world. Yet he is under desperate compulsion to resist any evidence or any experience that would make it appear less hateful; for his derogatory description of the world has become his chief justification for his own inadequate conduct of life.

The friend or relative to whom he makes his repetitive plaints may try to suggest some way out: may open up this or that opportunity; may offer to help him toward some new venture. But always the neurotic will see why the proffered chance is no chance at all: for other people, yes; but not for him. The more convincingly it is presented, moreover, the closer he will come to resentful panic in his rejection of it. He cannot accept a more spacious version of life than that to which he has made his painful accommodation.

A second type of self-trapped neurotic is the kind we speak

[1] Conrad Aiken, "The House of Dust," in *Selected Poems,* p. 117. New York: Charles Scribners' Sons, 1931.

of as a hostile personality. Such an individual holds within himself, as a carry-over from past defeats, an anger so unresolved and so inclusive that it attaches constantly to life itself and not, like normal anger, occasionally to some specific aspect of life. Thus he is against people and situations even before he encounters them—and in spite of any characteristics they may show.

As a personality trait, and not merely a response to some specific stimulus, hostility has various expressions: hypercriticalness, for example; readiness to belittle and disparage; a habit of nagging; a tendency to hold grudges; many-sided prejudice; cynicism; suspicion of people's motives; xenophobia; "patriotism" that seems to have no content except hatred for some enemy; a way of bringing every conversation around to something that can be deplored or viewed with alarm; quickness to take offense and to see personal opponents as public enemies; a readiness to exploit, humiliate, and intimidate; a habit of defining success in terms of status and power over others; and contempt for the "soft" enterprises of reconciliation.

The hostile person, in short, is ranged against the quietly exploratory attitudes; the remedial and nurturing ones; and those that search for agreements. Such an individual is at the opposite pole from the space-maker. Intent to corner lest he be cornered, and to liquidate lest he be liquidated, he simply cannot accommodate the thought that perhaps life holds room for all.

Beyond the self-pitying and the hostile are yet other types: the neurotically rigid, for example. Dorothy Canfield Fisher, in *Vermont Tradition,* tells a story that has come down in her family from the late eighteenth century; and we might borrow it here to describe the peculiar self-trapping of the rigid personality. Her great-grandfather, then a boy, was sent out one morning before breakfast to let the sheep out of the barn, so that they could reach the watering trough. Having opened the big door of the barn, he let down the bars of the sheepfold inside, and watched while the flock, "led by the majestically authoritative ancient ram," moved toward the barn door, with the dust raised by their pattering feet making a thin cloud around them.

"But they did not go out. When the old ram . . . came to the open door, he halted, shaking his great horned head in uncertainty. Behind him, all the flock stood still. . . ." [1] The boy could not understand it—until he pushed his way through the flock to a point where he could see what the ram saw: "the just-risen sun sent through a knothole in the barn wall a long ray across the opening of the door. In the dusty air of the barn it looked like a solid yellow bar. . . ."

The rigid personality, we might say, is as firmly held within a fixed pattern of response as was this ram; and the fact that nothing more resistant than a shaft of light blocks his road to freedom has nothing to do with the case.

So much for the neurotic. But what about the rest of us? We have all met emotional problems we have not known how to handle; and to the extent that they have deeply baffled us, we have carried forward on the ledger of our lives certain vulnerabilities and habits of self-defense. The barriers by which the self-pitying, the hostile, and the rigid are held back from the great venturings of the human spirit are barriers that halt and hamper every one of us at some point or another, in greater or lesser degree.

If the distortions our personality has suffered are limited enough that we can still, by and large, enjoy our human experience, believe in its worth, have a liking for those who share it, and accept its risks, we can—sometimes at least—

[1] Dorothy Canfield Fisher, *Vermont Tradition*, p. 189. Boston: Little, Brown and Company, 1953.

catch ourselves in the act of trapping ourselves; and can set ourselves free. It is this measure of initiative that distinguishes the person we call sound.

No one, of course, will always recognize the point at which he stands cornered by his own attitudes. But we can effect a measure of self-release if we realize even occasionally that what holds us back from experience is a barrier more like the shaft of light that trapped the ram than like a solid bar. Each time, moreover, that we thus set ourselves free we become more ready to suspect that the "bars" between us and further venturings are not as unpassable as they appear.

Taking ourselves as a case study, we would like to relate an incident from two summers ago on our Vermont farm. Early one morning we took a walk up the country road. By the time we returned, the sun had come over the Green Mountains and a flood of light lay across our lawn and perennial bed. The beauty halted us; and as we stood looking, there was enacted before our eyes one of the small mysterious dramas of growth. Responding to the warmth of sunlight, the swelling bud of an Oriental poppy dropped off one part of its three-part calyx; and the flaming, crinkled petal beneath unfolded a little. We went closer—close enough to lean over the bud with concentrated attention—and could actually see the petal's unfolding movement. The push of life was made visible before our eyes.

We waited, intent. Time passed. The sunlight grew warmer. A second part of the calyx fell away. By almost imperceptible degrees the bud was becoming an open flower.

Just as the last petal was uncrinkling, one of our farm neighbors came down the road on his tractor. He is a man who, as the Vermont saying goes, works from "can see to can't see"; and who, for all his long hours and hard work, can wrest from his worn and stony acres little more than a bare subsistence. Now, seeing us, he slowed his tractor to a stop to say good morning. "You're working early," he volunteered.

At this point, a peculiarly insidious temptation almost had its way with us: the temptation to say, "Yes, there's always a lot to be done." It was the temptation, in short, to assume that he, living in terms of work and more work, would respect us as early workers, but would feel only an astonished contempt for our actual reason for being there.

Happily, on impulse, we pushed the temptation aside: "Not working. We've just been standing here watching this poppy bud open. . . ."

His face, tired looking even that early in the morning, lighted up. "No fooling!" he said with interest . . . and withdrew from the gear shift the hand that had been about to reinstate motion.

We told him, then, how that first falling section of calyx had caught our eye . . . how we had waited . . . how the crinkled petals had become those of an open flower; and he, from where he sat on the tractor, turned his eyes to the poppy and looked at it quietly for what seemed a long time before he jerked himself back to the day's demands. "Well . . ." His hand went to the gear shift. He and his tractor went off down the road; and we looked after him, feeling humbly that we knew him a little better than before.

We recall this experience in all its detail because we so nearly missed out on having it. We came dangerously close to making a wrong guess—too tight and arrogant a guess—about a fellow human being. And, as the Duchess in *Alice in Wonderland* might say, the moral of that is that if we want to like the people around us, we had best give them a chance to be likable.

If we had acted on our first ready assumption that our farm neighbor could value nothing beyond the workaday "practical," we would have denied him the chance to offer us any contrary evidence. Also, we would have done an unnoticed second thing: *we would have set rigid limits to the types of experience we would let ourselves venture in his presence.* We would have denied ourselves room to move beyond the workaday "practical" when he was around.

Incidents of this sort may seem trivial in this world of clamorous hostility and gigantic issues. Yet what almost happened that morning was psychologically akin to more disastrous things we do as individuals and groups—under the illusion that we are protecting ourselves or being "realistic." We make assumptions about people that are too small to hold them; and then, having invited into the open only a scrap of their nature, we blame them for their mental and emotional poverty, and, at the same time, condemn ourselves to live and move among "smaller" people than are actually on hand as companions in thought and effort. Beyond our estimates of individuals, moreover, we make equally narrow assumptions about the kind of world we are in and what can be done with it; about life itself and what it holds in the way of possibilities. With each such fixed derogatory judgment, we unwittingly trap ourselves: set limits to what we will try; narrow the range of our experience.

What are some of the common ways in which we deny ourselves psychic space? One such way might be called that of keeping *down* with the Joneses—as we take the Joneses to be. We refer here to the all too familiar practice of saying that most people are stupid and then trimming down our own words and actions to the presumed dimensions of other people's understanding.

We think, for example, of the platform lecturer who, privately despising his audiences, makes his own public performance despicable: superficially smart, lazily slipshod, condescending, or vacantly platitudinous.

Or we think of a certain man we know who defines a friend as a person who is always around until you need him—and who then makes haste to be somewhere else. All friends, he likes to declare, are fair-weather friends. In thus describing them, however, he takes no account of the fact that he himself never talks with anyone about anything except fair-weather subjects. If he has perplexities, convictions, hopes, memories that go deep, and yearnings that would establish him as a member of the human fellowship, he keeps them proudly to himself: they are not to be shared with the herd. If, moreover, anyone else takes a conversational step beyond the margins of small talk, he quickly blocks this move with his flippancy, cynicism, or self-assertive dogmatism. The inevitable result is that even "friends" whom he has known for years remain strangers: strangers whom he chooses to call fair-weather friends.

Looking beyond such personal instances, we see how yet broader harm is done by our first making derogatory generalizations and then letting these pattern our actions. Our whole western world, for example, is today paying a high price for its past readiness to disparage Oriental peoples. Describing these peoples as inferior, western nations have sought to establish with them, for the most part, only such relations as might be suitable with inferiors: inferiors whom it would be proper to use, to "improve," to sentimentalize, or to patronize, but to whom it would not seem natural to turn for insight, and with whom it would not seem natural to work on a basis of equality for the building of a shared world.

One well-nigh disastrous result of such long derogation is now apparent: we have to cope with wariness and hostility at many points where we might have had friendliness instead. A second result, more subtle than the first, we often overlook: the fact, namely, that our own attitudes have hindered our own social and political maturing. We have not used the chances open to us for deepening and refining those practices of mutuality that we now make clumsy haste to acquire in a world that has become one world. We are not ready for the "great day" that has come. We are, in fact, so far from ready that our policy toward the Orient seems a constant grab bag affair: what is "pulled out" on any given day may be a destructive leftover from the past, a jerry-built product of our present fears, or a sound product of resolute new understanding. We are not psychologically ready, in brief, for the world we have technologically made; and one chief reason is that we have too long taken our lead from our own disparaging assumptions about Oriental peoples rather than from objective evidence.

A second form of self-trapping is all too common among us; and it is one that psychiatrists, having seen its tragic results in the lives of many patients, urgently ask us to understand. It is the form of self-trapping that takes place where the individual's definition of success is too small for his human nature: so small that it does not allow him to grow into full-statured maturity or to form any soundly based relationships with the people around him.

The self-centered, ambitious man on the make often claims that he understands other people because he has learned how to "get results" from them. In plain fact, he knows just enough about the intricate human being to reduce him to a sort of vending machine, which holds something that will minister to his comfort, enlarge his feeling of power, or advance his designs. The secret of life, then, for him, consists in knowing what "coin" to slip into what slot, and what lever to pull, to get the reactions he wants.

We recall here Marquand's character, Willis Wayde, who had "risen" to a position where most of his social and business entertaining could be done "either on an expense account or as a deductible item on his income tax." He "was at home now with the head-waiters and the captains. He knew just when to bestow a firm glance and the exact psychological moment to hand out a bill accompanied by a friendly handclasp. . . ." He knew these things and meditated upon them with neither qualms nor self-doubtings to disturb his complacency: "Each individual required a slightly different technique, but it was not difficult. . . . You had to realize that all these people had their problems and you had to know how to make allowances up to a certain point, because in a great democracy all men were brothers. It cost money and time to do these things in the right way, but most of it was business expense." [1]

Here, through and beyond the smoothness, we hear the flat ring of the counterfeit. Here, the human being is forgetting his human estate: is setting himself apart from his kind and using his limited knowledge of other people to avoid the emotionally demanding experience of learning enough about them to value their hopes and self-respects as he values his own.

We recognize another form of this "push-button" pseudo understanding in the political tactics of the demagogue. He too knows how to pull the levers of human emotion: how to release in a crowd of people the tide of unthinking loyalty he needs for his own purposes; or how to needle an opponent into becoming his own worst enemy by making a public fool of himself. Thus it is said of one demagogic figure of our time that his greatest strength lay in his uncanny awareness of how to reduce his political foes to a state of stuttering, impotent rage. This is, to be sure, knowledge of sorts; but it is the satanic type of knowledge that stops far short of being understanding. It lacks, we might note, both the generosity and the deep authority of understanding: it depends for its

[1] John P. Marquand, *Sincerely, Willis Wayde*, pp. 141–42. Boston: Little, Brown and Company, 1955.

"strength" upon the other person's making the proper push-button response, and shows up as glaringly weak where this response fails to materialize. There is probably no human figure that can shrink in apparent stature more abruptly than the demagogue who takes on as an opponent a person who does not rise to his bait: who regards him, for example, with quiet imperturbable humor.

Whatever his particular methods or motives, the person who feels successful only to the extent that he can manipulate others to his own ends is never likely to move into anyone else's emotional frame; for whatever the relation may be between a vending machine and the individual who pulls the lever, it is scarcely that of human fellowship.

Psychologically, one of the most curious things about a constant pursuit of self-advantage is its static character. The man "on the make" may appear to be on the go: "getting ahead," "climbing the ladder of success," "elbowing his way to the top." Yet in a deeper sense, he is going exactly nowhere; for he remains trapped within his own egocentricity. His emotional world is only large enough to hold himself *as defined by the limited aims he pursues*. It is not large enough to hold him as a full-rounded human being, nor large enough to hold him and others in mutual understanding. The wide psychic spaces where people can approach one another with interest and good will—and can become acquainted not only with one another but with their own deeper selves and with the range of human possibilities—are simply not for him.

One type of self-trapping is peculiarly tragic in both its nature and its consequences. It is a narrowing of the mind, or closing of the mind, on the part of an individual whose very way of life depends for its integrity upon the mind's remaining vigorously and generously open. Anyone who, like ourselves, has spent many years in academic circles and has, as a

citizen, cast in his lot with groups and causes broadly designated as "liberal," will recognize what we mean.

He will have encountered, for example, the paradoxical human being who will defend to the death *academic freedom*—
declaring that a university is nothing if not a place where
professors can teach the truth as they see it and can aim their
research in any direction where they think truth may lie—
but who will not, in his own field, lend a free mind to any form
of "truth" save the particular theory or "school" to which he
has attached his own reputation.

We might illustrate with one current instance of such voluntary fettering of the mind: an instance taken from our own
field of psychology. For more than twenty years, with constant
refinements of method and a highly responsible readiness to
submit his statistical and experimental procedures to the most
rigorous and critical of tests, Dr. J. B. Rhine has been carrying
on research in parapsychology at Duke University: research
in extrasensory perception, referred to "in the trade" as ESP.

Gradually, he has accumulated a body of evidence about
the reaches of the mind that would, if widely accepted, demand a major revision of various "classical" theories of psychology that have kept the mind well within the frame of
natural physical phenomena. Psychologists of the "natural
science" outlook have not been able to refute Rhine's evidence by any experiments of their own; nor have they been
able to prove his methods lack proper controls or exactitudes
of measurement.

By all normally accepted scientific standards, in brief, his
work deserves open-minded appraisal. He *may* have opened
up areas of reality never before entered and explored with
any comparable precision. We could reasonably expect, then,
at this stage, that many among the Fellows of the American
Psychological Association—regardless of their own "schools"
of psychology—would be lending to Rhine's experiments the

type of generous interest that scientists declare themselves obligated to extend to all responsible research.

Is this what we find? In 1952, Dr. Lucien Warner sent out to one-third of these Fellows—five hundred and fifteen of them—a questionnaire that enabled them to state whether or not they considered the investigation of ESP a legitimate scientific undertaking; what degree of acceptance they gave to the evidence so far accumulated; and on what type of contact with the research or with original reports of it they based their acceptance or rejection.[1]

While 89 per cent of those who responded to the questionnaire granted the scientific legitimacy of ESP research, and 78 per cent believed that such research properly came within the sphere of academic psychology, only 16.6 per cent of them were ready to consider that the occurrence of extrasensory perception was either established or a likely possibility. This might properly mean, of course, a well-considered rejection of Rhine's methods. That it did not mean this, however, was revealed by facts that the questionnaire brought out: namely, as Warner reports, that more than two-thirds of the Fellows *had never read an original report of the ESP research;* and one in three among those who rejected the evidence of extrasensory experience stated that he had made up his mind on *a priori* grounds, *without considering even secondhand reports or reviews of the evidence.*

We can guess that every one of these top-ranking members of a scientific profession had at some time told with relish the story of how the clerics rejected on *a priori* grounds the evidence thrust upon their reluctant minds by Galileo's experiments. What, then, persuaded them in their turn to do even as the clerics had done before them: to reject evidence with-

---

[1] Lucien Warner, "A Second Survey of Psychological Opinion on ESP," *Journal of Parapsychology,* 16 (1952), 284–95.

out weighing it because the acceptance of it would disrupt their theories?

One scientist has given a frank personal explanation of his attitude toward ESP and has stated his belief that he speaks for many of his fellows as well as for himself. He says simply that psychologists are still trying to find their way "out of the magic wood of animism" and that he, for one, rejects ESP, without regard to how accurate or convincing the evidence for it may be, "because it does not make sense." [1] That is to say, phenomena that will not yield to physical explanation are rejected out of hand: *rejected, not disproved*.

We are not primarily interested, here, in ESP. Our concern is with the scientific mind—the mind that claims to be open—behaving after the manner of the closed mind: shutting itself away from what it does not want to see. The free outreach of the mind is worth defending for one reason only: *because it is worth practicing*. In the long run, moreover, it can be defended by one means only: *by the consistent, and not merely expedient or occasional, practice of it*.

There is no reason to single out these psychologists for special reproach. Their "guilt" is of a type all too easy to illustrate; and few of us, perhaps, are wholly innocent. We think, for example, of the mutually acrimonious cliques and "schools" that often split English departments and Art departments into warring camps—with stereotyped approvals and contempts replacing that generous distinction of taste that enables the mind, if it will, to search for what is excellent wherever it is to be found. Or we think of the tenacity with which many medical schools—and their practicing graduates —have refused to make room in their minds for evidence that has pointed to emotional causes of organic symptoms.

[1] D. O. Hebb, "The Role of Neurological Ideas in Psychology," *Journal of Personality*, 20 (1951), 45.

We live in a time when freedom of teaching and freedom of research are having to be clarified and defended before the bar of public opinion; a time when anti-intellectuals seem, in many quarters, to be having a field day. But the exponent of the free mind will have to be willing, in the end, to be judged by whether or not his free exercise of the mind has made him a free person. The mind that has voluntarily cornered itself, and refused to move from its corner, is not the one best equipped to resist the efforts of outside reactionaries to crowd it into a corner.

It is not within our specialties only, however, that we often practice the very type of narrowness—and therefore of self-narrowing—that we deplore in others. As political and social liberals we have been firm in saying that democracy cannot defend itself by imitating totalitarianism. It must be distinctively, tenaciously, creatively itself: an "open" system that provides room for human variousness and human growth.

This means, on the one hand, we say, that all sorts of viewpoints must have a chance to try themselves out in the open market place of ideas; that conformity must never become the virtue by which the elect are singled out from the damned; that people must not be harried into corners by irresponsible accusations, official or unofficial, and there made to prove their innocence.

It means, on the other hand, that the errors of partiality to which we are all prone will be self-corrected by contact with other viewpoints that stem from other types of experiences. An "open" system, in short, is not distinguished from a "closed" system merely by the fact that differences are tolerated. It is distinguished by the fact that a cross-fertilization of differences makes for a constant enriching of the common life and prevents any one partiality from assuming the role of absolute. It must be distinguished, also, therefore, by those habits of integrity and mental courtesy without which

every meeting of opposed minds become a meeting of irresponsible angers and hostilities. The person who speaks most
convincingly for an "open" system—a free system—is one who
most deeply feels the drama of understanding.

This is the sort of thing we say when we talk in our role as
liberals: when we *consciously* talk in that role, defining what
it is that we believe and care about; what it is, to our minds,
that distinguishes the liberal from the reactionary or the
totalitarian.

Here, as elsewhere, however, it is by our fruits that we are
known; and the fruits harvested from a not inconsiderable
number of "liberal" minds today are those of a curiously inverted dogmatism. Many who pride themselves on their defense of an "open" system have taken up their own mental
and emotional residence, it seems, within a "closed" system.

Certainly they believe that democracy thrives on a free
exchange of ideas across lines of difference; but they would
scarcely be caught dead in the company of a person with
whom they strongly disagreed—except, perhaps, within the
respectable confines of an organized discussion group where,
for a span of time dictated by calendar and clock, they would
dedicate themselves to "mutual understanding" and the
"cross-fertilization of ideas."

Certainly they are opposed to the principle and practice of
guilt by association; but they would be inclined to look with
dubious eyes upon any fellow liberal who made a habit of
voluntarily exchanging points of view—except within an
organized discussion group—with conservatives or reactionaries. What was he up to? Had he been taken in by these
people on "the other side?" Had he sold out? Was he trying
to play safe by standing in their good graces?

Certainly the liberal believes that the democratic way of
life is sound enough—close enough to the deep realities of
nature—to risk being itself in all its practices. It is not weaker

than totalitarianism. It is stronger. It becomes weak only to the extent that it distrusts its own philosophy and its own methods and begins to imitate the totalitarians. The liberal is deeply convinced of this. Yet many, today, who think of themselves as liberals seem to doubt that a fellow liberal who puts himself freely and deliberately into a position to feel the impact of conservative or reactionary minds will be able to withstand that impact. He might indeed put himself into this position for sound liberal reasons; but sooner or later—so the fear runs—he would become an apologist for reaction. While a democratic nation, in short, should act with a firm, proud conviction of its own strength—a strength that only freedom can give—a democratic individual, according to this attitude, should not too often expose himself to the wiles and stratagems of undemocratic individuals: far from convincing them, he will not even be a match for them.

Certainly the liberal believes that the average human being is made of the sort of stuff that makes him capable of creating, practicing, improving, and preserving a free society. Yet many who think of themselves as liberal describe human nature in terms scarcely less derogatory than those employed by the dictator and demagogue. We ourselves have been startled, many times, to hear liberal defenders of democracy characterize the human race in general or the "average" human being in a manner that leaves no logical leg for democracy to stand on.

Certainly, moreover, the liberal believes in the responsible word—the well-considered and accurate word—and despises the whole miserable business of rumormongering, intemperate accusation, and stereotyped labeling. Yet many who call themselves liberals, and who have only contempt for those who brand liberals as Communists, run irresponsibly beyond the evidence in calling their opponents Fascists; and, with a sense of responsibility toward the spoken word that is scarcely greater than that of the rumormongers at whom they point with alarm, they too circulate about those whom they dislike "information" that they do not check for accuracy and that they cannot trace to its source.

Certainly the liberal knows that not all the answers are in; and that some of those that are in will turn out, in the end, to be no answers at all. The way of freedom is not the way of perfection. It is, rather, the way of trial and error—of error acknowledged and corrected; and of new trials based on new insights. Yet many who wear the badge of liberalism are as quick as any reactionary to defend their own errors; as stubborn, even, as any reactionary in standing pat on these.

We are not trying, here, to "discredit" the liberal. The plain fact is that we think of ourselves as liberals and that we have, nonetheless, caught ourselves in the act, many times, of forsaking the deep spirit and practice of liberalism for a type of inverted partisanship that would invite us to be anything but liberal. From these disturbing experiences of our own— these moments of catching ourselves in the act of trapping ourselves—we have looked up, as it were, and have been startled to see that we were not alone: that all too many of our fellow liberals were, like ourselves, making the mark of their liberalism *the side they were on with regard to one or another specific issue* and not the quality of mind and emotion that they brought to the handling of issues.

There is an old question that does not become obsolete: ". . . if the salt have lost his savor, wherewith shall it be salted?" If the good salt of liberalism, so essential to the sound growth of a free society, loses its savor; if it becomes not liberality of mind and emotion, but a constricted, angry partisanship in reverse, wherewith shall a free society be salted? How shall it build and preserve the firm bone structure of its being?

Gordon Allport writes that "the devotee of democracy

adopts a lifelong assignment in human relationships." [1] The words deserve to be underscored and lingered over: *a lifelong assignment in human relationships*. It is an assignment that can never be carried out by the self-trapped, the self-cornered; for it requires that the individual move out, as a free voluntary agent, into the wide open spaces of human give-and-take. It requires, most of all, a conviction that mutual understanding and mutual respect are possible between human beings at many points where they do not, at first glance, seem probable; and that such understanding and respect are important enough to be worth all the risks they may involve.

So intimate a thing is freedom, so intimate a thing is the liberality of spirit on which freedom rests, that on that summer morning when we two almost shied clear of putting to the test a farm neighbor's capacity to appreciate the drama of an opening flower, we almost, by that token, played safe at the expense of our own liberal faith. We almost said *No* in action to a way of human relationship to which we say *Yes* in words. We almost cornered ourselves within a pattern of caution too narrow for the types of experience we want to have in the company of our fellow human beings.

There is no need to go on laboring the point that the person who is mentally and emotionally trapped is all too often self-trapped. What we must recognize here, as in so many other cases, is that our redemption depends upon our being "born again"—and again and again.

Physical birth means the movement of the human infant from womb to world: from an environment of secure but rigidly limited and dependent experience to an environment that holds far more of both threat and promise. No human being lives and grows who does not, in some measure, make

---

[1] Gordon W. Allport, *Becoming*, p. 67. New Haven: Yale University Press, 1955.

himself at home within his post-birth environment and relate himself to it through his own developing capacities and
expectations.

Curiously enough, however, what we might call the *temptation of the womb* is never wholly outgrown. Again and
again we are tempted to make some one physical and psychic
environment into a place where we can feel secure and from
which, therefore, we do not elect to move even for the sake
of our own continued growth. The spacious world outside our
haven—our haven of already achieved knowledge, of already
earned reputation, and of established loyalties, convictions,
and group agreements—looks too dangerously spacious for
us to venture toward it. Therefore we choose to "hole up."

Only as we make an opposite choice, however—the choice
of *venturing toward*—do we experience the rebirth that
comes from entering a new environment, with its new body
of evidence about what life contains, and setting ourselves to
understand it. "Free men set themselves free," wrote the
poet, James Oppenheim. Psychologically, free men set themselves free only when they act as though they were free
enough to enter into new situations and relationships and to
try themselves out in terms of the perplexities and promise
these offer. If they make no such venture into the generous
reaches of psychic space, they are only self-trapped men who
call themselves free.

FIVE

THE DIMENSION OF KNOWLEDGE

WE HAVE dwelt, thus far, on a single aspect of our equipment for understanding. We have talked only, or chiefly, about our emotional readiness to make room enough for a fellow human being so that his experiences will not remain to us a closed book and he himself be a person on guard.

We have emphasized this factor because it seems to be a kind of *first*. Where such readiness exists, much can follow. Where it does not exist, experiences of outreach and of give-and-take are blocked at their source. The whole personality is readied for self-defense. It is held back from the venturings of understanding.

However, there is always a certain ambiguity in calling anything a *first*. "In the beginning," we say, and feel that we have pinned down a starting point from which everything else follows. But before long, we have to ask a further question: what was there before the beginning to make it possible for the beginning to begin? Translated into the terms of our present discussion: what makes a person ready with emotional readiness?

Success in reaching out toward our environment encourages us, we know, to further reaching out. But obviously there must be something within ourselves *to reach out with*. Even the infant soon moves out to his world with more than his aimlessly groping fingers. Very soon he brings to these hitherto "unknowing" fingers things that he has learned. More and more, as his learning goes on, he reaches out, not with fingers alone, but with memory, information, expectation, and purpose. In short, he adds the dimension of knowledge.

It is at this point that he truly enters upon his human estate. He "joins" his species by doing what no animal does: he not only "learns by doing" but he learns by learning—and he moves into relationships that give him a chance to learn. Thus, gradually, he borrows knowledge that extends far beyond his direct experience and works this into his way of looking at life.

As the years pass, such knowledge becomes more and more richly part of the growing child, determining his attitudes and behaviors. By the time he reaches adulthood—and indeed, long before—the dimension of knowledge has become for him a major factor in helping him to evaluate and decide.

What a person knows serves him, we might say, as a lens through which to look at his world and see beyond its surface appearances. Knowledge turns the opaque into the translucent or transparent, and gives the individual new materials for his response to life. To be sure—as we shall see later—it does not automatically do this; for he may carry within himself emotional resistances to what he learns. Or he may be using his knowledge as a compensation for failure in areas of human relationship, and may make it a wall between himself and his world, rather than a lens through which to see more deeply into the subtleties of life. Yet because knowledge does, in general, give new dimensions to our consciousness, it is one of the greatest of space-makers.

To take a very simple instance, we recall our own first experience of looking through a microscope at a cross section of cornstalk. We had seen corn growing all our lives; had planted it, walked down the rows, gathered ears; had driven between cornfields and called them beautiful. Yet until a friend, one evening, shared his microscope with us—and, later, his expert knowledge of what we had looked at—there was, we might say, a secret the corn was withholding. A further gift of sight was then bestowed upon us—so that we cannot drive past a cornfield, now, without seeing more than our eyes can see.

Moreover, what we thus see in the mind's eye carries its emotional charge. It serves to remind us that, in this universe of ours, we had best be careful about what we call *obvious*. More than once, since that experience, when we have started to "manage" a human situation without first troubling to understand it, or have found ourselves on the edge of treating some certain individual as an object to be easily catalogued, we have said, self-remindingly, "Cornstalk."

Perhaps this is as good a point as any at which to take stock of an additional fact that is often overlooked: namely, that a person's knowledge is that which keeps him actively and humbly aware of *what he does not know*. His knowledge tells him, again and again, where it leaves off and his opinion or his ignorance begins. At its margin, it impinges always upon the unknown; so that the more he knows, the more he encounters questions that invite him to say, "I don't know."

The ignorant person tends to be "closed minded," not only because he does not have enough facts at his command but also because he has not asked enough questions. For him, the answers are all in. What *he* knows is taken as equivalent to what is worth knowing. Therefore, he oversimplifies life with a tone of authority; belittles or condemns, with a clear conscience, those who search out new knowledge or who qualify their absolutes to make room for the complexity of the human situation; and even feels virtuous about refusing to learn anything that might upset the precariously balanced apple cart of his convictions.

It is sometimes said that knowledge, which comes through the intellect, is cold, while feeling, which comes through the heart, is warm. True as this seems to be in some cases, it is a highly misleading statement. It presumes that the knowledge we gain has no relation to what we feel. As a matter of fact, however, what we know about life and what we feel about it do not dwell in rigidly separate compartments. The wall between them is porous. They flow into each other, so that new knowledge tends to induce some new emotional response; and, conversely, a "change of heart" often prompts a search for new knowledge.

A concrete example will serve, perhaps, to show how knowledge and emotion, teamed together, can better our human arrangements. Speaking before a joint session of the Senate and House of Representatives of the State of Ohio, on February 16, 1955, Dr. William C. Menninger, of the Menninger Foundation, told a story about mental hospitals that he had been invited to tell. It was the story of how the State of Kansas had become the one state in the Union in which the population of mental hospitals had declined rather than increased over a five-year period. What he had to say was, in essence, a report on how the people of Kansas, and particularly the legislators, had opened their minds to knowledge not previously welcomed; how this knowledge had changed their feelings about the care of the mentally ill; and how, out of this fusion of new knowledge and new feeling, they had framed a dynamic question, "What needs to be done?"

At that time, all over America, legislatures were voting new appropriations to increase the size of state hospitals. This was a wholly orthodox legislative response to statistical evidence of overcrowding. It was an action that could be taken without the legislators' having to know what went on inside these institutions or what could more expertly and usefully be made to go on.

But in Kansas, thanks to an aroused governor and the cooperation of the Menninger Foundation, the Veterans' Hospital, and other individuals and groups that knew what the situation was with respect to mental health, something different happened: legislators set out to visit their state hospitals. They learned with their own eyes and minds what the conditions were. What they chiefly learned was that the most urgent need was not for more room—intolerably over-crowded though the institutions were—but for more and better trained medical and custodial personnel: "more brains" rather than simply "more bricks."

Then came the pay-off. Having learned this by their own voluntary efforts, these legislators did a far harder thing than the conventional one of voting appropriations for added space. They drew up a careful plan for increasing the number of hospital staff members and improving their training; and they put vitality into this plan by voting adequate appropria-tions for it. New knowledge, in short, awakened new emo-tions; and the fusion of the two got something done that ignorance and apathy would have left undone.

Psychologically, knowledge does something of quite special importance for the "opening out" of experience. In the first place, when we extend our knowledge, we extend, as it were, the "landscape" in which we feel at home. We become intimate with more phases of reality. We can move among them less awkwardly and guardedly. They become, we might say, part of our security rather than of our insecurity. We can therefore feel warm toward them rather than hostile or indifferent.

In the second place, knowledge—and particularly increasing knowledge—is one of the best guarantees we can have against the constricting, domineering power of the habitual and familiar. To learn something we have never known before about something we have "always known" is to re-enter the domain of surprise. In a profoundly redemptive sense, it is to become again as a little child.

Paradoxically, a sound and increasing store of knowledge is what makes us most comfortably, but also least complacently, at peace with our own ignorance. Anyone who is learning anything is constantly reminded that he does not know everything. Yet since he is, in fact, learning—not standing pat on either a pretense of knowing or a pretense that the unfamiliar is not worth knowing or would be "wrong" to know—he need not be afraid of being "found out" in his ignorance. By putting himself into the role of learner, he voluntarily announces the fact of his own desire to learn.

More than this: since the learning process brings him more and more broadly into contact—voluntary contact—with new questions and complexities, he is not likely to be driven into a panic every time his mind feels the feathery touch of the unknown. He knows the unknown is there. It cannot sneak up on him like a thief in the night; for he, with his interest alert and his already gained knowledge for company, is going forth to meet it.

Edwin Arlington Robinson has observed that

"The dower of ignorance is to distrust
All that it cannot feel . . ." [1]

The dower of the ignorant person is to distrust so many
aspects of life that he has always to be on guard. For him, the
"strange" is not something to be inquired about, wondered
about, approached with interest, and gradually incorporated
within the familiar. It is not something to be learned about
and then judged on its own merits. It is, quite simply, something to be feared if it cannot be avoided: something, therefore, to ward off, belittle, exclude, blame for whatever goes
wrong within the familiar scene, and even destroy.

What this comes to, we believe, is that an individual's
knowledge—far from being a kind of psychic mass within his
brain, as the phrase "body of knowledge" might seem to
suggest—is a permeative force within his personality. If it is
less than this—if it is reduced to an inert possession—it is
scarcely knowledge at all. To be *knowledge at work* it has to
be knowledge that is operating to stretch the individual's
area of awareness. It has to be a maker of psychic space and of
emotional hospitality.

Gerald Heard uses the word "childfulness" to identify one
trait that distinguishes man from the lower animals: namely,
the capacity to grow up without "hardening up" and "closing
in." [2] Such "childfulness"—which amounts to a sustained
power of mental and emotional growth—is, we would say,
possible to a person only as he goes on learning and as what
he learns is permitted to deepen and "warm" his daily responses to life.

Within a two-day period, recently, we chanced to hear two
curiously contrasted remarks made about two different

[1] Edwin Arlington Robinson, "The Man Who Died Twice," in *Collected
Poems*, p. 955. New York: The Macmillan Company, 1937.

[2] See Gerald Heard, *The Creed of Christ*, p. 10. New York: Harper and
Brothers, 1940. Copyright, 1940, by Gerald Heard.

people. When we put the two remarks together, they seem to point up with dramatic accuracy our human need to have both sound emotion and sound knowledge: the two operating as one.

One remark was made directly to us. We had suggested to a friend who was coping with a problem that he talk it over with a certain man who had, we thought, the very sort of knowledge that would help. Our friend demurred. "I'd rather not," he said with abrupt emphasis. We did not press the point, but may have shown surprise; for he continued, "I'll grant you, he knows plenty. But he's a cold fish." We had to admit the validity of his response. The man in question was well-informed: precisely and expertly informed. But he had a way of using his knowledge to widen rather than narrow the gap between himself and others: to establish, as it were, a kind of intellectual status system, with himself well "above" most other human beings.

The second remark we overheard in a restaurant. We do not know whom it was about nor what led up to it. It came to us as an isolated statement, suspended in one of those odd silences that punctuate the clamor of a crowded place. "She has all the good intentions and good feelings you could ask, but she doesn't *know* anything."

The two remarks, put together, state an important fact: namely, that neither "cold" knowledge nor "warm" emotion undisciplined by knowledge can rightly serve the practice of understanding. Understanding, it would seem, must be a fusion of appropriate feeling and accurate knowledge: the two made one. The practice of understanding, then, consists of bringing these two to bear upon one or another aspect of the human situation.

If we appraise the "childfulness" of a healthy and happy child, we can scarcely avoid being astonished at his aliveness. He is *alive with* the physical vitality of a sound young animal. Also, however, he is *alive to* his world. He is going forth to meet it, at point after point, to explore and handle it —and thus, in ways peculiarly human, to make it his own. He is demonstrating the fact that *to grow up* is *to grow out toward the environment*.

A newborn infant is scarcely larger as a psychological entity than as a physical entity. He has not, as yet, through any act of exploration or creation, staked out his claim to any portion of the world around him. But how large, as a psychological entity, is the ten-year-old boy who is at the "collecting" stage of life: who is making the whole wide world his own, we might say, by putting pieces of it into his pockets and other pieces of it into his mind?

How large is the adolescent? We do not mean the "problem" adolescent. We mean the normal, variously confused, but basically sound young person who is "pioneering" the strange mental and emotional landscape between childhood and adulthood, and whose long-range aim is to become a successful "homesteader" in the adult world.

He is large enough to contain an amazing reference store of knowledge and experience carried along from earlier years. Also, however, he is striking out into areas that were scarcely real to him when he was a seven-year-old or a ten-year-old.

He is exploring, for example, those relationships between man and woman that lead to the establishment of home and family life. He is exploring the structure of human society, filling with new content such abstract concepts as *right* and *wrong*, *justice* and *injustice*. Instead of merely obeying or disobeying *rules*, he is discovering what it means to live by *principles*. What he counts a matter of principle may not always be the same as the parental view; but where this is true, it is because he is *seeing things differently*, not because he is *disobedient*. He is acting out as best he can his own evolving value system.

In high school and college classrooms he moves far beyond the materials of his childhood learning. From a world of simple facts and procedures, he is moving into a universe of structured thought: from incidental stories to the encompassing of periods of literature; from simple arithmetic to algebra, geometry, and calculus; from a sampling of facts about earth and sky to the integrated disciplines of science; from historical incidents and heroic figures to an appraisal of historical eras, social trends, and political philosophies.

Finally—but by no means least—he is maturing his religious sense. No longer does he ask, as a small child asks, "Who made God?" and become impatient with any answer longer than the question itself. Instead, he lends his thoughts for sustained periods of time, and in genuine perplexity, to the immortal, unanswered questions that have to do with the meaning of life; and he tries to find a right focus for his own devotion. He does all these things—and becomes, therefore, psychologically large enough to do them.

How large, in mental and emotional terms, is the adult: the forty-year-old; the sixty-year-old? That depends. If *growing up* has meant for him chiefly *settling down*, he may, even in his middle years, be shrinking in psychological stature—as a very old person shrinks in physical stature. His "size" will depend, as it has ever since he was born, on whether or not he is growing out toward his environment. It will depend on whether he is still pioneering with his distinctively human faculties: still moving beyond the known into the unknown; still putting himself, *voluntarily*, into a position to be surprised, caught off guard by new aspects of reality, humbled by his own ignorance, stretched by new insight.

When we tie in the *venture of knowing* with that of our *trying to understand one another,* it is apparent that a readiness to learn and a readiness to grant psychic space to fellow humans are closely related. Quite simply, if our basic attitude is that of wanting life to tell us about itself, we will, by and large, give it a chance to do so.

We say "by and large"; for no one of us is wholly free from those hasty impulses to self-defense that block mutual understanding. At various points, in various moods, each of us shows himself more prone to ward off new knowledge and insight than to bid them welcome—and more prone to "catalogue" people than to listen to them. By and large, however— for at least three good reasons—the learning mind is a hospitable mind, a space-making mind.

For one thing, the knowledge it has already gained has given it "size" and elasticity, so that it is more able to accommodate the life that is lodged in other people than it could possibly be if it had remained small and rigid in ignorance or had learned, resentfully and reluctantly, only what was forced upon it.

In the second place, the learning mind has already, many times over, survived without disaster the experience of facing its own limitations—and it is not easily thrown into a panic by the prospect of facing them once again.

Finally, the mind that has learned much has savored the rewards of knowing: the tingling excitement of it, and the quiet reassurance. It has, in brief, savored the experience of adventuring and of feeling secure at the same time. Thus, it inclines to seek more of what it has already tasted and found palatable.

If all this is true, how shall we account for the presence among us of the person who knows plenty but remains "a cold fish"; and of the one who "has all the good intentions and good feelings you could ask" but who "doesn't *know* anything"—and who may even be flutteringly proud of "listening to the heart instead of the head"? More broadly, what has gone wrong in the all too many cases where knowledge and emotion do not seem to add up: do not fuse into a *taste for knowing*, on the one hand, and a *warmth of knowing*, on the other?

There are, of course, many kinds of ignorance that do not represent a rejection of knowledge. They limit the individual's understanding but do not reflect a distortion of personality. Thus, a child speaks as a child because he is a child. No matter how eager he may be, he does not speak as an adult because he does not have as yet an adult's knowledge and experience to speak from. Many times, moreover, ignorance reports what we might call *deprivation by circumstance*. Such deprivation is of two sorts: that of historical circumstance and that of individual circumstance. No one can rightly be "marked down" in terms of personality for not knowing what has not yet been brought within the human frame of knowledge—though his ignorance, shared by all other people, may well limit his capacity to cope with life's problems. Neither can he rightly be "marked down" for not knowing what he has never been given a chance to know—though his lack of knowledge may put him at a grave disadvantage among those who are better informed. It may even edge him into chronic self-defensiveness or inhibiting self-derogation if those around him mistake the nature of his lack, cataloguing him as deliberately ignorant or congenitally stupid.

What chiefly concerns us here is a different type of inadequacy. It is the misuse of knowledge or, it may be, the rejection of knowledge. What has gone wrong in those instances where knowledge and emotion do not fuse into understanding because the individual does not let them do so—is even on guard against their doing so?

Here, for example, is the type of "intellectual" who does

far more than any anti-intellectual to bring the human intellect into bad repute. Prodigiously informed in many areas, or minutely informed in some one area that he seems to regard as the only one worth while, he uses what he knows to widen the gap between himself and others. Instead of using his knowledge to bridge the inevitable separateness of our individual, self-conscious humanity, he uses it to exaggerate that separateness. His whole manner divides the "herd" from the "elect." He makes more of one small error in what another person says than of all the truth it may contain. He is alert to every chance, it would appear, to show other people up, put them on the spot, make them feel more clumsy and inadequate than they are; to ridicule the beliefs they live by; or simply to overmaster their hesitant opinions with his own "superior" certainty.

Here is another individual who seems to offer the sharpest possible contrast to the "intellectual." He is, in fact, avowedly anti-intellectual; and the "intellectual" despises him as such. His current conviction is that all intellectuals are Communists or fellow travelers. When a certain speaker whom he regards as "red" comes to town, he goes into action. He assembles "facts" and offers to the group sponsoring the speaker—or to the public at large through the letter columns of the local paper—what he calls "documentation." So far so good: it would appear that he respects facts and takes the stand he does only because incontrovertible evidence makes him do so.

Yet what happens when he is offered counter-evidence that cuts through the fabric of his charges and that is too solid for him to refute? *He rejects it without a hearing.* He rejects it, moreover—and this is the significant point—with his raw emotions showing through the veneer of his "factuality." From being a person who has claimed an interest only in "well-documented evidence," he turns abruptly into one who is determined not to be proved in error. Where his "documentation" leaves off, he forges ahead with declaration pure and simple: people like this speaker, he warns, are smart enough to pull the wool over the eyes of ordinary honest people, so that all seeming proof of their innocence or even of their active anti-Communism should be discounted. The fact that they have their "proof" all ready just shows how smart they are, and how much the Communists have learned about putting things over on the public.

Or we might take a third type. Not long ago, we had reason to try to judge the reliability of a certain radio commentator on a local station. His reporting of the news was ostensibly impartial. Yet it consistently invited the listener to arrive at a far from impartial conclusion. We sought information about him from a friend whose fairness we trusted and who, as a resident of the community, had listened to the program over a sustained period of time. "Well," he said, in answer to our question, "I call him a half-truth man." The phrase caught exactly the character of the commentator's work. Starting with a half-truth, he managed to end up—after a period of "hard-hitting frankness" and subtle innuendo—with what seemed a whole truth but which was, in effect, a falsehood; and what he planted in the mind of the audience was consistently, but not quite libelously, a derogation of certain individuals and minority groups.

Or here is a person who is a liberal—and a dedicated, courageous liberal—in the sense of his being invariably on the liberal side of social, economic, and political issues. He is *for* life in the vitally important sense of wanting to extend opportunities and to help people everywhere to help themselves. Moreover, he "knows his stuff": has facts and figures to undergird his good will. Yet there is a point where his readiness to know leaves off and his determined antagonisms take over. With clear and creative eyes, and well-equipped mind, he can see that much good can come out of groups, lands, and peoples that have long been among the earth's excluded and depressed. But if someone in the American scene whom he is accustomed to regard as an opponent of all that is generous and just supports one of his "causes," he is more dismayed than pleased. He shows no interest in learning more about this opponent's viewpoints or reasons. Rather, he asks, in effect, "Can there any good thing come out of Nazareth?"—and answers "No," without waiting upon the evidence. If he is forced to see that good *has* come out of "the other side," he still prefers to count his opponent's action as opportunistic rather than honest. For, paradoxically, even though he wants *the human race* to be converted to his viewpoint, he does not want *his chosen opponent* to be converted. His personality structure is such that he experiences as "letdown" anything that blurs his "devil-angel" theory of the human situation. He is happiest when waging a "good fight," with the enemy unmistakably known and unambiguously evil. He does not, therefore, welcome facts that show the enemy to be a mixture of good and evil—and on some counts, at least, a friend. He wants to prove his case, and to win support for the causes he believes in; but emotionally he cannot afford to have people agreeing with him at random, all over the place.

Finally, here is a woman who "just naturally understands people"—and who resists all evidence about them save that provided by her own "intuition." She resists it, moreover, with a "sweetness" that is both stubborn and complacent. Psychological knowledge, to her mind, is "cold": an intellectual intruder upon the domain of the heart. She grants it at best the limited virtue of being useful, perhaps, to those whose insight is less warm and immediate than her own. One fact about her "understanding," however, is painfully and exasperatingly plain to those who have felt the brunt of it: the fact, namely, that her "intuition" always justifies her treating the people around her in the manner that best fits her own convenience and her own ego-image. Because she "knows" that her son is not really in love with the girl he wants to marry, she manages, "with only his happiness in mind," to break up the relationship. She "knows" that her husband would be happier in a different job that would carry more prestige; that a quiet neighbor "ought" to get out and join things even though she thinks she is satisfied with her home-making job and her personal friendships and interests; that Negroes are "nature's children" and happiest when "kept in their place."

Instances of knowledge misused or rejected could be multiplied endlessly. But their multiplication would only underscore more heavily a single point: that the transformative, space-making power of knowledge is not automatic, but can be made non-operative where the individual's tactics of ego-defense or ego-aggrandizement are ranged against it.

Does this tell us anything we need to know about our own readiness to create the sort of psychic space in which the drama of understanding can be enacted?

It invites us, at least, to take stock of our mental hospitality. Do we welcome unexpected and unfamiliar facts when, so to speak, they arrive on our doorstep? Do we let them come in and state their case? Or do we peer at them through a cautious peek-hole and tell them to be off, and not to come back, unless they seem likely to support us in what we want to believe?

How do we act when we are proved mistaken: when a judgment we have made upon another person or upon some human problem is shown up as unfounded or unfair? Do we bow to the facts, acknowledge our misjudgment, and if necessary make amends for it? Or do we, to keep our ego-defenses intact, contrive some makeshift reason for rejecting the facts?

Even more vital, perhaps, is a different sort of question:

are we still voluntary learners? Have we taken the state of being *grown up* to be a finished state: one in which we can *settle down?* Or are we still *growing up* by the process that has emancipated us, stage by stage, from the limitations and constricted views of infancy, childhood, and adolescence: namely, that of moving out toward the not yet known?

Any individual who is psychologically alive is, in a sense, a constant pioneer. He is striking out, with his mind and emotions, on one road after another; and like all pioneers, he is setting himself to learn what he must learn if he is to feel at home in his new, broader environment: not fearful of it, nor fearful of moving beyond it, but at ease with its problems and possibilities.

What we learn can properly remain, on many counts, a matter of individual choice. But certain directions of our pioneering seem to be pointed out for us by the age we live in. Our age has posed drastic new problems in the area of human relations and mutual understanding. If we make no effort to know what must be known for the solution of these problems, we are likely to become, through our words and actions, a reason why they are harder to resolve than they need be. Also, happily, our age has been marked by swift, unparalleled developments in the very areas of knowledge most relevant to our current problems: areas that have to do with the nature of man and, specifically, of *man in society:* interpersonal man. If we let our individual minds pioneer along these fronts where some of the best pioneering of our age is being done, we may well achieve a kind of knowledge that will not only make us feel more creatively at home in the world we have to live in, but that will also make us able to give the people around us room to realize their own potential selves.

SIX

TO ERR IS HUMAN

WE HAVE spoken earlier of man as a mistake-maker. The word "man" in this context applies to every one of us—man, woman, and child. Since it is something we all have in common, the fact that we make mistakes ought, it would seem, to encourage mutual understanding and sympathy and a wish to set right what has gone wrong. That it does not always do so is apparent.

Instead of being honest about our own mistakes, and doing what we can to straighten them out, as often as not we defend or excuse them. Instead of being generous toward other people's mistakes—even when they are no worse than ours—we become angry. In no uncertain terms, we tell the mistake-maker off. Or—which may be worse—we nurse our hurt feelings in silence, letting them show through that silence just enough to keep the other person uneasy. Or we "forgive" —but do not forget. We keep the past alive in us as a grudge. Or we bring it up to the other person, time and again, harping on it until what was genuine regret on his part turns into self-defensive resentment at our unwillingness to let bygones be bygones.

Wherever human relationships, whether between individuals or groups, have become strained or hostile by reason of misjudgments or wrong behaviors on anybody's part—or everybody's part—one question seems most of all proper to ask: namely, how do we best undo what has been done, or best alleviate the unhappy results of it, and put our relationship back in working order for a fresh start? How can we best treat the blunders of the past *as past and done with*—and then go ahead?

Wherever we turn in today's world, it seems, we find human beings who look guardedly or vengefully at one another across barriers of old mistakes: mistakes that have never been openly acknowledged and that are still, in many cases, being defended; mistakes that, even where an effort has been made to straighten things out, have never been forgiven—much less forgotten.

Thus, at a myriad family tables and a myriad conference tables, we might say, the past sits in as a present troublemaker; and because the past sits there, those who most need to think and talk their way toward mutual understanding are unable to do so.

We have many things to learn in this age. But there is nothing, perhaps, that we more drastically need to learn than how to call an episode finished when it is finished. This is the art of rescuing the present and the future from the tyranny of the past. Unless we can learn it, and practice it with more interest in moving beyond old errors than in perpetuating the memory of them, the world's future—which is also our personal future, and the future of those we most intimately cherish—may be a sorry affair.

If we are to be realistic about taking old mistakes out of circulation, so that they cannot continue to distort our lives and our relationships, we will have to face a number of hard facts.

The first is that certain individuals and groups have no intention of letting "the dead past bury its dead." For such as these, the old wrongs and antagonisms that divide people and make them hurt one another are not something to be set right. They are something to be constantly stirred up, magnified, and capitalized. Other people's fears and hostilities are their stock in trade: the very thing they can most handily use to consolidate their own position of seeming advantage or power.

We all know the village gossip and the office trouble-maker: the person whose own ego-importance and strategic position are maintained by setting others against each other and then making sure that they are kept far enough apart by well-planted rumor and innuendo, that they are not likely, in simple good faith, to get together, compare notes, and check up on facts.

Today, we note an equivalent type in the person who attaches the label Communist or pro-Communist to someone whose "disloyalty" consists in his being on the other side of the political fence—or in his being simply an "intellectual," a dissenter, or an object of envy. In communities all over the land, and even within halls of government, this sort of trouble-maker has capitalized on our national uneasiness. To-day, happily, in most places his influence is on the wane. The period when he thrived was from the late 1940's up through 1954: the period when we as a government and as a people were being startled into tardy awareness of the power and recalcitrance of world Communism and had not yet got our bearings with regard to the problems thus posed. Even to-

day, however, this "village gossip writ large" is a force to be recognized and reckoned with. Most of all, recognized—by the tell-tale fact that when he has accused someone, or has set group against group, he shows himself committed to preventing those in whom he has thus induced mutual fear and hostility from getting together to compare notes and talk things over.

Individuals, however, are not always acting as individuals when they stir up or perpetuate dissension among us. Often they act as representatives of groups. Thus, there is the type of labor leader whose face is set like flint against any form of labor-management co-operation that might dim labor's memory of old exploitations. Even more familiar is the type of politician who never lets any member of the opposing party live down a past misjudgment—and who is adroit in making every past misjudgment appear to have been deliberate corruption or disloyalty. Within every religious, racial, and economic group there are—and always have been—those who speak for an unhealthy, opportunistic segment of the larger body: a segment that sees in every deep-seated fear and antagonism, and particularly in every new fear and antagonism that can be stirred up, a chance to increase their own power.

The individual rumormonger, we have noted, makes a tacit bet with himself that those whom he has turned into enemies will not risk coming close enough to each other to become friends. In like fashion, these power-seeking segments of larger groups—political parties, economic classes, and the rest—make a tacit bet with themselves. They bet that if they can spread fear broadly enough and make it intense enough, they themselves, as defenders and saviors—or as an element too dangerous to be crossed—will be able to get away with methods that would not otherwise be tolerated. They will thereby be able to assume a leadership role for which they would not, in an atmosphere of normal good will, be even remotely considered.

They make a bet with themselves, we might say, that if they create enough smoke, and persuade enough people to watch the smoke with acute anxiety, they can do two further things: get across the idea that the only thing to do, in such circumstances, is to fight fire with fire; and establish the notion that they, having shown themselves "realistic" and "foresighted" about the fire's presence, are the natural ones to lead the fighting.

At this point, often, they can go further. They can make a seeming virtue out of their own lack of squeamishness about methods and can, by their willingness to do the dirty work, ease the not too exacting consciences of those who are ready to have done in the name of necessity what they are not themselves ready to do. It is by this process of first creating a crisis and then "bravely" taking on the burden of it that even a small segment of a larger group can negotiate itself into a position where it has, with regard to the making and executing of policy, a sort of majority status. The most striking examples of this, in our time, are provided by the totalitarian regimes: by the manner in which, in both Nazi Germany and Communist Russia, an "elite" minority has assumed a role of absolute power by first writing the word *crisis* in gigantic letters across the majority consciousness and then setting itself up as defender and savior of that majority. For us to recognize this tactic as practiced by these regimes is not, however, enough: we have to recognize it wherever it is practiced —even among ourselves.

Next to be appraised are groups that, in their entirety, are geared to the spreading of fear and hatred—and are organized for no other purpose. Religious and racist "hate groups" are of this type. Marketing their wares with destructive shrewdness, such groups not only prevent old hurts being

healed and old antagonisms being reconciled, but they plant
new seeds of fear and rancor. When what they have thus
planted is full grown, the seeds from it often blow on today's
winds of uneasiness to lodge in the minds of many who would
never knowingly be associated with "hate groups" and their
nefarious works. It is thus that the general climate of opinion
may become so infected that a vicious minority exercises a
majority influence.

Uppermost today to be reckoned with, among the forces
that capitalize hatred, is totalitarianism. Fascism and Communism alike represent grudge on a grand scale: grudge hal-
lowed as virtue; grudge raised to the level of absolute
philosophy and all-embracing policy. In the way that Communism, for example, keeps alive in the memory of Asian
peoples every worst aspect of western colonialism, while
practicing a new colonialism itself, we confront an arrogant
determination not to let anyone forgive and forget.

Perhaps the most appalling thing about Communism, in
moral terms, is precisely that it will not tolerate the thought
that every human being is a creature of error and every human
society the structured product of both wisdom and folly. To
the Communist mind, one side has a corner on rightness. The
other side is absolutely wrong; and has, therefore, to be
liquidated. To forgive its mistakes, or come to any sort of
honest working terms with it, would be to license it to enact
more error. When the western nations stand baffled before the
utter recalcitrance of Communist powers that must somehow be lived with but that refuse to work out in good faith
any plan for the gradual bettering of relationships, what they
are confronting is a philosophy that declares one portion of
the human race to be infallible and that enthrones as virtue a
refusal to forgive any past wrong or to let processes of growth
take care of any past misjudgment.

Here, then, is a first hard fact for us to hold in mind: that
the wish to have old errors and grudges taken out of circula-

tion is by no means a unanimous one. We have to expect, in
a period of many tensions, that various unhealthy, cynical,
and self-serving types will exert an influence after the nature
of their own make-up—just as we have to expect that looters
will come out of the cracks of our society wherever fire, flood,
or other public calamity has created confusion. But just as
the forces of law and order can prepare to handle the problem of looting, so the forces of law and order—and of common sense and decency—within our own minds can take on
the job of not letting the obsessed or opportunistic trouble-
maker make too much trouble.

The second hard fact we have to deal with is the presence
among us of a considerable body of people who cannot forgive and forget; or who, more precisely, cannot forgive because they cannot forget. These are the neurotics. In them,
the past—their personal past—lives on as a constant incitement to fear and anger.

The neurotic may be starved for affection and may reach
out for it as best he knows how. But his very personality
structure is built in the image of his own most painful past
experiences: of fear, humiliation, loneliness, rejection, failure. Thus dominated by the past, he cannot forgive himself
for being himself; nor forgive those who have been, or who
seem to him to have been, the authors of his defeat. He is
equally unable to forgive those in the current scene who
defend themselves as best they can against behaviors of his
that they experience as unjust, spiteful, callous, demanding,
possessive, or domineering, but that he—from where he emotionally stands—feels to be natural and called for. Even
more broadly, he is unable to forgive life itself for being the
sort of thing it is.

To be unable to forgive and forget what has taken place in
the past is to be unable to give the present and future their
due. The neurotic's tragedy is that he never can give the

present and future their due. This becomes the essence, also, of his tragic influence upon other people's lives.

It goes without saying that many such individuals are to be found among those who form or join "hate groups"—as they are to be found in any set-up, large or small, that enacts totalitarianism. They are drawn to such movements by their anxious preoccupation with status and by the fact that they have a surplus of fear and hostility to "invest." Their own total make-up, moreover, bids them see the world as menacing and therefore renders them susceptible to the demagogue's tactic of specifying some enemy as the source of danger.

Most neurotics, however, do not act out through mass movements their inability to forgive and forget. They simply act it out wherever they live and move among their human fellows. They act it out not only toward those who have really committed some offense, but—by a hang-over from the past—toward those whom they merely associate with their own dissatisfactions and defeats.

In how many homes, for example, does a wife take out on her husband a grievance against her father—a grievance generalized into a conviction that no man can be trusted? In how many homes, classrooms, and offices is authority being exercised as irresponsible power because someone, at the deep levels of his being, has never forgiven or forgotten the defeats he himself has suffered at the hands of some hated authority?

Housman put his finger on a sad truth when he wrote,

> "I see
> In many an eye that measures me
> The mortal sickness of a mind
> Too unhappy to be kind." [1]

[1] A. E. Housman, *A Shropshire Lad*, XLI, p. 58. New York: Henry Holt and Company, 1932.

Too unhappy, we might say, to let bygones be bygones; and unhappy because unable to let bygones be bygones. This is the vicious circle of neurosis. And again the fact we have to face stands clear: namely, that our best efforts to take out of circulation old mistakes and the hostilities they have bred may be brought to nothing by neurotic resistance. A neurotic inability to treat the past as past may prove as solid a "road block" in one situation as a deliberate wish to capitalize old fears and angers may prove in another.

A third hard fact comes very close to home: the fact that few of us are wholly free from the characteristics of either the "public" rumormonger and opportunist or the "private" neurotic. If those of us who make up the healthy majority were less like those who make up the unhealthy minority, fewer human relationships would be distorted by unacknowledged and uncorrected mistakes and unforgiven wrongs.

Psychologists have, in a general way, made us aware that we all have some neurotic traits. We all carry around some "undigested" portions of our past: experiences with which we have never deeply come to terms, so that they can still catch us off guard. When some outside stimulus reaches through, as it were, and lays its finger on one of our touchy spots, we over-react as though a raw wound had been touched. We show ourselves to be more timid, irritable, or belligerent than the occasion justifies.

We sometimes speak of the neurotic as *panic prone*. By this we mean that he carries around enough constant anxiety to experience even a moderately dangerous situation as overwhelmingly dangerous. This is why he adds more than his share to any wave of hysteria. But all of us are prone to make certain disproportionate reactions—and therefore to add more than our share of emotional coloring to various situations. One person, for example, may remain unperturbed by the bad manners of a pompous individual who is dominating a conversation: unperturbed, or mildly irritated or amused. Another person, however, who is also listening may be stimulated to the point of rage—because of what he has unconsciously added to the situation out of his own past.

Part of the time at least these neurotic tendencies of our "healthy" selves are likely to take the form of determined self-excuse or self-justification with regard to our own mistakes and of grudge or self-righteousness with regard to other people's mistakes. The chances are, in brief, that every one of us has made his contribution, large or small, to the store of uncorrected errors and unresolved conflicts; and that he has done so because of what he unwittingly has in common with the person he calls neurotic.

While many of us are more or less ready to acknowledge that the individual with neurotic traits is not always somebody else, most of us have scarcely begun to notice what we have in common with the types we count most dangerous to human relationships in our time: the rumormonger; demagogue; extremist; big or little totalitarian.

Yet one reason why these types have been able to do so much harm has been that our own behavior in opposition to them has not presented an unalloyed contrast to theirs. We, too, have had our "favorite enemies": specified individuals or groups whom we readily designate as responsible when things go wrong; whom we are reluctant to credit with any virtue; whose past mistakes we keep alive in the public consciousness as much as we can; whom we talk about in derogatory stereotypes; about whom we circulate unverified stories; and whom we simply do not approach with any will to sort out important disagreements from unimportant, to check up on our facts, or to search for possible bases of understanding.

Almost all of us, in short, think and act today in terms of irreconcilable "in group" and "out group"—which is precisely the sort of thought and action upon which every rumor-monger, demagogue, and totalitarian has learned to rely for his success. So long as we can be persuaded to stay far enough apart from one another, in clique or faction or party, that we see one another only as faceless shapes or as caricatures; and so long as each group actually enjoys retailing its own pet exaggerations, and rationalizes as realism or virtue its own reluctance to take one reconciling step toward those whom it has cast as "the other side," we can be told almost anything about one another—by local extremist, self-serving demagogue, or unrecognized Communist—and will be inclined to believe it.

So much, then, for some of the obstacles that make difficult even our best efforts to correct old errors, heal old hurts, and move constructively beyond them. To know what these obstacles are, however, is only a first step. We need also to know what it takes to keep the present and future from being tyrannized over by the past.

For one thing, it takes the power to distinguish between a mistake and a sin. If we treat every error and misjudgment as a deliberately perpetrated wrong, we stand small chance of living together in any state approximating good will. The person who self-righteously "forgives" or grimly "refuses to forgive" another person's error in judgment is, so to speak, mixing his categories. We must let one another correct mistakes; live them down; relegate them to the past and be done with them. But this does not mean that the mistake-maker is to be regarded as a "sinner" to be forgiven—or to be denied forgiveness.

We might take a case that involves a husband and wife and, indirectly, their children. Years ago, the husband, who wanted to go into business for himself, thought he saw a good chance to do so. In the face of his wife's reluctance, he took that chance—investing most of their savings in a project that did not pan out. His failure, in plain fact, resulted less from misjudgment than from outer circumstances: the building of a new highway made his location obsolete before his business was well enough established to survive such a setback. He did, however, lose most, though not all, of what he had invested; and the job he then had to take meant his starting over at a lower wage than he had been earning before the venture.

His wife, treating his misjudgment as a deliberate sin against herself, has never forgiven him; nor has she ever permitted the children to forget that things might have been easier for all of them if he had not been too "pigheaded" to listen to her. Far from forgiving him, indeed, she now makes his unfortunate choice of an enterprise seem far more stupid than it was; and her own insight, which was as much timidity as anything else, far clearer than it was. Also, she leads the children to believe that the money lost would have supported a far higher standard of living than even the happiest of investments would have made it support.

Thus the marriage drags along, and the children grow up, in an atmosphere of nagging and needling. The husband, through the tired years, has become a sort of walking apology; the wife, a walking reproach. Both are emotionally stunted by a refusal to forgive where, in actual fact, not forgiveness but the valor of understanding was called for.

What such a case illustrates is that a person can do monstrous wrong by simply adding, as this wife did, *an unwillingness to let the past be past* to *a magnified sense of having been in the right*. Whatever initial rightness of judgment this wife could claim—if, indeed, her reluctance was that of right judgment—has been dwarfed by the colossal wrong she has done to herself, her husband, and her children—condemning all alike to live out their lives in mutual acrimony under the shadow of one mistake; and denying to all alike the self-confidence and companionship they might have earned by exploring together the possibilities that lay beyond that mistake in judgment—or, as we might prefer to say, remembering the relocation of the highway, that accident of circumstances.

It would be comforting if we could dismiss this wife's behavior as wholly extraordinary: if we could say that most people do not thus confuse mistakes that have had unfortunate consequences with sins that call for forgiveness. In fact, however, all too many of us, in big ways or small, act after the manner of this wife. If we are hurt or inconvenienced by another person's error of judgment, we assume the role of a person who has been wronged. We then act as though the "wrongdoer" must properly wait upon our emotional bounty —grateful for the forgiveness we elect to hand down; or patient before our decision that his "sin" is unforgivable.

Nor is it only in our personal dealings that we thus mix our categories. Many of the angers and recriminations that today confuse and weaken our society stem from this tendency to treat misjudgments—whether in national or international affairs—as deliberate wrongdoing: as wrongdoing, moreover, that cannot be forgiven or lived down. "Judgment is mine, saith the Lord." It is unfortunate that so many of us, so many times, feel righteously qualified to say instead, "Judgment is mine"—and let it go at that.

There are cases, needless to say, where people actually wrong one another—and cases where whole groups of people have wronged one another. After simple mistakes in judgment have been taken out of the picture, we still have cause to explore the art of forgiving as we would be forgiven. The extension of forgiveness between human beings is both an art and a necessity. If it is not practiced, or is grudgingly or self-righteously practiced, a great many relationships are bound to remain distorted.

The truly forgiving person is not one who employs his power of forgiveness only on an emergency basis: when some specific wrong has been done him. Rather, that power is in constant operation as part of his personality structure. He is able to forgive specific wrongs because he accepts life, with all its limitations, as well worth living. We might say that he, in contrast to the neurotic, forgives life for being the mixed up sort of thing it is. He forgives it because he likes it so much. As a corollary to this attitude, he accepts himself and other people, with all their limitations, as worth living with: worth being involved with in the human enterprise.

Thus believing in life, he can forgive the specific wrong-doer, when occasion requires—and can do so in a manner that puts the relationship back in good working order. He can thus forgive because he has known, all along, that life is imperfect—and has taken it for granted that he, in the course of living, must expect to encounter his share of its imper-fections. He can forgive, also, because he keenly feels how fine a thing it is to be alive when understanding and con-structiveness are the order of the day.

When he practices forgiveness, in brief, he is not doing some grim or self-righteous duty—any more than he is when he, in his turn, asks forgiveness. He is doing what, at the deepest level of his being, he wants to do: getting a derailed relationship back on its proper track, so that it can go ahead.

For such a person, time spent excusing and defending his own mistakes and time spent in berating someone else, nurs-ing a grudge, or planning revenge would alike be time wasted: time lost from the companionable, constructive business of living. He would, therefore, become as bored with the process of heaping endless recriminations upon a person who had wronged him, or of brooding in conspicuously hurt silence, as he would become with having such recriminations or such hurt silence directed at himself. He asks forgiveness and grants forgiveness in the same spirit: because his deep and spontaneous wish, when things have gone wrong between himself and someone else, is to straighten them out as best he can—and write *finis* to the episode. Mutual acrimony is not, for him, what life is about. Rather, it is an interruption of life, and is to be dealt with as such.

Precisely here, we believe, is a clue to why some people can relax in the presence of an affront when others would "tense up" and retaliate. It is a clue, likewise, to why they show far less strain than most of us do in the act of asking or granting forgiveness. The essence of the matter is that *they are being themselves.* They are not straining to perform an act that goes counter to their normal make-up or that sets up an inner conflict between the sound and the neurotic aspects of their own nature: between their conscious wish to forgive and their deeper unacknowledged impulse to make the wrongdoer "eat crow." Even in the moment of affront, the soundly forgiving person knows *with his whole personality* what his own long-range wish will be: that is, so to handle the unfortunate situation that it can be relegated to the past. Even in the moment of crisis, he remains himself; and as soon as possible, he forgives—and *forgets*.

It is the person for whom forgiveness represents a struggle against opposing aspects of his own nature who "forgives"— but whose forgiveness has to be put in quotes, so to speak, because he does not forget. Even when the issue has ostensibly been resolved, he experiences residual inner tensions that attach to it. His ego still feels diminished and in need of self-assertion. His wish to make the wrongdoer "eat crow" is still surreptitiously alive. Again and again, therefore, he will be likely to bring up the past; and even if he does not openly bring it up, he is likely to nurse enough of a grudge to mar his future relationship with the person in question.

The truly forgiving person does not act out his forgiveness according to rule or tactic. What he does, in effect, in the most constricting of all situations—where human beings face each other as offender and offended—is to make room for things to be set right. How he does this we can perhaps best see by noting certain things that he does not do.

He does not make a prolonged exercise of placing the blame. We recall, in this connection, a recent remark made to us by a friend whom we regard as wise about the things that deeply matter in life. In the organization where he holds a position of authority a peculiar crisis had been generated out of a series of misunderstandings, wrong decisions, conflicting wills, and, finally, self-defensive angers. It looked for a while as though one valued part of his program was in jeopardy. What struck us most forcibly was the quiet way he went about setting things right: sizing up the problem and fitting the pieces together in much the same spirit that an expert mechanic shows when he is tinkering a machine back into shape.

When we saw him again, a few days later, and asked him about it, he said, "Oh, that came out all right." We asked a further question: "Did you find out how it all started—who was to blame?" He shook his head: "I didn't try too hard—because I didn't need to know. As a matter of fact, I suppose I *do* know; but nothing would have been gained by putting the man on the spot. He was upset enough without my jumping on him. The important thing is that we located several points in our set-up where misunderstandings could easily get started—and where people could pretty easily get on one another's nerves. I don't think we'll have any more trouble of that sort."

Then, as an afterthought, he added, "The longer I work with people, the less interested I am in making an issue out of who's to blame for what. Whenever you start placing blame, I've come to believe—and making a lot of it—you also start oversimplifying your problem. While you're glaring at one individual, and holding him to account, you're not giving your attention to the over-all set-up of which he's a part. By the time you're through with him, moreover, you've probably made him a less useful member of your organization. You've made him afraid of you. Or you've left him with a rankling sense of injustice: of having had more blame piled on him than he deserved. No: as far as I'm concerned, it's enough to get matters straightened out. If I can do that, most of the people involved will straighten themselves out."

In the second place, the truly forgiving person *does not go in for melodramatic emotional "scenes" of repentance and forgiveness*—even though he may, under certain circumstances, have to operate in situations where emotions are at high pitch. He tries to establish an atmosphere in which people can use their heads. Certain neurotic types, we know, "specialize" in melodrama. They initiate quarrels—with a marriage partner, or a friend—for the sake of making up: and making up in a state of teary forgiveness. This is not the way of the sound human being.

Again, *he is not self-righteous in forgiving*. He does not place the offended self on a pedestal and, from that superior vantage point, condescend to the "sinner": "I forgive you." He inclines, in fact, to shy clear of saying in so many words, "I forgive you." For he recognizes that the phrase sets the *I* and the *you* too far apart for the emotional health of either: too far apart, with virtue too exclusively lodged in the *I* and error in the *you*.

The person wise in forgiveness is likely to be wise, also, about human nature and its odd sensitivities and vulnerabilities. He suspects, therefore, that it has taken some inner struggle on the other person's part to expose himself to whatever reaction an admission of blame may bring forth. He recognizes, in brief, that anyone who acknowledges a fault is, in subtle measure, putting himself at the mercy of the affronted human being's personality structure—and that this structure may show itself to be mature or immature, sound or unsound, generous or vengeful.

Even more importantly, he knows that the person who has faced his own mistake has, in the process, had to face himself as the maker of that mistake; and that this encounter with a painfully unflattering self-image may have left him raw on the edges.

Knowing these things, he knows further that when he says "I forgive you," the implied gap in righteousness between himself and the "sinner" may be filled with a sudden inrush of self-defensiveness on the other person's part; so that the other's energies, in the very moment when he is trying to correct his error, may be diverted from the constructive business of growing beyond error. In spite of himself, and in spite of his honest wish to set matters right, the mistake-maker may find himself under such compulsion to protect his diminished ego that his energy system readies itself for "fight or flight." A great many human faults, certainly, have been given a new lease on life by the obtuseness of the individual who has "forgiven" them.

A person of deep generosity toward life knows, in brief, that any sound act of forgiveness has to be an act of healing. He does not refuse to the other person a decent chance to express regret and set things right if he can. He does not brush off the other's apology as of no importance, nor hurry past it as though it were an embarrassment and nothing more; for the mistake-maker, as a self-respecting individual, has a right to put his house in order. But his reception of apology and redress, when these have been made, is a healing reception. Often, therefore, it is on the casual side. It aims to lower tension, not heighten it; to prevent self-defensiveness from blocking new insight; to move as swiftly as realism permits beyond the weighing of error to the weighing of new possibilities; and, most of all, to get the interpersonal relationship back on the plane where the pronoun *we* is easily spoken.

It is significant, in this regard, that the great prayer of our tradition says explicitly, "Forgive us our trespasses, as we forgive those who trespass against us." The words may be repeated by a congregation in unison or by an individual in private; but throughout the prayer, in either case, the pronouns that have human reference are *our, us, we*. No human being is here set apart from others in righteousness or fault. The needs are common needs; the fallibility is no less common. The person wise in forgiveness is one who spontaneously enacts the spirit of this prayer.

There is one final thing he does not do. *He does not enlarge his condemnation of a specific misbehavior until it covers the wrongdoer as a total personality.* It is no sound practice, we have learned, for a parent to say to a child who has done something wrong, "You're a bad boy; and you know I can't love you if you're a bad boy." The wise parent confines his negative judgment to the specific misbehavior. He singles this out, so to speak, from the general company of behaviors and makes it stand clear as unacceptable. He rejects it, but he does not reject the child. Neither does he drag up from the past all the mistakes he can think of that the child has ever made, framing out of the whole a covering generalization: "You always . . ." What the wise parent does not do in the handling of a child, we, if we are wise, do not do in any of our human relationships.

Talking with us one day about some of the problems of our troubled time, a friend of ours used the phrase, "the corrosive consequences of incivility." He went on to say that, to his mind, many of the relentless antagonisms that now divide and weaken us as a people are the product of initial mistakes compounded by bad manners—and more often than not, by the deep incivility of those who will not permit others to acknowledge their mistakes, correct them as best they can, and *be done with them.*

The deeply civil person knows life as imperfect—flawed, limited, self-contradictory; as unfinished—often immature, raw on the edges, unfulfilled; but as remarkable in fact and possibility, and as structured for growth. With all these aspects the truly civil person feels at home.

He is not, therefore, readily stampeded by human shortcomings. For he has known all along that they exist—and that we all take our turn at feeling the impact of them. Yet he knows that they *are* shortcomings: for he has also experienced the presence of good and is in a position to feel the difference in quality between good and evil. Thus, his civility expresses itself in a subtle fusion of attitudes. He is reconciled to the existence of limitations and of evils; but not passively reconciled. His devotion is to the excellent and to those unfulfilled possibilities of life—in every human being and every situation—that are, we might say, the raw material of excellence.

This devotion to what is sound and generous in human behaviors and relationships will express itself in many different ways. When occasion requires, it will express itself as readiness to correct his own mistakes as best he can or, as the case may be, to give other people a chance to correct theirs.

For such a person the arts of apology, restitution, and forgiveness are simply part of the business of living. Because he deeply feels the drama of life's transcending, even in small ways, its previous limitations, he does not want growth to be halted overlong by stubborn hostilities or by preoccupation with faults and mistakes.

We have spoken of the "corrosive consequences of incivility." Here, we might well pay tribute to the redemptive consequences of civility. If we do not harvest figs from thistles, neither, happily, do we harvest thistles from fig trees. Civility no less than incivility will tend to produce after its own kind. Where civility sets the pattern for human relationships and behaviors, it is not likely that mistakes of the past—no matter who has made them, nor how grievous they seem—will be allowed to dominate and distort the future.

SEVEN

GRATITUDE: THE MATURE

EMOTION

ALL THROUGH the human centuries, no doubt, people have exhorted other people to be grateful. We would question, however, whether anyone has ever actually felt gratitude because he was told to feel it.

Countless persons, being thus exhorted, have doubtless tried to summon up the proper emotion—and have felt guilty when it would not come. They have identified as gratitude what has, at best, been a sense of obligation. They have performed by rote, as it were, such actions as are commonly taken to express gratitude; and have reproached themselves when they have slipped up on these. But it seems improbable that anyone has ever by command, or by his own determination to feel what he ought to feel, experienced the rich sense of "overflow"—"My cup runneth over"—that can rightly be called gratitude.

We bring up this matter of futile exhortation, reproach,

and self-reproach because we feel it is highly unfortunate that gratitude—one of the most rewarding emotions we experience—should so often be regarded as on the "ought" side of life: "You ought to be grateful"; or, condemningly, "You're ungrateful. You don't appreciate all I've done for you."

The fact is that gratitude is an emotion that no human being feels, or can feel, until he has grown into it; and the emotions we arouse in a person—particularly in a small child— when we demand that he feel gratitude are the very ones most likely to prevent his growing into it. A baffled sense that he has somehow "been bad," anger at himself, a sense of guilt, resentment at being nagged at and made to feel inadequate, a stiff preoccupation with keeping up pretenses: all these make for an in-turning attention; a focusing upon the self. Gratitude is felt only to the extent that an out-turning attention has become a natural way of life.

A small child—still on the receiving end of things—takes the bounty of life for granted. It is the only way he can take it; for he has, as yet, no power to estimate, and therefore appreciate, the efforts that others put forth in his behalf. He can be glad to get things, and can show impulsive warmth toward the giver; but he cannot, in any accurate meaning of the term, be grateful.

By the same token, a child takes the frustration of his wishes as an inexplicable and deliberate affront. To his mind, all adults—and his parents in particular—are people who can give him what he asks for if they will. Their valid reasons for refusing him one thing and another, or for taking out of his hands what he has appropriated to himself, cannot by his standards be good reasons. Denial of his wishes thus amounts to both *deprivation* and *affront*. To the pain of not getting what he wants is added the angry sense that it is being deliberately withheld. So long as the experience of wanting and getting, or of wanting and not getting, is interpreted in these rudimentary terms, it is not an experience roomy enough to hold gratitude.

A child can be, and should be, instructed in *behaviors* that make him an acceptable human being. He can be taught not to grab everything in sight; to say thanks for what he is given; not to throw a tantrum when he has to wait his turn; and, gradually, to give as well as to receive. As these behaviors become for him easy and natural, he will less often experience angry tensions between himself and other people and will have more chance to grow into affirmative emotions by the simple process of liking and being liked. He can, in brief, be helped to learn *how to act*. Also, he can have his attention drawn to the fact that back of the gift he receives is the giver: "Mrs. Smith made these cookies for you and brought them over"; or "Did you thank Uncle John for your new sled? He made it himself because he knew you wanted one."

How to act and *what to notice in the relationships of giving and receiving:* a child can be initiated into these. But he cannot be told *what to feel*. His emotions will mature as his understanding matures; and gratitude—which, in its authentic forms, is a fairly late comer—is an emotion he will feel and express, not by command, nor by rote, but on his own spontaneous terms, when he has grown up enough to feel the intricately rich pattern of give-and-take by which life is supported.

We remember, years ago, hearing a young bride make fun of a wedding present she had received from a distant relative: an elderly widow. It was a cake plate that did not, in truth, fit into any scheme of things that she would choose. It was ornate—gilded and beflowered. Also, in price-tag terms, it was undeniably cheap. With her friends clustered about her at the wedding reception—where a long table was heavy with "suitable" presents—she held up the plate for ridicule. Caricaturing in a few stiletto words the elderly—and almost desperately poor—woman who had sent it, this bride seemed wholly unaware of what she was reporting about herself: namely, that she was still a child; and a spoiled, undisciplined child, at that. She was scarcely more ready for marriage, parenthood, or any other of the privileges and responsibilities of adult life—in a world where all relationships are "for better or worse"—than would have been the tiny flower girl who, a few minutes earlier, had scattered rose petals before her in the wedding procession.

True, she did not throw the plate on the floor and break it, as a child might have thrown an unwanted gift. But unmistakably she showed herself to be still at the stage of life where only the gift, not the giver, was real to her; and where other people were "good parents" or "bad parents" according to whether or not they gave her what she wanted. She was pleased with most of her gifts: proud to show them. Yet the way she handled that one plate revealed the fact that she was not *grateful* for any of them; for gratitude has no place in the make-up of the individual who does not spontaneously see the giver behind the gift.

It was significant to realize, as we watched this episode, how many different stages of psychological growth can be revealed in a group of human beings all of whom are approximately of the same chronological age. For the bride was not the only one who "showed her age." Among the young women gathered around her there were two who laughed with her and who added their own wisecracks about the plate and the uses she might make of it. But there were also those who looked uncomfortable and embarrassed. There was one who turned away, picked up another present, and studied it more intently than need be. And there was one who reached out, finally, and took the plate from her hands—putting it back on the table as tenderly as if her fingers were touching, and comforting, the little old woman who had bought and sent in good faith what was to her a gift greatly to be wanted.

This is the crux of the matter. Gratitude is never felt, and never can be felt, except by those who have grown up enough to feel the reality of other human beings. We have many times been told, in proverb and precept, that "the gift without the giver is bare." Perhaps we need to tell a related truth: namely, that the receiver who accepts a gift but has no warm sense of the giver is barren of gratitude.

It may be that one reason why we do not better understand gratitude, and its role in human experience, is that we rarely think of it except in relation to some specific gift or word or act of kindness or helpfulness. In deeper truth, gratitude is an aspect of personality. Just as we noted in the preceding chapter that the power to forgive a specific wrong—to forgive and be done with it—roots in the power to forgive life itself for being the imperfect thing it is, so we must note here that the power to feel grateful for a specific gift or service is rooted in a more pervasive attitude. It expresses something far more profound than the fact that the individual is pleased because he has got something he wants. It expresses the fact that he feels privileged to be in on the mutual processes of give-and-take. Gratitude is thus a warm sense of being included in a pattern of reciprocities.

What forms of appreciation does a person, in fact, grow into if he soundly grows up? One basic form, we would say, is appreciation of those who know how to do what needs to be done: gratitude, in short, for the many kinds of expertness that keep life going.

A child's toy is broken; and with it, his heart. Comes the

older boy, or the father or mother, and in a miraculous sort of way the broken toy is made whole. What the child could in nowise do for himself another person has known how to do—and has done willingly. Experiences of this sort are a kind of preface to our adult awareness that no human being goes it alone: that where our individual knowledge and skill leave off, someone else's knowledge and skill have to take over—and can take over.

While we were writing this chapter, we took time out, one morning, to stand at a window and watch a surveying crew at work. They were doing for us what we would not have known how to do: locating and marking the corners of our tract of woodland. As we watched them plunging through the winter woods and then, each of them in his place, going to work with plumb bob and precision instrument, we were grateful: to them for their knowledge and skill; but also to the long line of surveyors and instrument-makers who stood back of these particular men; and to the human race that has oddly learned to solve one problem after another by parceling out, so to speak, jobs to be done.

Another example. One summer evening, at our farm, the electricity went off, and we and a friend who had been visiting with us became to one another only voices in darkness. We fumbled for matches and candles and a flashlight.

Seeing that neighbors' windows were as dark as our own, we settled down to wait, sure that it would not be long till the trouble shooters would be on the job. It seemed only a matter of minutes before we heard cars and then voices, and realized that they were focused around a near-by pole that held the transformer. We went out to watch the proceedings.

Three men were at work. One, already up at the top of the pole, was fixing into place a block and tackle with which the others, at work on the ground, could bring within his reach a repaired connection. We stood and watched, with the admiration that expertness always evokes. These men knew what they were doing. They went about it with swift, co-operative precision. Sooner than we would have thought possible, they were through: ready to reassemble their gear and put it back in the truck.

To the man who seemed to be in charge we voiced our admiration of their sure workmanship. He smiled, but as though surprised. "It's our job," he said.

Our appreciation, which had been extended to the competence of these men, now found a wider focus. It embraced their attitude toward their work. They did not need to "talk big." They had their job to do; accepted it as theirs; and performed it with a responsible accuracy that made them self-respecting members of the human enterprise.

"Doctor, lawyer, merchant, chief"—to these, and to others in multitude, we turn for help and for the satisfaction of needs and desires; and they, on occasion, turn to us. Gratitude for being in on such human give-and-take seems to us as natural as breathing. Yet it does not, we know, come as naturally as breathing. It is the product of our experience of living. Time and again, in the presence of one expertness and another, we have watched something being done that has solved some problem; eased some friction; brought light into physical, mental, or moral darkness; or added to the richness of life. On such occasions, our position has not been too far removed from that of the child who stands by while father or mother fixes the broken toy or makes a new one.

Not too far removed; and yet very far removed. For we, unlike the child, have had years in which to learn that back of every taken-for-granted object and service, and back of every product of insight and devotion, lie knowledge and effort.

Also, as adults, we have a privilege that the child cannot have in any equal measure: that of knowing what it feels like to be included in the reciprocities of expertness. As adults, we have had time to earn our own right to say, "It's our job."

A second form of gratitude seems also to come as a product of sound growth. This is gratitude for the amazing common decencies of most people: for the simple fact that most people, most of the time, take the brunt of circumstances without falling apart; that most of them, given half a chance, are friendly rather than hostile; that most of them would rather help than hurt.

Recounting the story of one group among the human many that have pushed into unknown lands and suffered the hardships of their venturing, Archibald MacLeish writes:

"Before us are other lands and a new winter . . .

Nevertheless we go on: we are not returning:
Strange as it is that men: wanderers: wretched:

Deceived often: misled: their way lost: thirsting:
March on in the sun! But so the desire has
Strength over us . . . and the love the love of this earth. . . ."[1]

No small child is in a position, as yet, to value the tenaciousness with which mankind as a whole, and most individual men, have tacitly said in the face of adverse circumstances —or, simply, in the face of endless chores, "Nevertheless we go on: we are not returning."

In one sense, of course, there is no other choice. No way of return lies open. But in another sense, as psychiatric case studies make plain, there is a way of return: the way we call *regression.* Human beings of any age can slip back into attitudes and behaviors appropriate only to children: into dependence, irresponsibility, quick anger at not getting their

[1] Archibald MacLeish, "Conquistador," in *Collected Poems 1917–1952,* p. 295. New York: Houghton Mifflin Company, 1952.

own way, the habit of judging others only by how these others minister to their wishes. People *can* thus retreat from the everyday chores of life, and also from its larger hazards and griefs. But most of them do not. Most of them, in steady, unobtrusive, friendly fashion enact "the love of this earth."

We cannot expect that a child will, in any profound sense, feel gratitude for simple human behaviors that are, on the whole, decent, courageous, and helpful. He has no way of knowing, as yet, how tired people can be—and still go on about their jobs. He has no way of knowing how many lives are chiefly expended in "chore work"—in doing things "over and over that just won't stay done." [1] He can see in the darkness of his room, at night, shapes that are not there; and can fear these enough to go pattering off to his parents for comfort. But he has not yet lain awake at night staring at broken hopes and plans and at a future that seems wholly dark; and then got up, in the morning, and gone on about his business —"making do" with what he has to work with and what he can find within himself in the way of reasons for going on.

We expect that a child, though keenly aware on his own terms of the world around him, will be obtuse with regard to much that grown-up life involves. If an adult, however, has no eye for the common decencies that are enacted all around him; if he is chiefly cynical, or chiefly proud of his "superior" capacity to belittle and debunk, we can suspect that he is emotionally stunted in his growth: he has taken on size and age without taking on an appropriate awareness.

Part of mature life, once more, is gratitude for all experiences of mutual understanding. The truly grown-up person does not take the good will of other people as his natural

[1] Robert Frost, "A Servant to Servants," in *Collected Poems*, p. 83. New York: Henry Holt and Company, 1939.

due. Nor does he take friendship for granted, nor love, nor compassion, nor the bolstering tolerance extended to him in his least likable moments by those who understand that he is not, at those moments, liking himself very much either.

The mature person knows enough about the vulnerabilities of our human stuff to know how easy it is for self-defensiveness to block understanding. He knows enough about the isolating effects of simple preoccupation, and enough about the body-enclosed and experience-enclosed separateness of each individual to be grateful for every occasion when, transcending such separateness, mind meets mind. He is grateful for the responsive smile that announces friendliness; for the sudden lighting up of interest in another person's eyes; for all moments of companionable silence; for the readiness of another to listen attentively across barriers of disagreement; for the warm power of another to recognize for what it is the shyness that makes him, at times, wordless when he wants to speak, or more blunt and abrupt in speech than he intends to be; for all chances to explore with others the questions, needs, and hopes that lie at the deep levels of our common human experience; and for all efforts that are made by anyone, anywhere in the world, to replace antagonism with understanding.

The small child has no way of knowing that all mutual understanding is a kind of miracle. To him, his own feelings are so obviously "right" that he cannot think of himself as hard to understand. Nor can he know how complex and various other people are. He can, and normally does, respond very early in life to a show of friendliness; but as he answers smile with smile, he has not the slightest sense that he is enacting one of the unique and triumphant powers of his species. He has a lot of growing to do before a permeative gratitude for all experiences of mutual understanding and affection can become part of his character structure; and he may never do this requisite amount of growing, even though he lives to be old.

Yet another basic form of gratitude is that felt for all energies and insights that have maneuvered mankind out of primitive helplessness and ignorance into some measure of civilization.

Whether we pick up the most ordinary tool, or feel the texture of one of the new "wonder fabrics," or appraise the institution we call the public school or the one we call a court of law, or take down a book from the shelf, or put a pan of rolls in the oven to bake, or listen to a symphony, we stand in the presence of the human tradition—and many of us learn to stand gratefully. We are on the receiving end of that distinctive power that makes it possible for us to borrow knowledge from those who have gone before us and to move on from where they left off; and also for us to borrow courage, holding ourselves to the line laid down in words spoken long ago; and to borrow standards and ideals by which to set the compass of our lives.

Some people seem constantly amazed at human shortcomings but never amazed at human insight and wisdom. These they take for granted. They may be petulant or querulous in their readiness to blame; or proud of their ability to pick flaws in what is commonly regarded as admirable; or, in the face of one or another human blindness, they may ask in repetitive astonishment, "How dumb can people be?" But they seem never to be surprised at what mankind, initially helpless and ignorant before the raw forces of nature, has managed to learn, make, and pass along as science, technology, art, law, political and social institutions, and general standards of civility. They are, in effect, still children who

take for granted the goods that come to them and who feel
not only deprived but affronted when things do not fit their
pattern of what should be.

A related form of gratitude is the type we feel to all who
have helped us grow in body and mind. This normally means
some measure of solid gratitude toward those who fed,
clothed, and kept us warm through the stages of our infant
dependence; who comforted us when we cried for comfort;
who first inducted us into patterns of behavior that have
since kept us from being blatant or shrinking misfits among
our human fellows; who helped us to learn that disappointment, loss, and grief can be survived; and who, by words
and contagious actions, helped us gradually to put some content into such abstract terms as truth, justice, mercy, integrity, and love.

Occasions for this type of gratitude, however, do not end
when we are supposedly grown-up; for the "grown-up" human being still has growing to do. As long as he lives, he has
occasion to add knowledge. As long as he lives, moreover, he
remains variously shortsighted, confused, and ego-centered.
As long as he lives, therefore, he has reason to be grateful
to those who somehow stir him out of apathy, complacency,
narrow specialization, and stereotyped thought into some
new learning.

Recently, we were visiting in a home where a very new
mother had just survived—barely survived, she said—the
ordeal of giving for the first time without help a bath to her
first baby. Exhausted from the slippery encounter, she sat
with her feet up on a hassock and relaxed. "Boy," she said,
"am I an infant when it comes to taking care of an infant!
And am I grateful to that nurse for what she taught me
about what to do!"

To feel grateful for experiences of growth is also, as a rule, to feel grateful for the gift of life; and gratitude for the gift of life has a way of turning into gratitude for being able to give as well as to receive.

Edwin Arlington Robinson writes of

> "Two kinds of gratitude: the sudden kind
> We feel for what we take, the larger kind
> We feel for what we give." [1]

Once we have learned this larger kind of gratitude, he goes on to say, we have learned a truth that has "been told over to the world a thousand times," but that the world has never rightly understood.

This truth, underscored alike by men of spiritual insight throughout history and by men of psychological insight today, is: *that the sound direction of growth for every human being is away from the infantile state of merely receiving, and of taking what he receives for granted as his due, toward the mature state of both giving and receiving—and of being grateful for the chance to do both.*

The emotionally disturbed individual—the "problem person" in whom we so often discover our common shortcomings writ large—can never be truly grateful either in receiving or giving.

He cannot be grateful *in receiving* for two good reasons. In the first place, his anxious and angry self-concern prevents his ever coming close enough to other people to feel their problems as just as real and just as difficult as his own. From where he stands, their lives look easy. Therefore, it is right and natural, in his judgment, that they should minister to his needs. For them not to do so is plain selfishness.

[1] Edwin Arlington Robinson, "Captain Craig," in *Collected Poems*, p. 115. New York: The Macmillan Company, 1930.

Such sympathy as the disturbed individual can offer tends to be reserved for whatever people he has, so to speak, incorporated into his own ego: those with whom he has so closely identified or upon whom he has become so dependent that their troubles are felt as a threat to his own frail security. His anxious concern about them is not unlike an insecure child's concern about a parent: a child who can feel panic fear that something has happened, or will happen, to a parent but who cannot enter into that parent's genuine problems nor extend to him a selfless consideration.

The second reason why the emotionally disturbed person cannot be truly grateful for what he receives is that what he is given can never do for him what actually needs to be done. What he needs is a basic sense of security and self-respect. Nothing that anyone can give him *from the outside* can, for long, satisfy his inner lack. He can pretend gratitude, and even feel a brief semblance of it. But when his inner problem resumes command over him—when his deep insecurity and anger at life surge back—he will translate his lack of satisfaction into a feeling that he has not been given enough: that he has not been given what is properly due him. The sense of having been given a raw deal by someone or something, or by virtually everyone and by life itself, is simply not compatible with gratitude for receiving.

Neither is it compatible with *gratitude for the chance to give.* The deeply disturbed person is, in emotional terms, so needy a person that he can establish only a bargaining relationship with others; never a relationship of genuine mutuality. Giving is, for him, a kind of exigent *quid pro quo.* He does not give out of a profound appreciation of what he has received from life. He gives in the hope of receiving. He may give money, gifts, praise, flattery, attention, obsequious service, patient "chore work," blind loyalty. Yet he gives to receive: a sense of power, answering gifts, praise in return, affection, security, a sense of virtue, a feeling of importance.

This is why such an individual can never truly enact what we call in religious terms a "sense of stewardship." A sense of stewardship can be experienced only by those who have grown into a deep gratitude for both receiving and giving; for it is, in essence, a conviction that something of great worth has been given to them to use with respect, to care for, to improve if they can, and to pass on to others.

We discover here a reason why the person who is mature in gratitude seems, often, to have such effortless power to make other people want to do the best they can. He does not diminish them nor what they have to offer. For his sense of the reciprocities by which life is supported goes deep enough to make him endow with value and meaning much that is ordinarily dismissed as commonplace. Just as a few threads of color in a fabric may be important if they are part of the over-all plan that makes a room warm and inviting, so, to the grateful person's mind, even the "widow's mite" is important as part of the whole: the whole life that the human race *as a whole* is living on earth.

EIGHT

THE SPACE-MAKING PERSONALITY

WHAT QUALITIES in a person make him able to give other people room to be themselves? We have already considered a number of these. Yet the covering question may still be easier to ask than to answer; for we find that most of what we need to know about these qualities cannot, so far, be learned from the psychological sciences.

Gordon Allport has pointed out some of the reasons for this in his searching analysis of the prospects and present limitations of these sciences.[1] The rigorous aim of the psychologist, he shows, has been to bring his science into line with physics and mathematics. Therefore he has a "preference for visible externals." But much of what goes on in a personality is neither external nor visible. It is deeply hidden. Hence it cannot be demonstrated by laboratory experiments. Also, it is unique to the individual and therefore not, as scientific demonstration should be, repeatable.

This puts most of what we need to know about a person-

[1] Gordon Allport, *Becoming: Basic Considerations for a Psychology of Personality*, pp. 12–13. New Haven: Yale University Press, 1955.

139

ality outside the domain of "rigorous psychological science." And this is precisely why, Allport goes on to say, "so many psychologists fail to take an interest in the existential richness of life. . . . In their desire to emulate the established sciences, psychologists are tempted to tackle only those problems, and to work only on those organisms, that yield to acceptable operations." It is for this reason that they are especially averse to "problems having to do with complex motives, high-level integration, with conscience, freedom, and selfhood."

To be sure, clinical psychology and psychiatry have had to go deeper than laboratory psychology into the subtleties of human nature. But they, because of their therapeutic task, have been more concerned about the disturbed individual— the one who habitually feels cornered and who, in turn, often corners others in his effort to make himself secure— than they have been about the individual who has achieved "high-level integration." It is precisely this latter type, however, that we are here trying to discover: the one who has achieved such "at-homeness" with life that he can make room for others and invite them to feel at home and, in their turn, to make room for yet others.

In short, after we have assimilated the best insights the psychological sciences can give us, we still must search beyond them, in a direction which, we believe, psychologists will more often take in the future than they have in the past.

To put it briefly, we need to get as intimate a look as we can at what the individual feels and does when he is in the presence of certain other people, and *because he is in their presence*. This turning of attention to life that is being lived is, we note, the major thesis of Gordon Allport's book to which we have referred. It may well become the major thesis of an increasing number of psychological studies.

Such "research" will still fall far short of the stringencies of exact science. But it can bring us very close to ourselves. It invites us to appraise our person-to-person responses as accurately as we can, but not to dismiss them as irrelevant because they are personal and private.

Such person-to-person responses bring us closer, in plain fact, to certain aspects of psychological reality than does any other kind of evidence we know. Through them we are on the inside of life: we know what life feels like to at least one organism—the self. In short, our experiences of confident reaching out or of wary drawing back are themselves indubitably part of reality. To contend that, because they are intimately our own, they can tell us nothing we need to know about reality seems patently absurd.

It is equally absurd to discount what others report about their intimate experiences. Sometimes they report these voluntarily, in words—spoken or written. Often, however, the report they make is involuntary and nonverbal. Thus, when a shy person becomes visibly more shy than usual, he tells us, in effect, that he is experiencing his psychic environment as inhospitable. The person who bristles suddenly and converts a quiet conversation into an argument makes a similar report. He may outwardly be talking about almost anything under the sun; but what he reports is that inwardly he feels threatened, cornered, forced to defend himself. Why he feels this way is another story; *but that he does feel this way* is a fact made public by his behavior. It is, therefore, a fact objectively available to us not only in our own dealings with him but in our effort to discover what it is we do to one another that makes us bristle into self-defense or, in contrary fashion, open up in unguarded response.

It would, of course, be folly to confuse this type of evidence which we can draw from personal experience and literature with the type that disciplined, impersonal science

has to offer. But we need not make an *either-or* choice between the two. Our proper objective is to try to understand
the make-up of reality; and our personal responses—however elusive, wayward, and irrational they may appear—*are
reality.* They are drained of neither their reality nor their
relevance by the fact that they do not readily submit to the
external, repeatable methods of laboratory research.

We return, then, to our question: what qualities in a person make him able to give other people room to be themselves? And we find an answer quite simply by thinking of
individuals we have known in whose presence we have, in
one way or another, been made to feel the roominess of life.
From among a host of these, we select, almost at random,
a certain tax accountant who is also, we think, a very special
kind of human being. He cannot seem to look at the figures
of a tax return without seeing the individuals and the family
whose hopes and anxieties they report. Often we have lingered in his office far longer than necessary. We have done
so because we have learned that, in some mysterious way,
we would go out from his office more "civilized"—more
ready to practice civility—because we had been there. Our
own horizons would be wider, and our sense of life more
perceptive, for having listened to this man think aloud about
people and money.

If he had moralized about these, we would have attended
to our business as expeditiously as possible and been on our
way. If he had viewed the behaviors of "economic man" with
aloof tolerance or aloof contempt, we would have found ourselves another tax accountant. What has many times held us
there in his office has been the unobtrusive but unmistakable
affection he has extended to those whose annual successes
and failures, foresights and follies he has embalmed in tax
returns.

Without ever violating the privacy of any client; without ever naming a name, or giving any clue by which an individual might be identified, he has introduced us to fellow humans and has tacitly reminded us that they—all of them —are to be taken into account in any generalization we may shape up about "humanity."

The men and women he has talked about have had to remain for us types without names or faces; but they have not been stereotypes. They have been earners and savers; spenders and misers; gamblers and investors. They have been people of plan or of hasty impulse; people building up a business or—by reason of shiftlessness, fatigue, lack of basic interest in it, or old age—letting it slide; people honest only by the precise and narrow letter of the law or honest by the broad spirit of that law. As he has talked about them, they have risen and walked as human beings. They have walked into our minds—and we have had to make room for them.

This accountant illustrates, we believe, one basic quality of the type of personality we are trying to understand. This quality is the power to feel other human beings as real and alive. He has never told us what we "should" feel about anyone. He has simply thought aloud with us, his eyes holding the memory of faces he has looked at across his desk; and he has made our own world more spacious by inviting us to make it large enough to hold people as people.

A point here needs to be underscored. The genuine spacemaker, we have found, never provides room only for the person he happens to be with at a given time. He is, rather, able to provide it for this one person because he provides it for others also. His basic attitude toward life—reflected in what he chooses to say and how he says it, and even in his silences when he is thinking things over—is generous and inclusive rather than niggardly and exclusive. The person who happens to be with him feels this attitude as warmth and hospitality.

He is able, therefore, to release himself for the ventures of understanding.

We quoted earlier the line from James Oppenheim's poem, *The Slave:* "Free men set themselves free." The space-maker does not give freedom to anyone. What he does is to enable the other person to make it for himself. He creates an atmosphere in which this other person feels reassured enough to be able to risk behaving like a free human being; and in the process of thus behaving, he can stretch the margin of his world.

There is a second quality of the space-maker. We had this called to our attention recently by the description given of a certain doctor in Isabel Smith's book, *Wish I Might:* the moving story of her twenty-one years as a tubercular patient —and for the most part, a bedridden patient—at Lake Saranac.

Among the many persons who helped her keep the upper hand of both her unutterable boredom and her deep despair, Dr. Francis Trudeau, she writes, stood out as a mountain of strength. Yet what he did for her was so simple we could easily miss its significance. What he did was merely to be at once exacting and sympathetic; flexible and firm. At one and the same time, he extended to her a compassionate, personal, supportive warmth and, equally, an imperative expectation that she would bear up—not slump into self-pity or despair.

In spite of her best resolution, there were times in those long bedridden years when she did fall into black despair. But, she writes, it "wasn't comfortable or safe to fall, for if there was anything Dr. Trudeau hated, it was to find me huddled up under the bedclothes looking as if I had lost my last friend.

"At such times he'd stand towering over me in the doorway.

'My land, Izzy,' he would say, 'what's the matter? Lying there as though the end of the world had come.'"

Suddenly, however, having thus established the fact that her slump was nothing short of disgraceful, he would change his manner:

"'Are you sunk, girl?' he would ask. 'Come on now, tell me all about it.'

"That was all the encouragement I needed. Shamelessly I would lay my sorrows, a bursting bundle of them, right in his lap. . . . We faced the thing, whatever it was, head on; and once we had faced it together it seemed to shrink, to assume less terrifying proportions, even when there was nothing, actually, that could be done about the matter."[1]

The doctor might have been a "softy"—saying cheery nothings that, to a patient made hypersensitive by long suffering, would inevitably have sounded phony. He might have been a brisk disciplinarian, saying sharp words that made her shrink still more deeply into her despair. He might have been a "cold" personality to whom the ups and downs of her moods, like those of her temperature chart, were merely facts, not anything that aroused his concern; and to whom she herself was more an object than a person.

He was none of these. He was a man who knew both his medical job and human beings—and who profoundly respected and cared about both. As one who knew his medical job, he was aware of the stern requirements he had to set for a patient. As one who knew human beings, he was aware of the patient's deep longing for comfort. He knew, moreover, that a patient had to keep on good terms with himself if the interminable trial of illness was to be endured without permanent damage to the character structure. Therefore, he had to require the sort of behavior that would, in the long

[1] Isabel Smith, *Wish I Might*, pp. 64–65. New York: Harper and Brothers, 1955.

run, keep the patient's self-respect intact. To do less than this would be no kindness. But to do this *without kindness* would be impossible.

Dr. Trudeau, in brief, did not employ "effective tactics." He gave his knowledgeable and responsive self. His severity was balanced by sympathy, his firmness by flexibility; and in the creative blend of the two, terrors became less terrifying, resolution was strengthened, and space was even made for impossible hope.

When we came upon this passage in *Wish I Might*, we lingered over it long enough to put by the side of Dr. Trudeau a certain high school teacher.

We first sought the acquaintance of this teacher because of what her principal and several of her students and ex-students told us about her. To her principal, she was a teacher in whose classes one "problem student" after another was surprisingly remade. To her students—who were remarkably unanimous in their judgment—she was one who did not make things easy, but who was always fair; and who made them feel she liked them.

Translating the students' verdict into psychological language, we might say that she *structured* the classroom situation and then, within this frame of fair rules and of respect for "quality performance," made each student, in spite of his mistakes and shortcomings, feel accepted.

We would say that she thus provided the right sort of psychic space for her students to thrive in. That space was not so unmapped that they never had any idea where they were going; nor was it full of unexpected pitfalls put in their path by arbitrary authority; nor was it so untamed a wilderness that their own undisciplined impulses could run wild. It was *structured*, but not *constricted*. Within this reasonable frame of order, students did not feel trapped; did not have to be on guard. Gradually, therefore, they could practice the skills of moving out beyond themselves—toward one another and toward their studies. In short, they had the kind of room necessary for growth.

The normal individual, child or adult, does not want always to be indulged or to have his own way. When he is struggling with a problem, he does not want someone else simply to take it out of his hands and solve it for him. Neither does he want to be smothered in unexacting sympathy. He may accept indulgence if it is offered; but he will like neither himself nor the overindulgent other person any better on this account.

What the normal individual wants is to gain self-respect by finding his way around within his allotted portion of reality. He wants to measure up to what is called for by the various situations he meets. Exaggerated indulgence and sympathy invite him to stop short of delivering the goods himself—and short, therefore, of earning either enough self-confidence to go ahead toward what comes next or the type of self-respect that is based on accomplishment.

Exaggerated harshness similarly makes him stop short. It forces him to care less about earning self-respect by accomplishment than about defending himself. If his only chance to preserve what little sense he has of being a person depends upon his being constantly ready to attack or escape, he will scarcely grow toward wiser and more durable versions of selfhood.

There is this much, then, to be definitely said about the maker of psychic space. He not only releases people *from* entrapment, but releases them *into* a sense of actual roominess. The world into which he invites others contains the known and the yet to be learned; the familiar and unfamiliar; the simple and the complex. It is a world that is at once orderly and open—and therefore conducive to growth.

One type of situation in which space is all too commonly denied is the one in which there is a strong difference of opinion about what should be done. So commonly, in fact, does disagreement of this kind lead to mutual "crowding" that if it does not, we do well to ask why.

If, for example, we propose to someone that a certain thing be done, put our case as strongly as we can, and have our proposal rejected, we will normally suffer some sense of rebuff: of ego-diminishment. If we experience no such sense —and therefore no need to go on the defensive—we can guess that the person who has rejected our proposal has been a good space-maker.

We can illustrate with a recent experience. Talking with a certain man in an administrative post, we suggested— even strongly urged—a particular course of action with regard to a certain problem. He rejected our idea: decisively. Yet we felt neither affronted nor belittled. As we walked away from his office, we had no impulse to say, "Well . . . that's the last time we'll go to *him* with any suggestion!" On the contrary, we felt more confirmed than ever in our freedom to approach him with any ideas we thought worth while.

Why did we feel this way? We tried to answer that question; for our own state of mind told us that the way this man had treated us was a sound way for human beings to treat one another. What had he done? He had considered our idea before rejecting it: had listened with unhurried attention, with his eyes warm and thoughtful. And when he rejected it, he gave specific reasons: laid before us facts we had not known. Stating these facts objectively, and basing his decision upon them, he kept the situation from deteriorating into subjectivity: into an open or veiled competition of egos.

Also, there were things he did not do. He did not, after the manner of the emotionally insecure person, push off our suggestion as though it were a threat. Nor did he waver timidly between his judgment and ours, as though he could not trust his own except where it was bolstered up from the outside. Nor did he treat us as children who had to be wheedled into giving up our idea—as though it were a favorite "toy." In other words, he did not ease us into the experience of being turned down by pretending that our idea was "almost good" or had "great merit."

Being in a position to know what was wrong with our proposal, he did not have, nor did he pretend to have, high regard for it. But he respected us enough to keep the discussion of it on an adult level—and openly on an adult level, not taking easy refuge in "secret information." Also, he respected the untried possibilities of life enough to weigh honestly any idea honestly offered. Finally—and not least—his whole manner took it for granted that we were capable of being interested in facts and of bowing to the imperative they laid down.

When we left his office, we knew we had met a considering mind. At no point had we felt cornered. On the contrary, we had been given all the room we needed to walk around the problem and look at it from new angles.

Yet another quality of the space-maker calls for appraisal. Stated negatively, it is the power not to make the first ego-assertive gesture that it seems "natural"—or tempting—to make. It is a quality, however, that is best defined by being recognized in action.

In the course of a desultory conversation with an acquaintance, we brought up the name of a friend of ours, saying, "We understand you know So-and-so." The man to whom we were talking came to sudden, interested attention. "Yes. Yes, I know him." He waited for us to say more; but since our mention of this friend had been wholly casual, we added only, "He said he knew you." The man's interest deepened even further: "Did he tell you how we met?" Then, before we could say "No," he said to himself: "No. Of course, he wouldn't. But I'll tell you. . . ."

For a moment he sat reflectively silent. Then: "Our acquaintance goes back four years or so—maybe five—to a day when he walked into my office and introduced himself. The mayor had appointed him, shortly before that, as chairman of a citizens' committee to look into playground conditions. I didn't know anything about him. He was just a name to me. But I had been pushing another man for that chairmanship; and when I heard who had been appointed, I began shooting my mouth off to anyone who would listen. Not knowing what he had done to qualify him for the job, I said he hadn't done anything: that the mayor had appointed a Nobody—and probably wanted a Nobody who would see to it that the committee would make a few appropriate noises and then call it a day. . . ."

Again, he sat briefly silent, remembering; and then went on: "I was eloquent. Not very reasonable. Not informed, certainly. But eloquent. . . .

"Then one afternoon—when I had said my say all over town—he came into my office. Not angrily. He was more diffident than angry. He just came in and introduced himself; and as nearly as I can recall it now, he said, 'I'm told you think the mayor has made a pretty poor choice. I'm not sure you aren't right. But I don't think I'm as bad as I'm told you think I am . . . so I thought I'd come around and ask about your objections.' That was the first time I saw him give that shy, quizzical smile of his: you know it if you know him at all. 'It's not too late for me to resign if you can convince me,' he said—and waited for me to take up the ball. But I didn't even know where the ball was by that time. I could only mumble something about not knowing his qualifications. . . .

"He didn't say—as he might have—'You could have kept your mouth shut till you found out about them.' He just nodded and told me about his experience in public recreation: told it not in a way to show me up as an ignorant fool, but as though I had a right to know. . . .

"Almost before I knew what was happening, then, the whole business of what I had said about him was simply put behind us and we got down to talking about the real problem: how to get decent playgrounds in certain depressed areas. Before he left, he asked me to serve on the committee; and it wasn't any sense of civic duty that made me say *Yes*. I wouldn't have missed the chance to work with him . . . get to know him . . . find out what made a guy tick that could come in the way he had. . . ."

In psychological essence, what he thus told us about our friend was that he was able to postpone ego-assertive and ego-defensive gestures long enough to make it unnecessary to make them at all: long enough so that he could, instead, treat a situation as something in which the other person— even the opponent—also had a stake.

It may be worth returning, here, to a point made in Chapter I: to the fact that a competition of angry prides, once started, is hard to stop; and that if it is continued long enough, it is often the force that turns *conflict limited* into *conflict unlimited*. Blessed, therefore, we might say, is the person who does not make out of every slightest provocation a reason to hurry into angry self-defense: the person who can, instead, take time to establish a relationship in which no one—neither himself nor anyone else—feels compelled to prove himself by throwing his weight around.

It was out of another experience that we gained a further insight into what a person has to be in himself if he is to be a space-maker.

We shall not easily forget an evening spent with a friend

who had just come through a grueling investigation. It had been grueling in its duration and its publicity—and also in what had seemed the deliberately harassing manner of certain of the investigators. He had come through it, however, with success and dignity—and with no sign of bitterness.

We knew him well enough to ask what might have seemed a prying question: how had he steadied himself throughout the ordeal? what resources had he called upon?

He gave no brisk or flippant answer. Before he answered at all, he got up and walked around the room a couple of times. Then he said, "I called on everything I had . . . and needed it all."

Fragment by fragment, then, during the next couple of hours, he told us the psychological story of how he had lived through the hearings. With one part of his mind he had listened with all the alertness he could command to the questions put to him, and had framed his answers. But with another part he had called upon his inner resources.

In the terms we have been using, he thus made space for himself. At one time and another, he told us, he privately called upon the memory of Socrates and the remembered image of the Grand Tetons against the sky. With a split-second vividness he had relived a certain moment that came back to him out of the depression years. His father had come home to report the loss of his job. At the news, his mother had sat down on the nearest chair—and had continued to sit there, in a terrible silence, for long minutes. Then she had roused herself, got up, touched her husband's shoulder gently as she passed him by on her way back to the stove, and remarked, "Well, we're not dead yet."

As the hearings dragged on, he had called upon remembered fragments of poetry and the long look of a country road between wheat fields; upon the remembered decencies of people he had known and heroisms he had admired in life and history. "I came through all right," he said finally, "but I couldn't have done it alone."

That, perhaps, is the essence of *inner resource*. It is experience which the individual has made deeply his own in the process of living. It therefore returns to him, in time of need, to support him, to establish for him standards for his own conduct, and to surround him with a goodly company. At the same time, it enables him to push back the walls of immediate circumstance and to move as if the universe were lending him its spaciousness.

Just as Socrates observed long ago, when told that he should prepare for his death, that he had been preparing for it all his life, so this friend of ours might have said that he had been preparing for those hearings all his life. All his life, in one way and another, he had been learning how to make room for himself. Also—or therefore—he could make room for others: for their mistakes, confusions, mixed motives, fears, hostilities, honest blunderings, and plain bad manners. Thus he eluded not only the trap of outer circumstance but that of inner circumstance as well: he did not imprison himself within walls of bitterness.

On that evening, moreover, he made room for us: room that was serene and wide; hospitable to anything we might want to say. We remember how, as the hours passed, it seemed as natural as breathing to draw out of the private corners of our own minds our own "emergency resources" and put these into the good company of his.

Finally—because this catalogue of traits must come to an end somewhere—there is one further quality we have learned to associate with the person who can offer this gift of hospitality. Clarence Day once described it: "The test of a civilized person is first self-awareness, and then depth after depth of sincerity in self-confrontation. . . . 'Risky?' Yes;

like all exploring. But unless you are capable of this kind of thinking, where are you? No matter how able or great, you are still with the animals." [1]

He wrote this in tribute to a man who fell far short of being a model of virtue and wisdom. He was moody, excitable, often bombastic. But Day was willing to forgive him his many faults because of one virtue: *he always saw through his own stories.* No matter how convincing he made the tall tales of his own exploits, he did not fall into the trap of believing them.

This may seem an odd virtue to single out and credit with redemptive power. Yet most psychiatrists would, we think, agree on its importance; for the disturbed individuals who come their way are precisely those who have built up well-nigh impenetrable defenses against self-seeing and who, at one or another level of consciousness, have come to believe whatever they must believe to bolster their egos. Most psychiatrists would agree, also, with Day's afterthought: "The tricks of self-deceiving are too many and ingenious for most of us. . . ."

From the point of view of our present concern, we would say simply that the more prone a person is to self-deception, the less able he is to make space for others. He cannot grant them room to be themselves because he has to keep them in whatever roles he has assigned them in his own drama of ego-defense and ego-assertion.

Thus, among the self-deceived, there is the mother who "loves" her daughter too much to let her marry and leave home; the reformer who "loves" mankind, but can scarcely endure most people; the "efficient" person who scarcely notices the difference between a fellow human being and a piece of furniture; the "patriot" who finds no other service to his country quite so much to his liking as that of bearing

[1] Clarence Day, *After All*, p. 221. New York: Alfred A. Knopf, 1930.

witness against his neighbor—witness that he does not too carefully check for truth or falsity; the professor who, year after year, builds his own reputation for scholarship by publishing as his own, without thanks or credit, the researches of his graduate students; the delinquent youth who proves himself "brave" by acts of violence against helpless victims; the partisan—liberal, reactionary, Fascist, Communist, or whatever—who puts what is useful to the "Cause" above what is true; the government administrator who extends the definition of "top secret" to cover anything he would rather not have to explain to the public; the demagogue and the dictator who identify the common welfare with whatever advances their own power. These are but samples of the many who develop an almost unlimited capacity to believe what they tell themselves and who, with self-deceptions to maintain, become inevitably cruel.

Perhaps a word of caution is here called for: not everything that passes for self-awareness and self-examination has redemptive power. As C. S. Lewis has observed, it is altogether possible for a human being to indulge in long self-examination "without discovering any of those facts about himself which are perfectly clear to anyone who has ever lived in the same house with him or worked in the same office." [1] Those who live and work with a person know him *by how they are made to feel when he is around*. But he, for all his self-examination, may have discovered in his own motives and behaviors only what he went looking for: evidence to support his determined self-excusings, self-approvals, or self-seekings.

The person who grants psychic space to others—and who does so in a manner that leaves them unirritated and unobligated—may or may not have long deliberate periods of self-

[1] C. S. Lewis, *The Screwtape Letters*, pp. 20–21. New York: The Macmillan Company, 1943.

examination. But he is almost certain to have many moments of self-illumination: moments when he is surprised and humbled, and probably amused, to discover how truly he himself is described by the descriptions he is accustomed to give of the human race.

Self-awareness and self-confrontation are not, for such a person, exercises to be performed like a sort of daily dozen. They are not—to borrow a further phrase from Clarence Day—"heavily flavored with moral intentions." Neither are they a form of disguised self-indulgence. They are simply parts of his allover experience—his warm, interested, individuated experience—of getting on to the hang of things: himself included. His granting of space to others, in brief, is a natural, unself-conscious extension of his taste for reality and his willingness to let life itself be roomy.

As we said earlier in this chapter, our own firsthand contacts with people who make us feel that we have room to move will not yield us insights that fit into the same category as those derived from accurate scientific researches. In this intimately personal area, our experiences will and must remain impressionistic rather than precise and measurable. They will come to us, moreover, when they come. We will not be able to produce them, on laboratory schedule, as predictable and repeatable phenomena.

All this, however, is not to say that they are irrelevant to our understanding of what puts quality into life. So long as we do not pretend that they are more than they are, they can make a contribution not made by the more exact psychological researches or by the therapist's investigations of disturbed personalities.

In a recent letter, a friend of ours tried to pin down the peculiar contribution of a certain individual. He spoke of the understanding this person helped to bring "into the bruised egocentricities of other people's lives." To bring such understanding is, perhaps, as high a privilege as any one of us could ask. It is also a signal accomplishment—one that is not possible except to the individual who can grant "living space" to himself and others within a frame of reality that he himself takes to be spacious.

PART TWO

OUR STRUCTURED
RELATIONSHIPS

FUNCTION OF A LIFE ROLE

WE ARE INTERPERSONAL selves. We live our lives in human situations: in contexts. We can try, experimentally, to think strictly private thoughts about the self— "I myself"—as an independent and isolated entity. But we are likely to discover, very soon, that the alternative to having our minds go completely blank is that of thinking about ourselves *in relationship to:* to child, parent, husband or wife, friend, neighbor, fellow worker, competitor, or even stranger; to someone who reminds us of someone else; to someone we admire; to someone who gets on our nerves; to someone we wish we could feel less awkward with; or to plans and activities that involve other people.

Herman Melville wrote in *Moby Dick* that if you were to set the most absent-minded of men on his feet, and start him going, he would somehow find his way to water. We might say that if you were to set a man's thoughts "on their feet," and start them going, they would, by however direct or circuitous a route, find their way to another human being.

It is never enough, in short, for the individual to pronounce a definitive, world-excluding, "I am." He cannot know himself as an abstraction in limbo. The only way he can know himself is as a person living a life in one or another setting.

That we must learn to think about ourselves *in context* is one of the chief assignments laid down for us by modern psychology. It is an assignment, moreover, that is interestingly in line with all the major developments of twentieth-century science—not in the field of psychology alone, but in virtually every field.

Thus classical physics yielded to modern physics at the point where it gave up the concept of separate particles of matter able to pull and push one another without being internally changed in the process. The study of electromagnetism forced the development of a quite different concept: the "field theory." For that study made it evident that what goes on "between" particles is not one thing, while their inner structure remains unalterably another. The inner and outer were revealed as mutual modifiers. If the particles were to be truly understood at all, it was discovered, they had to be conceived of as involved in a field of force, not in terms of some once-for-all "inner" reality.

In the biological field, experiments in embryology dictated a similar change of concept. Whereas it had long been assumed that each cell of a living body performed a function irrevocably set for it by its inner structure, it was proved that cells could be induced to change their function when given a different environment. Thus, for example, an immature cell grafted into the eye region of an embryo surprisingly became eye tissue; but the same kind of cell took on a different function if it was grafted into the region of the ear. There, it became ear tissue. Thus, the very cells of the body were shown to *be themselves* only as they were *part of*.

Their functions indicated not their inviolable inner character but an involvement in the body's structure.

In psychology—where the pioneering work of Kurt Lewin and his associates has yielded invaluable insights—it has become more and more clear that it does not make sense, but only elaborate nonsense, to characterize any human individual out of context as an "isolate," with no reference to his "life space."

Developments in the field of psychiatry have taken a similar direction, and certain earlier assumptions have had to be left behind. According to those earlier assumptions, it was "obvious" that a mental patient carried within himself, so to speak, the pattern of his illness. As the number of case studies and therapeutic interviews have increased, however, a different picture has unfolded.

For one thing, it has become strikingly apparent that the "same patient" is not the "same person" with different therapists. The things he says are different. Such emotional symptoms as laughter and tears take on a different pattern, a different rhythm. He utilizes different mechanisms of self-defense. His whole conception of himself and of human society may apparently change. For another thing, it has become unmistakably clear that any patient comes to the psychiatrist's office out of some human context in which he has undergone certain emotional experiences; and it has become equally clear that when he leaves the psychiatrist's office, he will have to "be himself" in some other context. All this has led to the conclusion that diagnosis "must be diagnosis *in situ*, or *in vivo*—not the specification of a disease, but the specification of a disturbed relationship." [1]

[1] Gardner Murphy and Elizabeth Cattell, "Sullivan and Field Theory," Chapter V in *The Contributions of Harry Stack Sullivan: A Symposium*, p. 164. Edited by Patrick Mullahy. Hermitage Press, 1952. Copyright, 1952, by the William Alanson White Institute of Psychiatry, Psychoanalysis, and Psychology. We are indebted to this chapter not only for this specific quotation but for many of the details of the trend we are here describing.

In five terse words, Harry Stack Sullivan summed up the vital new orientation of the psychological and psychiatric sciences: "People behave in interpersonal fields." [1] Stated as a principle of therapy, this insight has progressed out of the clinic and psychiatrist's office into our everyday spheres of behavior and mutual influence—there to become part of our "new common sense."

It has been in the light of this insight that we have, in earlier chapters, dealt with the making of psychic space, or the denial of such space. We have been sizing up the many respects in which we are makers of one another by virtue of our being "environments" for one another.

To the word "influence" we thus restore something of its original meaning of "in flow"—though not its ancient meaning of a one-directional "in flow" from the stars to mankind. What we are coming to recognize is that the society of man can best be understood as a complex of mutual—and mutually transformative—"in flows." We can speak figuratively of our being pushed around—as though we were the separate, impenetrable particles of classical physics. But we speak a deeper truth, it seems, when we talk of a "field theory" of personality—thus taking account of what we become through mutual interaction.

In emphasizing in earlier chapters this fact of our mutual influence, we have dealt chiefly with specific occasions on which one person's attitude has determined the "space" another person has been able to move in—thereby helping to determine the kind of person he would be on that occasion.

In the present chapter, we wish to explore the web of sustained relationships we build with our world—or fail to build; and how these determine both what we become and

[1] Harry Stack Sullivan, "The Study of Psychiatry," *Psychiatry*, 10 (1947), 355–71.

what we count for in the human scene. We wish, in brief, to think about the roles we play.

The phrase "the roles we play" may evoke some resistance. It may seem to suggest "theatrical" ways of behavior that are "put on," contrived as a pretense. Both the dictionary and current psychological usage, however, grant the phrase a second meaning: that of any function that a person performs. It is in this sense that we shall be using the word *role*.

An individual may, at a committee meeting, act in the role of chairman; and for long years of his life, that same individual may act in the role of farmer, college professor, lawyer, or mechanic. He will probably act, also, in the roles of parent, neighbor, fellow member, fellow worker, friend, stranger among strangers. He will act in the role of citizen; and, more broadly, as a member of what we call western civilization; and still more broadly, as a resident of the modern world—rather than the ancient or medieval world.

The richness or poverty of our lives, their stability or instability, their integrity or lack of integrity, are not only conditioned but also expressed by the roles we assume and how we assume them. Each role puts us into a certain context. There, it operates in us as a *selective force*. It invites us to selective behavior: this action would be fitting; that would not. It invites us, also, to selective seeing: this is relevant; that is not.

We remember watching a seasoned traffic officer in New York City induct a beginner into that role. The two stood together in the middle of an intersection. The older man not only let the younger practice his new role but also, we noticed, in quiet intervals, called his attention to situations to which he would need to be alert. He inducted him, in brief, not only into fitting behaviors but also into selective seeing —and selective ignoring. He helped him to establish one kind of relationship with one aspect of reality: a traffic officer's relationship to pedestrians and cars. He probably did not urge him to take note of a certain face in the crowd that might hold an artist's attention; nor of another face that a doctor might look at a second time, reading in it the signs of illness.

Or we might take the role of discussion leader. There are certain things that a discussion leader does not do—or if he does, we can properly say that he has got his roles crossed. He does not deliver a lecture—though he may, in other contexts, be a lecturer; nor impose his opinions upon the group —though he may, in other roles, have firm convictions and speak up for them. He does not so abdicate his function as leader that the discussion wanders aimlessly. Yet on other occasions—in the role of host, for example—he may let people talk as they will on any subject to which the conversation happens to drift.

As his behavior is conditioned by his role, so is his seeing. Thus, he will be alert to notice that a certain hitherto silent person wants to speak up; but he will not absorbedly study, over the heads of the group, a map that happens to hang on the wall—though in a different role he may be a collector of maps.

Any role that we assume calls, in brief, not only for appropriate skills and alertness, but also for appropriate restraints and self-disciplines. It says to us both "Thou shalt" and "Thou shalt not." This is true of even a very specific role we take on only for one brief interval. It is demandingly and rewardingly true when the role is broad and sustained: the vocational role, for example, or the parental. It is most of all true when the role is life-embracing: when it is that of *believer* in some overspanning conception of life.

We might here give further thought to Gordon Allport's statement, quoted earlier, that "the devotee of democracy adopts a lifelong assignment in his human relations." This is to say, in effect, that for such a devotee the performance of all sub-roles—in the home, on the job, in the community, at the polling place—will have to be consonant with the democratic definition of human nature and of man's relationship to man. Whether directing traffic or driving in traffic, whether listening to a small child tell breathlessly of what she saw in the park or negotiating a dispute between labor and management, he will act in the role of democratic man —not of totalitarian man.

Or we might consider another statement by the same psychologist: "A man's religion . . . is his ultimate attempt to enlarge and complete his own personality by finding the supreme context in which he rightly belongs." [1] *The supreme context*—that which overspans all lesser contexts: this is the religious individual's proper frame of reference; and his role is that of enacting, in every smaller context, what his religion has to say about life.

Harry Emerson Fosdick has said that vital religion is like good music, in that it needs not defense but rendition. The role of the truly religious person is that of "rendering" his belief—without letting too many jangling discords mar the performance: discords that will appear if he, for whatever reason of expediency or convenience, steps out of his religious role when he steps into one or another sub-role: domestic, racial, vocational, political.

The roles we take on, by choice or circumstance, locate us within "fields of force." They determine the points at which we will be "environment" for other people, while they are "environment" for us: the points of our mutually transformative "in flow."

[1] Gordon Allport, *The Individual and His Religion*, p. 142. New York: The Macmillan Company, 1951.

As we come to understand what this means, we gain a new way of looking at both the tragedies and the possibilities of human experience. We note how commonly failures in life are failures to find proper roles or to live up to such roles. More happily, we begin to see that our best way of being useful to other people lies not in our coercing them into "proper" behavior, nor in telling them how to run their lives, but in our helping them in any way we can to locate themselves within roles within which they can, by sound performance, achieve both self-respect and a happy sense of belonging. What we can do for ourselves, moreover, to enrich our own lives, is of like sort: we can move into new contexts, learn what they rightly ask of us, and become more rewardingly ourselves as we lend ourselves to roles that are big enough to grow on.

Certain types of human failure that are, in essence, failures with respect to role, deserve special attention.

Thus, the neurotic individual—or in an even more extreme case, the psychotic—is one who sees himself in a role that is not, objectively, the one that is his. His behaviors, geared to his unrealistic self-image, are simply not those that fit the realities of his context.

We spoke earlier of the victim of neurotic self-pity. Let us look at him again from the angle of roles. The role in which such a person sees himself is that of one who is "put upon"; unappreciated; never given a chance. His words, tones of voice, behaviors, attitudes toward other people, all become expressions of this role. Not even goodwilled overtures or words of warm appreciation and gestures of affection will make him abandon his role as abused person; for this has perversely become for him a kind of haven. So long as he stays within it, he can feel right with himself—for whatever has gone wrong with his life can be attributed to an outside cause.

Therefore he has to be grudging and niggardly in his responses even to friendly and generous behavior. He has to see to it that his emotional balance sheet will show him always in the red: what comes to him from others must never be accounted enough to match what he needs or deserves. For if it were enough, he would be thrown back on the necessity of explaining to himself why he has not achieved inner security and outer significance in terms of accomplishment. When Rollo May singled out self-pity as the emotion that had never done anyone any good, he was underscoring its peculiar power to make an individual see himself as no one else sees him—or can be expected to see him in terms of his behaviors and objective circumstances.

The person who thus takes on the role of "victim" or "martyr" may make life miserable for only his family and neighbors. But he is emotionally kin to a far more destructive type. In *King Jasper*, Edwin Arlington Robinson writes of a certain zealot who would tear society to shreds in order to "reform" it,

> "Young Hebron has a grievance; and for those
> Whose eyes are lighted with a brain on fire,
> A grievance is a mission, a religion. . . ." [1]

We need scarcely elaborate the picture. Our twentieth-century world has come all too painfully to know "Young Hebron": the individual who moves from seeing himself *victimized by society* to seeing himself *as appointed to overthrow society*.

Emphasizing that the roots of mental illness lie, not within

[1] Edwin Arlington Robinson, "King Jasper," in *Collected Poems*, p. 1451. New York: The Macmillan Company, 1937.

the tissue system of the individual, but in the interaction of that individual and his life situation, Harry Stack Sullivan said that the final effect of therapy should be such that "the patient as known to himself" would be "much the same person as the patient behaving with others." [1] In terms of our present concern, we might say that the roles in which a healthy individual sees himself are ones that he can *act out* without either walling himself away from objective reality or coming into constant destructive conflict with it.

The neurotic and the psychotic are tragically fated to claim roles that either keep them in perpetual conflict with reality or compel them to insulate themselves against all challenging "in flow." The neurotic bully who never takes on an adversary of equal strength, and the insane person who sees himself as the resurrected Christ, have alike adopted roles that will not stand the test of objective reality.

Some individuals who have never felt happily at home within their human context retreat into the extreme isolation of the neurotic or psychotic role; others take a different course. They join some gang or movement that offers them a role that they find, or hope to find, emotionally palatable: *that of repudiating with strong companionship and support, and within a frame of justifying agreements, the world that has repudiated them.* These individuals are of intense concern to us today because of their tendency to show up in criminal and delinquent gangs, in hatemongering organizations, in irresponsible pressure groups, and among those who join totalitarian movements.

This dangerous tendency is well illustrated by certain findings of one of the research groups at Princeton University's Center of International Studies: a group which, under

[1] Harry Stack Sullivan, *Conceptions of Modern Psychiatry*, p. 117. Washington: William Alanson White Psychiatric Foundation, 1947.

the leadership of Gabriel A. Almond, devoted four years to a painstaking study of the appeals of Communism.

The group studied, on the one hand, the Communist media of communication—from Party "classics" to mass media—to learn how Communism was presented to different segments of society and to different levels of adherents, and what appeals were deemed to be effective for each group. It also studied susceptibility to these appeals as reported by 221 ex-Communists: "Of these, 64 were American, 50 were British, 56 were French, and 51 Italian. One hundred and fifteen had joined the party before 1935, and 106 in later years; 111 were working-class and 110 were middle-class (primarily intellectuals) in occupational background; 51 had held top party posts, 73 middle and low positions, and 97 were rank and filers. The great majority were persons who left in the 1940's and later." [1]

The study shows that no single stereotype fits the Communist Party. Yet there is strong evidence—particularly in the case of the American respondents—that those to whom the party appealed most strongly were individuals who had not found within their regular environments roles to which they could devote themselves with any assurance of winning an affirmative response from the people around them. In one sense or another, they were outsiders looking in—wanting terribly to be insiders; and they saw the Communist Party as a body within which they could become insiders in the double sense of having significance and having companionship.

Some were "self-made intellectuals" who, by studying on their own, had become mentally estranged from unintellectual families and associates without finding a substitute "home" within any regular intellectual community—or had,

---

[1] Gabriel A. Almond, *The Appeals of Communism,* p. xxi. Princeton University Press, 1954.

perhaps, established a "livelihood" relationship to such a community without really establishing a "life" relationship.

Some were young students who were more bookish than most and not at ease among the fellow students. To many of these, Communism seemed to offer not only friends with whom to do "scientific" thinking about social problems, but also a chance to be confirmed in their own feeling of superiority to their normal associates.

A significant number were foreign-born and first-generation Americans who seemed, emotionally, to belong nowhere: they had rejected one culture in their effort to become wholly "Americanized" and had themselves been rejected, or less than fully accepted, by another. Some belonged to minority groups, and felt themselves cast in the role of inferiors and menials regardless of their individual deserts.

A startling percentage of them were people who projected upon society the hostility that had been fostered in them by their own parents and other authorities. "More than 30 per cent of the American cases saw the party . . . as a means of gratifying their own desire for rebellion. . . ." [1]

Yet others—a number of them middle-class intellectuals —felt mentally and spiritually homeless: attached to no "neighborhood" save that which they and their kind made out of shared derogation of the *status quo.* They hungered for some channel through which they could express at once their resentments and their ideals, their contempt for "babbitry" and their wish to belong to "the people." Communism invited them into a fellowship of hard work: the Marxist millennium was to be an "earned utopia." Also, it invited them to despise for ideological and "idealistic" reasons what they already resented for personal reasons.

Regardless of backgrounds and types, most of the respond-

[1] *Op. cit.,* p. 103.

ents emphasized that, as Party members, they were in a role that not only permitted them to hate, but obligated them to hate. Many pointed out, also, that they were encouraged to feel themselves hated. In the words of one British respondent, "You maintained your devotion by being a persecuted minority with all the world against you."

All the world—but specifically those designated in the Communist "demonology" as the enemy: "The kinds of antagonists against which the hatred of the party was directed vary to some extent from one political setting to the next. For example, the Catholic Church appears to be a commonly perceived target of hatred in the Italian party. This is true to a lesser extent among the French respondents, and hardly appears at all among the Americans and British. There are certainly other specifically local antagonists such as the Tory Party in England, the Christian Democrats in Italy, governmental agencies such as the FBI and the Department of Justice in the United States." [1]

It is significant, however, that of all objects of hatred, the one most to be despised was the "turn-coat": the ex-Communist. The Party member, in brief, was not only assigned a role but was, to the extent that indoctrination could accomplish this effect, *chained to that role by his own emotional involvement.* He was so conditioned to accept loyalty to the Party *as an absolute* that he would have to pay high in the coin of self-doubting and self-hatred if he withdrew from it—and even higher if he withdrew and became an "informer." Despicable roles were thus defined for members as vividly and precisely as were "idealistic" roles.

In stressing this study of the appeals of Communism, we are pointing up a lesson we all need to learn if we are to be ready for the long pull against totalitarianism: namely, that

[1] *Op. cit.*, p. 131.

a society is vulnerable to the fanaticisms of resentment—
Communist, Fascist, or otherwise—to the extent that individuals and groups within it have been unable to find roles to
perform that both let them see themselves as worth while
and let them earn some matching approval from the people
around them. The perverse genius of Communism has lain in
its power to offer seemingly significant roles to strikingly
divergent individuals.

Perhaps we can best illustrate this power of the Communists to provide roles for the role-hungry by quoting five
different respondents who cooperated with the Princeton research group: "I didn't worry through the thick books on
Marx. I joined the party when it moved a widow's evicted
furniture back into her house. I thought it was right. That's
why I joined." (p. 101) "A political outlook based on a
Marxist and dialectical materialistic approach appealed to
me as an attempt at a scientific approach to politics . . . I
was young and restless and wanted to be positive about
something. . . ." (pp. 101–102) "There was so much that
you shared together that you understood, and didn't have to
argue about. . . . Then again, friendships were deeper because you were aware of the hostility of the outside world."
(p. 119) "The CP is a wonderful outlet for hostile and contemptuous feelings. You can be hostile without guilt because it's for something bigger than yourself—and not for
personal reasons." (p. 122) "I became the 'doer' instead of
the 'receiver' . . . I did things to other people. I learned to
do to other people what had been done to me. I acquired a
'knowing smile.' I learned to 'develop' people." (p. 143)

David Morton spoke for the psychologically homeless no
less than for the physically homeless when he wrote about

"Waifs of the roofless century, beaten and blown
    By winds veering and violent, smelling of war. . . ."[1]

[1] David Morton, *Housing Project*. Chattanooga *Times*, Dec. 4, 1952.

The proper mental and emotional home for the human being is a human context within which his personal qualities
are valuable and valued. Lacking such a home, he may only
feel, in the words of the old folk song, "It looks like I ain't
never going to cease my wandering." Or he may cease his
wandering: he may move into some spiritual slum that calls
itself a new housing project for the spirit of man.

Among the malcontents and extremists of the right we
find many who, in a different sense, feel excluded from their
proper roles. These individuals are far harder to classify
than are the Communists because they have no coherent
political philosophy; nor do they submit as a group to any
orderly discipline. Even though they seem to lay great stress
on conformity, conventionality, and submission to authority,
their emotional and political responses are basically anarchic.
Thus, it is highly misleading to call them fascists; and because of the potentially destructive rage that animates many
of their words and behaviors, it is even more misleading to
call them conservatives. They elude, indeed, all standard
ideological labels. In an effort to pin down their characteristics, Leonard Boasberg has called them *radical reactionaries,*
while Theodore W. Adorno and his associates, in *The Authoritarian Personality,* uses the term *pseudo-conservatives*
—as does Richard Hofstadter, borrowing from them. What
these various writers and social scientists thus try to capture in a name is the self-contradictory make-up of these
right wing extremists.

"The ideology of pseudo-conservatism can be characterized but not defined, because the pseudo-conservative
tends to be more than ordinarily incoherent about politics.
The lady who, when General Eisenhower's victory over
Senator Taft had finally become official, stalked out of the
Hilton Hotel declaiming, 'This means eight more years of
socialism' was probably a fairly good representative. . . .

So also were the gentlemen who, at the Freedom Congress held at Omaha . . . objected to Earl Warren's appointment to the Supreme Court with the assertion: 'Middle-of-the-road thinking can and will destroy us'; the general who spoke to the same group, demanding 'an Air Force capable of wiping out the Russian Air Force and industry in one sweep,' but also 'a material reduction in military expenditures'; the people who a few years ago believed simultaneously that we had no business to be fighting communism in Korea, but that the war should immediately be extended to an Asia-wide crusade against communism. . . ." [1]

Such inchoate political demands are not to be viewed with either amusement or contempt; for they point to acute psychic misery. "The restlessness, suspicion and fear manifested . . . give evidence of the real suffering which the pseudo-conservative experiences in his capacity as a citizen. He believes himself to be living in a world in which he is spied upon, plotted against, betrayed. . . . He feels that his liberties have been arbitrarily and outrageously invaded. He is opposed to almost everything that has happened in American politics for the past twenty years. . . . While he naturally does not like Soviet communism . . . he shows little interest in, is often indeed bitterly hostile to such realistic measures as might actually strengthen the United States vis-à-vis Russia. . . . He wants to have nothing to do with the democratic nations of Western Europe, which seem to draw more of his ire than the Soviet Communists, and he is opposed to all 'give-away programs' designed to aid and strengthen these nations. Indeed, he is likely to be antagonistic to most of the operations of our federal government except Congressional investigations, and to almost all of its expenditures. . . ." [2]

[1] Richard Hofstadter, "The Pseudo-Conservative Revolt," *The American Scholar,* Winter 1954–1955, pp. 11–12.
[2] *Op. cit.*, pp. 12–13.

Here again we do well to realize that we are dealing with "waifs of the roofless century." Nothing that any political party within an organized frame of government could do would satisfy them for long. Their demands and denunciations are not, in any true sense, political even when they are couched in political language. Rather, they represent, within an atmosphere charged with political issues, the desperate attempt of individuals to find objective explanations for their own acute anxiety and unhappiness.

What these extremists of the right chiefly tell us—no matter what they may seem to be talking about—is that they do not know where they belong within our society, which is also *their* society, and that they feel their personal world to be going from bad to worse. They hunger for status; but they have no secure sense of role.

Their very preoccupation with status is, indeed, a kind of key to their problem. To such anxious and alienated minds, we know, three questions are of vital importance—and remain forever unanswered: who am I? how should I feel about other people? what accounts for my not having the life I want and deserve? The emotional turmoil generated by these unanswered questions almost inevitably makes the individual wish for a system of order in which the answers would be automatic and dependable: in brief, a status system. A status system says to each individual, in effect, "You are So-and-so. You belong in this niche." It says also, "These other people belong here . . . and here . . . and here. Therefore, you'll be doing all right if you treat them thus and so." Finally, the person preoccupied with thinking about status has an answer to why things are going badly: the wrong people are on top.

Various studies that have been made of these extremists of the right suggest that their resentment stems from the fact that changing social and economic conditions have "robbed" them of a status that "once rightly belonged to them" or people like them, or that they "once rightly expected to achieve."

We have to make this distinction between "once rightly belonged" and "once rightly expected" because within pseudo-conservative ranks we find two very different types. We find individuals of old American stock whose fortunes have declined and who are under strong emotional compulsion to account in some ego-sustaining way for society's "change for the worse." But also we find many individuals of recent immigrant stock. Their emotional problem is also that of explaining to themselves a discrepancy between what they experience and what they feel they deserve.

While members of "old families" tend to join the pseudo-conservative ranks when their fortunes are declining, members of these "new families" tend to join when their economic fortunes are rising. For it is at this stage that certain emotional problems become acute—problems that they have hitherto assumed would disappear with the achieving of "success." Having shown themselves "good Americans" according to the formula laid down in the "American dream" —that of status earned by effort—they feel that they deserve not only what money can buy but also what money cannot buy: a secure sense of belonging and of significance. This is often denied to them—in part, because they are still treated as "almost ousiders" by the very groups they think of as most American; and in part, because, within their own minds and their own family circles, they are unable to achieve a comfortable harmony between the culture they are trying to cast off and the one they are trying to take on. To have succeeded in practical terms after long, self-denying effort, and then to find the emotional fruits of success still out of reach, is to be virtually compelled to find some explanation that bolsters rather than threatens the already diminished ego. The "logical" explanation is that society has changed for the worse— and that someone is to blame.

The *pattern of fear* in these extremists of the right is interestingly different from any that seems common among those who have found Communism appealing. Communists despise their adversaries as "soft," decadent, inferior in understanding of economic and political processes. Also, they believe—and are insistently taught—that history is on their side. Their fears are therefore, we might say, short-range, immediate, and practical. They are afraid of being found out—and therefore interrupted—in the activities assigned them by the Party; and they are afraid of being charged with "deviation" from the Party line. But they are not afraid of the ultimate outcome: the triumph of Communism is, for them, already set down in the book of the future, but not yet precisely dated.

On the other hand, although extremists of the right often despise their adversaries as "inherently" inferior—by reason of race, class, or what not—they simultaneously fear them as "smarter" than themselves; and their deepest fear is fear of the future—fear that they and their kind are "on the way out."

Because they feel that change has somehow been put over on them, they see the enemy as sinister and devious. Under present conditions, this almost guarantees their being anti-Communist—at any cost to our own way of life. Communism has provided them ready-made, we might say, the very type of "enemy" they emotionally demand: a conspiratorial enemy that works in the dark; and an enemy, moreover, that would put the "wrong" people on top. The trouble with anti-Communism of the extreme right, however, is that it is too much like Communism in its devil-angel pattern of thinking, in its disregard of personal liberties, and in its destructive preoccupation with tearing down rather than building up. We might almost say that these rightists are anti-Communists not because of what Communism is but because they themselves are *anti-:* more often than not they are anti-intellectual; anti-scientific; anti-labor; anti-Semitic; anti-foreign; anti-Negro; and, as the case may be, anti-Catholic or anti-Protestant. They are, in brief, against any group that can be represented, in one way or another, as responsible for our society's "change for the worse"; as having profited by that change; or simply as being "strange," "sinister," or "upstart."

It is pitiful, at times, to see how the sort of extreme rightist we are here describing will carry the ball for an entirely different and far more cynical type: the individual who has no compunction about exploiting the fears and tensions of our time to his own advantage. Such an individual—in contrast to those we have been talking about—is commonly one who enjoys a mounting sense of power: demagogic power, or extreme sudden wealth. Far from seeing himself as dispossessed, he says, in effect, "I am the State—or I soon will be." His counterpart among the Communists is the cold, cynical, manipulative leader: the one who says, "I learned to 'develop' people." He, like that leader, sees the future as his for the taking; he is on the offensive, not the defensive. Like that leader, again, he uses whatever language of appeal serves best to rally the support he wants—and among those whose support he finds useful are the frightened pseudo-conservatives who see themselves as about to be liquidated by the leftists. Anyone who wants to make a study of today's strange bedfellows might well take a look, for example, at the make-up of some group that is loudly proclaiming the income tax amendment to have been the work, if not of the devil, then at least of socialists and Communists. Communists are not the only ones who have been served by "dupes" and "fellow travelers."

We have lingered over these "cultural waifs" who join extremist groups of the left or right for three different reasons. In the first place, they point up the danger to personality inherent in an individual's lacking a sound sense of role: in his not knowing where he belongs nor how to make himself valued for what he is.

In the second place, they point up the danger to a free society inherent in the presence of a great many individuals who feel "lost"; and who, lacking a sound role, are driven to seek a substitute. Such persons, as we have noted, feel *unjustly deprived*—though they would be hard put to it, often, to state in rational terms who has deprived them of what. Their dominant emotions are anxiety and hostility. These emotions, therefore—not reasonableness nor good will—determine their choice of groups to join; and because their lives are inherently disordered, they are strongly drawn to the artificial, status-minded orderliness of totalitarian groups.

In the third place, these "waifs" put a peculiar challenge to the rest of us—and specifically to those of us who are trained to think in the areas of psychological and social science. We have to make sure that we ourselves do not, with regard to these exasperating and destructive types, get our own roles crossed. It is temptingly easy to do just this. As scientists, for example, we may try, in all objective sincerity, to understand the emotional make-up and obsessive problems of the pseudo-conservative. But all too often, when we are not specifically occupied with our analyses, we stop being scientists altogether and talk about these same pseudo-conservatives in the current stereotypes of our political, social, or intellectual fraternity. We are even tempted, many times, to exploit our scientific insights. We convert them, as it were, from *tools of understanding* to *tools of belittling*. We use the objective language of science for our own subjective purposes.

The inner confusions that make the pseudo-conservative what he is—and that make him anti-intellectual—also make him temptingly easy to show up as ridiculous. With the right

scientific terms at our command, it is no trick at all to dispose
of him and his inchoate political diatribes; or to hold him up
as an object on a pin to be coldly analyzed; or simply to
enjoy the reassurance of feeling superior to him. To the extent that we thus indulge ourselves, however, we too, in a
subtle but destructive way, become anti-scientific and anti-
intellectual.

It is no easy business to recognize human types as dangerous to the common welfare; to learn how to diminish their
influence; and to remember, all the while, their humanity,
their suffering, and their peculiar need. Yet this, it would
appear, is what our present situation and our emerging
knowledge require of us.

In addition to these we have mentioned, there are many
other types of defeat that report the individual's lack of a
proper role or his failure to grow up to its performance. But
all such defeats and failures that invite our understanding
and compassion simply point up what we said earlier in this
chapter: namely, that the human being is a creature of roles
and contexts.

A friend of ours wrote us, last summer, about having served
as co-ordinator of program and personnel for a ten-week project sponsored by one of the social agencies: "It was a most
demanding job while it lasted—24 hours a day. But I feel
happy about it, because I do know that I filled my role sat-
isfactorily." There, plainly stated, is one persistent clue to
human well-being: a sense of role worth performing—and
well performed.

As we have already noted, it is never enough for any one
of us to say, "I am." He has also to be able to say, "I am part
of. . . ." Or, differently stated, "We are." The "we," moreover, cannot be merely a device for magnifying the "I" or
making it feel more secure and important in opposition to

some excluded "they." It must be the sort of "we" that profoundly testifies to our being members one of another.

It does not necessarily take an unusual or "important" role to insure both the individual's sense of integrity and his sense of belonging. We recall, for example, in the old song, the buoyant Miller of the Dee who sang as he worked because he felt like singing. Questioned about the reason for his happiness, he replied, "I love my wife, I love my work, I love my children three." He felt good, in brief, about the way that he fitted into the human enterprise.

Or we think of Robert Frost's French Canadian friend, Baptiste, who, working on an axe-helve,

". . . knew how to make a short job long
For love of it, and yet not waste time either." [1]

Or of Sandburg's fish crier, on Maxwell Street, in Chicago, whose

"face is that of a man terribly glad to be selling fish,
terribly glad that God made fish, and customers to whom
he may call his wares from a pushcart." [2]

Or we think of a host of people we ourselves know: women who are, in Sandburg's phrase, "terribly glad" to be mothers to their children and wives to their husbands; teachers who, after long years in the classroom, are glad they went into teaching; musicians for whom the fact that music exists, and that they are privileged to compose it and play it, is an unending amazement; men in public office who hold that office to be a trust; garage mechanics whose fingers "love" the machines they work on; men and women who, beyond their vocations, have taken on one or another role within

[1] Robert Frost, "The Axe-Helve," in *Collected Poems,* p. 230. New York: Henry Holt and Company, 1939.
[2] Carl Sandburg, "Fish Crier," in *Complete Poems,* p. 10. Harcourt, Brace and Company, 1950.

their communities, and experience that role as a calling rather than a chore.

The role itself may seem ordinary in the extreme; or it may "concern the welfare and happiness of millions yet unborn" —as did the role of those who shaped our nation. But wherever the relationship between an individual and his role is a sound and happy one, we seem to discover a fivefold testimony of this fact: the individual willingly learns what he needs to learn to perform the role; he willingly disciplines his own passing impulses sufficiently to keep these from getting in the way of his proper performance; he willingly does the job better than he would have to do it just to "get by"; his feeling for his work is affirmative and affectionate; and he exhibits a comfortable, self-confident sense that he is "paying his way" in the human scene—making his contribution; doing something worth the effort it takes.

TEN

ROLES CHOSEN AND UNCHOSEN

MANY OF THE roles within which we make ourselves happily at home or remain lonely and resentful misfits are not of our own choosing. We are born into them; grow into them; are willed into them by our society; or are propelled into them by circumstances.

They may even represent half-choices on our part: choices made because they seemed to be, at the time, the only ones, or best ones, we could make within a given situation. Vocational choices for most people are probably of this sort: within a certain frame of necessity or opportunity, a decision is made and then lived with; and habits, attitudes, and relationships are built in terms of it.

Sometimes our roles are unanticipated by-products of choices we have made: unanticipated and even unwanted by-products, but nonetheless ours to live with. Thus, a woman we know married a specialist in land reclamation. In marrying him she committed herself to one role she did not really envision at the time and for which nothing in her young years had prepared her: namely, that of being homemaker—and human being—in a long succession of brief, makeshift, temporary homes in some of the most barren places on earth.

In any case—and this is the point that must be made—the free person is by no means one who is privileged to enact only, or even chiefly, roles of his own choosing. Primarily, he is one who has learned to move *with the mental and emotional outlooks of a free person* within the limits of "fated" roles and, in effect, to push back the constricting limits of these by exploring the possibilities they hold. In addition, he may also devise new roles for himself. But creativeness within and beyond our assigned roles must depend, it would appear, upon our having come to workable terms with ourselves in relation to these assigned roles.

No one—to start at the beginning—asks to be born; nor does he ask to be born a member of a certain household, sex, or race. No one, however, is likely to live a happy and fruitful life if he goes through his years reiterating the plaint that he did not ask to be born; or if his sustained attitude toward his family, sex, or race is one of bitter resentment.

Once having been born, moreover, each individual carries within himself—not by his choice—those urgencies of growth that will normally cast him, as time goes on, in the roles of child, adolescent, adult, and, if he lives long enough, old person. Moreover, the society that counts him a member will, at each stage, underscore his age-level by assigning him various roles, turning *child* into *school child; young man* into *member of the armed services; adult* into *worker, tax payer, citizen; old person* into *retired person.*

The individual may be ready or unready for any given role when the time comes for him to enact it. He may move into it willingly or reluctantly. In extreme case, he may even resist an assignment, his whole personality structure being ranged against it. He may say *No* to it deliberately, as the conscientious objector, for example, says *No* to military service—and accepts, by that decision, whatever alternative role his society prescribes. Or he may say *No* to it as a disturbed child says *No* to the role of *school child,* by becoming functionally ill on school mornings; as a grown man may say *No* to the role of *earner* by clinging fast to that of adolescent playboy; or as an elderly woman may make what we might call a cosmetic rejection of her role, disguising herself, in her own eyes at least, as the girl she once was.

It is significant to note, here, the difference between rejection of some specific role for reasons of conscience and neurotic rejection of the role appropriate to a next stage of life. Some of the noblest figures of our century are those that said *No* when the role of collaborationist was held out to them by a totalitarian invader of their country. Because of another role that they chose to enact in the full conscience of maturity, these individuals said *No* to a role they felt to be wrong—and assumed, deliberately, the burden and hazard of their decision. It is a very different matter when the victim of neurotic fixation or regression holds back from what comes next in the way of normal responsibility and opportunity.

Thus, the sullen, querulous, or explosive anger of the neurotic can often be understood as an insistent rebellion against the fact that he cannot simultaneously enjoy the comforts of regression—into dependence, irresponsibility, self-indulgence, tantrums—and the rewards of progression. His anger is, in effect, a demand that the people around him protect, placate, and pamper him as though he were a child but, at the same time, respect him and be companionable with him as though he were an adult. Wanting the benefits of two incompatible roles without the pains of either, he is constantly at odds with life.

Perhaps another distinction is also worth making: that between the habitual, angry regression of the neurotic and the occasional restorative "regression" that even the most mature individual allows himself—and must allow himself—from time to time. Residual immaturities, we know, dwell in all of us as long as we live. Every normal person, then, tends on occasion to forsake the role set for him by his current age-level and to reassume, briefly, some less responsible role that he has put behind him. In ways that do no harm to anyone, he plays hooky from his grown-up estate—and is wise in doing so. For it is a safe guess that anyone who is consistently trying to meet the daily demands of life as best he can will have moments when he feels like saying,

"My body is weary to death of my mischievous brain;
I am weary forever and ever of being brave. . . ." [1]

The difference between the sound person and the neurotic is not that the former *always* stays within the role "assigned" him at one or another age-level, while the latter repudiates that role. It is, rather, that when the sound person "regresses" he knows it: he simply takes time out from the thoughts and obligations of which he is "weary to death." Renewed, then, in body and mind, he voluntarily re-enters his accustomed role and goes ahead with the business of living.

He differs from the neurotic in another vital respect also: affectionately and without resentment or recrimination, he grants to other people their turn at "regression"; for he knows that in them, no less than in himself, a residual child lives on—and has a right to live on.

There are many roles that we assume, not because we have initially chosen them, but because we have been born

[1] Elinor Wylie, "Nebuchadnezzar," in *Collected Poems,* p. 48. New York: Alfred A. Knopf, 1933.

into them or have grown into them within one or another cultural frame. The decently responsible enactment of such roles constitutes for each of us a basic curriculum of living.

These are by no means, however, the only roles assigned us without our asking for them. Fate, accident—whatever we may call it—also plays a part in our lives and sets demands for us to meet. Thus, on a single day, recently, we received word that one friend of ours, hitherto a happy wife, had been cast in the role of widow; and that another friend —because a drunken driver failed to see him in a pedestrian crosswalk—had been cast in the role of permanent invalid.

Around the world, in any direction we look, we see those who have been thrust by accident, war, famine, flood, illness, or other disaster into painfully exacting roles—there to contrive, as best they can, a way of life and a reason for living; and there to exhibit, also, whatever quality of life is embodied in their personal make-up. The load of sorrow and loneliness and pain that rests upon the world today makes it imperative for us to understand how it is that human beings who enact their "fated" roles with dignity and courage go about doing so.

Last summer, we received a letter from a woman—a stranger to us, except that she knew us through our books —which began with these words: "This may be one of the last letters I will ever write. I am going blind. The diagnosis is conclusive; and it won't be long now. Before the darkness closes in, however, I want to say thanks to a number of people—you among them—from whom I have borrowed thoughts that will go with me into that darkness, to keep me company there."

She then went on to tell us, with no word of self-pity— but in words that left us humble and grateful—just what it was she had found in certain passages of our books that she felt would be of permanent use to her. She shared with us, also, some of her other "borrowings." She had gathered and memorized, for example, certain vivid lines of poetry because, she said, "As long as I can quote these to myself I will still be able to see moonlight on water and leaves falling in autumn." She was not, she made clear, intending to spend the rest of her life with her hands folded in her lap and her blind eyes remembering past beauties. She planned to find her way, as promptly as possible, into new skills and relationships—and most of all, into new ways of being useful. "But meanwhile," she wrote, "all I have learned and loved will stand by me."

We think, again, of a couple who telephoned us one evening to ask whether they could drop around and see us. They were acquaintances only, people with whom we had crossed paths a few times in professional circles. But they came and sat with us for long hours, before the fire; and when they left we were proud to know them. They needed, the husband said on arrival, to talk themselves out to someone who would just let them talk. They had been forced, that day, to accept with grim finality a fact that they had earlier refused to credit: namely, that their only child was mentally deficient. What they did, in effect, while we listened, was to define for themselves a parental role far different from the one they had deeply hoped to enact. They defined that role; accepted its painful demands; explored its possibilities; and tacitly promised each other the type of support that the long pull would require. Then they went out together into the night; and we, watching from the doorway, saw them as figures of more than individual courage. We could not help seeing them as part of the interminable procession of human beings who have taken on their fated roles and carried them through.

We might recall here, in different context, the story told

us by the friend of whom we spoke in Chapter VIII: the one whose mother, back in the depression years, had received the word of her husband's loss of job by first sitting, for long minutes, in a terrible silence; and then, as she returned to her work, touching her husband gently on the shoulder and saying, "Well, we aren't dead yet." In this story, perhaps, we find a clue to what it is, psychologically, that human beings do when they face the problem of shifting from a wanted to an unwanted role—as this woman had to shift from being *wife of a man with a job* to being *wife of a man out of work*.

It may take a person long minutes of "terrible silence," or sometimes long months and years, to come to terms with a role that he resists with all his make-up and yet knows he must accept with all that make-up if he is to maintain the integrity of his relationship to life. No matter how long the time-span, certain stages apparently have to be worked through. First, the stage of accepting the reality of the new role: letting it into consciousness instead of warding it off, so that it is not only known to exist, but felt to exist. Then, the stage of going deep down into the privacy of the self, there to rally whatever resources of strength and perspective have been built into the self "for keeps." In the third place, there is the stage of turning again toward the world in which a new enactment of permanent values has to be contrived.

This third stage of turning out toward the world again seems itself to involve two aspects: that of lining up specific things that can be done; and that of reaffirming unity, in one way or another, with fellow human beings. This is the stage at which the isolated, lonely "I" begins again, in word and action, to practice saying "we." In terms used in the preceding chapter, the individual puts himself, emotionally, back into a human context and accepts the fact that he is involved with others in a mutually transforming "in flow."

There would seem no need to labor the point further: the individual whose life is to be a "quality" performance, and not merely an endurance test or a study in self-indulgence or erraticism, has to make it that kind of performance by the way he enacts a multitude of roles he has not chosen for himself—some of which, at least, he would all too gladly change if he could.

The fact that we have or have not chosen a given role does not keep it from being ours—as long as we are in it. It does not alter the fact that we are, in that role, part of the mental and emotional environment of other people: people who, like ourselves, are having to "make do" within many unchosen roles. Nor does the distastefulness of the role alter the fact that if our performance of it, while it is inescapably or properly ours, is resentful and slipshod, the habits of thought and action thus established in us, and the distribution of energy thus determined, will tarnish our performance of even our chosen roles. Just as an individual can never become a truly cultivated person by being courteous only to "important" people, or to those from whom he wants something in return, while the rest of the human race bears the brunt of his incivility, so we cannot shape a sound life by performing well only those roles we have freely elected as ours.

Some of the imperatives, in brief, that pattern our human existence can be grim and painful affairs. Yet there is no way in which we can reject them without courting a still more tragic defeat than they impose. This is the testimony of religious seer and psychologist alike—and of countless ordinary human beings who have said in word and action, "Well, we aren't dead yet."

There are two Biblical passages that seem to us to be peculiarly relevant in this connection, because they point up two different aspects of our human obligation and privilege.

The first is that rending passage in which Jesus, facing the final agony of his life, prays that he may, if possible, be allowed to escape it, but then concludes, "Nevertheless not my will, but Thine, be done." Here we see, as it were, the archetype of an attitude which, wherever it shapes behavior, lifts it above mediocrity. The parents, for example, of the mentally deficient child spoke in the spirit of this passage as they sat with us that evening before the fire. They told how they had refused to believe the dreadful evidence of deficiency; had sought every type of test and counseling that might help them contradict that evidence; had gone through a stage of feeling that they could not face the role cut out for them and that they would simply have to make some arrangement for the child that would let them ignore and "forget" its existence. Yet, in the end, they bowed to the dictates of that role—because they cherished values that would, in the long run, have made the rejection of it unthinkable. They did not say in so many words, "Thy will be done"— at least, not to us; but they did say a kind of modest and prosy equivalent: "Well . . . if that's how things are going to be. . . ."

The second passage is the one in which James, defining religion that is pure and undefiled in the sight of God, makes it embrace the visiting of widows and orphans in their affliction: in brief, standing by other human beings when they have been cast in stern roles not of their choosing. Here again, we know, is a pattern of behavior that redeems life from mediocrity; for it constitutes a willing admission that whatever our human enterprise is within the universe, we are all in it together.

The person who has learned, with some fair measure of skill and happiness, to handle the basic roles assigned him by birth and growth; and who has further learned, with strength and tenderness, to deal with the fact that there is not much for a human being—whether himself or another—to do with a painful yet inescapable role except see it through as best he can, has his reward. He is also the person who is most likely to create, and happily to enact, roles of his own choosing that are good both for himself and for those who come within his sphere of influence.

The neurotic, of course, who rejects every demanding and distasteful role as not for him—or whose resentful enactment of such roles, when he cannot escape them, is in the spirit of "Why should this happen to *me?*"—may also create roles for himself. Some of these he may act out only in hostile daydreams. Others he may act out by maneuvering himself into one or another form of dependence and helplessness, so that someone else has to carry his load. Or he may make a role out of resentment pure and simple and see himself as big and brave in the enactment of it, as the bully does; or the criminal; or the dictator. But every role he creates will bear the trademark of his distortion: it will intensify, not modify, his own self-deceptions and self-justifications; it will consolidate, not relax, the fear-anger focus of his energies; and it will widen, not narrow, the gap between himself and his human fellows.

The person who is most free to create for himself, and to enact in the world of reality, roles that have the stuff of health in them is the one who is least fearfully or resentfully preoccupied with warding off "assigned" roles—whether these be the normal roles that go with the various stages of growing up, or the abnormally exacting roles thrust upon him by one or another disaster. The freedom of such a person is, in effect, a *freedom of attention.* Having liberated himself, in fair measure, from the emotions that wall a human being off from the world around him and turn him in upon himself, he is *at liberty* to explore the possibilities of his situation. He is also *at liberty* to move toward other people with understanding and good will.

We might return here, briefly, to the climactic episodes in the life of Jesus, and do some hypothetical thinking about them. He was betrayed into the hands of his captors almost immediately after he had said, "Thy will be done." He might conceivably still have won his reprieve by renouncing his beliefs. Or, doomed beyond reprieve by the fears and angers these beliefs had already generated, he might have gone to the cross fighting his fate at every step of the way: screaming, blaspheming, protesting, denouncing, pleading. That is to say, he might have done so except for one thing: namely, that he had meant it, with every fiber of his agonized being, when he had said, "Nevertheless not my will, but Thine, be done." Having thus accepted his role, he was able to turn his attention outward toward others. He was able, at the end, so to feel the reality of these others that he could say, "Father, forgive them; for they know not what they do."

Again we recognize an archetype in the area of behavior. Whenever a human being, whether happily or in agony, accepts *as his own* a role "assigned" to him by life, he earns the privilege of turning his attention away from himself and perceiving with new vividness what reality offers him as raw material for his understanding and appreciation.

The ways in which sound individuals create roles for themselves are well-nigh limitless in number and variety. In the vast majority of cases, what they actually do is to create roles within roles: within the established frame of their daily work, they put the stamp of their own spirit upon that work, so that it becomes uniquely theirs—no matter how many other people may be listed in the census as doing the same kind of job.

We might recall, for example, from the chapter on the

space-making personality, the teacher whose classroom was by no means just one more classroom. It was a place to which she herself had given unique identity: a place where "problem" students, one after another, could experience order, freedom, fairness, and affection so that they could progressively lend themselves to learning and enacting what life calls for. The role she happily created for herself, in brief, was that of making an environment in which students who had formerly cast themselves as enemies of all schooling—and, for that matter, of organized society—could find both means and incentive to change their roles and take on ones more conducive to healthy growth.

Or we might take another example. We have more than once heard it said of a certain member of a Congressional committee, "He's called the conscience of the committee." We have been struck, each time we have heard the phrase, by the tone of respect and even affection in which it was spoken. This would not have been true, we have realized, if the speaker had felt himself impelled to say, "He has set himself up as the conscience of the committee"; or "In his own eyes, he's the conscience of the committee." What was quite apparent was that the label was being voluntarily granted to him by others: others who were themselves men of conscience and who had watched him in action.

We set ourselves to find an explanation. A wide variety of individuals have, within recent years, come and gone as members of Congressional committees: men who have variously seemed worthy or unworthy of the tasks assigned them. What had this one man—who had not even been chairman—done to command unique respect and affection? How did he see the role that was his to perform?

The answer, as we began to piece it together, had no dramatic fanfare about it. It appeared to lie in the fact that this Congressman, modestly and tenaciously, and often in

anxiety of spirit, was treating his role as committee member
as one that influenced other people's life, liberty, and pursuit
of happiness.

We learned how invariably, for example, his treatment of
witnesses—even recalcitrant and obstreperous witnesses—
was civil treatment: the sort called for, not by their being
co-operative or otherwise, but quite simply by the fact of
their being human. We learned how tirelessly he had worked
for the bettering of committee procedures: for rules that
would not put the work of the committee at the mercy of
witnesses cynically intent on blocking it, but that would
guarantee fairness and minimize the erratic or self-interested
play of personality upon the processes of objective investigation.

We learned of one case where a very young witness,
rubbed the wrong way by some word or action on some committee member's part, turned abruptly stubborn, and proceeded to conduct himself in a manner well-nigh guaranteed
to put his future in jeopardy. When the witness had been dismissed by the committee, and had left the room, this Congressman excused himself and followed, followed almost on
the run, to catch the young witness and his wife—the latter in
tears—at the elevator. He talked with the young couple until
the wall of hurt stubbornness crumbled and an occasion was
set up for the straightening out of a human record.

Why, it might be asked, should a Congressman of the
United States virtually run down the hall to give a recalcitrant witness another chance? Why should he virtually plead
with that witness not to make disaster for himself and his
wife out of hurt pride? Or a very different question might
be asked: Why should he *not* do these things if his conception of his role as committee member was large enough to
make room for them?

The point here, we think, is that most human creativity

in role-making is usually exercised by people whose roles in life are broad enough to encompass many different interpretations of function. The term *doctor*, for example, may suggest a certain kind of training and activity, not suggested by the term *deep sea diver, housewife, policeman, taxicab driver, reporter*. In itself, however, the term does not tell how any individual doctor sees or enacts his role. It does not tell, therefore, whether he "corners" his patients, emotionally speaking, or gives them room to breathe and to grow. Does he see his own role as a tiresome routine? Or as a financially profitable line to be in? Or as a chance to belong to the human fellowship deeply and warmly, by ministering to people at the points of their anxiety, grief, and pain? We might say, "Albert Schweitzer is a doctor." But we would barely be opening up the subject of what he is; for we would, as yet, have said nothing about how he sees his medical role and what he has uniquely made of it.

Just as creativeness may be at work under such labels as teacher, lawyer, clerk, and Congressman, so it may be at work under such labels as widow, cripple, invalid, refugee. The terms suggest roles shaped and limited by "fate"; but do not tell what any given individual has made of his assigned role.

Many forms of creativeness that enrich life and give it distinction have to do with how roles are enacted by persons who put upon them the stamp of their own insight, devotion, and, often, their own sheer "aliveness": their blithe and resilient refusal to let circumstances get them down.

Other forms of creativeness, however, can best be understood as *extensions* of roles. We noted in the previous chapter that a role we take on, even briefly, operates in us as a force that makes for selective seeing and selective ignoring. The roles we take on day after day, year after year, naturally exert a potent influence upon what catches and holds our attention, and stirs our mind into action, even when we are not on the job. A man whose speciality, for example, is handwriting tells us that he can *never* look at a signature or at a written document without seeing the words through the lens of his skill. He cannot read even a letter from a friend or a member of his own family without having the experience—to his own amused exasperation—turn into a sort of "busman's holiday." Similarly, a trial lawyer tells us that he rarely meets and talks with a new acquaintance without soon finding himself trying to estimate how this person would be likely to act on the witness stand.

Such specialization of seeing may, of course, mean chiefly a narrowing of it. It may skew the individual's vision to the point where it skews him as a personality: where it almost dehumanizes him. But specialized vision may also be sensitized vision. It may, in its influence upon the person's relationship to life, have less to do with what is *ruled out of consciousness* than with what is *ruled into consciousness*. Where a basically sound human being looks at his world with the eyes that his knowledge and skill have given him, he is likely to see with his selective vision not only what is, but what might be—and what needs to be. This is why so many of the significant roles that people have created for themselves within our society have been logical extensions of vocational roles they were already enacting.

So numerous are examples of this sort of thing that we can pick them almost at random. We might take the case of Ernest Coulter who, back in 1904, was acting as clerk in the newly established children's court in New York City. Day after day, in his vocational capacity, he saw youngsters in trouble; and as he appraised the pattern that repeated itself in case after case, he began to realize that these youngsters in trouble characteristically were youngsters without warm, close relationships to fine adults. Having sized up things as they were, he looked beyond the courtroom with the eyes of his knowledge and caught a glimpse of what might be. What he thus saw moved him to take on a new role—and to draw others into that role. On a December night, in 1904, speaking to a men's club in a New York church, he told of the plight of the children who were brought to court. "Can nothing be done?" asked one member of the audience, when he had finished. Ernest Coulter had his answer ready: "Yes. If each of you forty men here would be a friend to one boy, forty boys would have their chance." "I'll take one," said the man who had asked the question. "And I"; "And I. . . ." So the Big Brother Movement came into being.

Or we can take another example. At a naval hospital, in 1945, two wounded sailors made a modest request: would it not be possible for them to have music lessons? The request was brought to the attention of Fritz Kreisler—and of others like him, who had both the expertness and the emotional capacity to respond to it: to respond to it by taking on a new role, and by inviting others to enact that role also. Since that time, the Hospitalized Veterans Service has provided more than 200,000 individual and group music sessions to veterans and servicemen at their physicians' requests. As a leaflet printed by the group points out, "It is far more than an entertainment resource. Its contributions to the rehabilitation teamwork process are now widely recognized, and the demand for extension of these services to more hospitals and more veterans greatly exceeds the organization's resources." When we read such a report and note on the cover of it, "Fritz Kreisler, Chairman," we know we are witness to one more of the countless cases in which our society has been enriched—and human suffering alleviated—because a person has looked at a situation with the eyes of his expertness and what he has thus seen has made him create a new role and take on its disciplines and obligations.

Kreisler himself writes, "In a long life devoted to music, nothing has moved me so much as the opportunity to serve some of our veterans who suffer from service-induced disabilities. . . . To see a boy, shut away in a Veterans Hospital, forgetting his personal tragedy and reaching for health through the healing rewards of music is truly inspiring."

The initial phrase, here, is of key importance: "In a long life devoted to music. . . ." Another person, explaining why he had assumed some different sort of voluntary role, might say, "In a long life devoted to teaching . . ."; or to law enforcement, or to the ministry, or to the study of nutrition, or to the park service, or to banking, or to road building, or to housing or city planning. In any case, he would be stating a fact that any one of us with a field of knowledge to call his own can try out for himself: namely, that an individual who views his world with the selective seeing his specialty grants him, plus the emotional warmth appropriate to his human estate, is likely to discover some point where a new role is called for. He may also discover within himself an incentive to create and assume that role.

There was a time when we ourselves were mildly irritated by the cultural habit of labeling people by role: chiefly, by vocational role. It seemed to us that it did not say much about the strange totality of a human being to say, off-handedly, "He's a mechanic"; or "She's a secretary"; or "He runs a hardware store." But we have, of recent years, come to feel differently about this. We have come to realize that the consistent roles people enact—roles chosen, unchosen, and half-chosen; roles vocational and "extracurricular"; established roles within which they find a place and new roles they create for themselves—are, in effect, the paths by which they make their journeys into the midst of life.

Thus, when a man goes, day after day, down to his store or his office, *he goes into the human situation by way of that store or office.* He enters a certain frame of experience within which to employ his basic habits and attitudes; within which, also, he will be progressively persuaded to do certain types of selective seeing and selective ignoring; and within which, finally, he will establish interpersonal relations with various fellow humans. In plain fact, then, we are saying something fairly significant about a person when we say, "He's a radio commentator"; or "He's a plumber." We still do not know, to be sure, whether he is a sound or a shoddy workman; a mature or an immature individual. But we do know something of importance about the "field of force" in which he and other people are involved, for better or worse, in a mutually transformative "in flow." We also know something of importance about the opportunities that are open to him for being the kind of person he believes in being.

We have come to feel thus about the significance of human roles and the manner of their enactment by simply acknowledging how deeply and willingly we ourselves belong to certain roles that ostensibly belong to us. But we have come to it also by realizing that most of the friends we value are closely identified in our minds with the roles they perform. "By their fruits ye shall know them." We know these friends by the way they handle the roles they call theirs. Many of them we met, in the first place, in terms of these roles. We have heard them talk about what they do—and what they see still to be done.

Thinking thus about the people we know, we sat down one recent evening with our address book for company. This book is, for us, a kind of "Who's Who" in the area of our interpersonal relations. It is by no means merely a list of names and street numbers. It is a reminder of experiences we have enjoyed, through the years, in many different parts of this country, with many different people: people whom we have met and come to know, for the most part, as fellow members, fellow workers, fellows in concern.

We sat down, then, with our address book. Opening it again and again at random, we simply took the top name on each page and thought about the individual in terms of the roles we know him as performing. It was like having an orchestra seat from which to watch, appreciatively, the enactment of the human drama. Radio commentator; staff member of the National Council of Churches; worker with Camp Fire Girls; teacher; psychiatrist; carpenter; owner of a restaurant; newsman for the Associated Press; landscape architect; artist; YWCA secretary; Director of a University Extension Division; representative of an electrical appliance company; consultant on human relations in industry; minister; librarian; college professor; housewife; photographer; member of the staff of a settlement house.

By way of these roles, these men and women make their useful and self-respecting entrance, day after day, into the broad field of responsibility and mutuality. But we know many of them by other roles, also: roles that they have elected, or created, or had thrust upon them. The housewife, for example, was program chairman of a local AAUW group at the time we first met her. We know the carpenter not only because he has, in that capacity, worked on our house, but also because he is the moving spirit of a certain folk dancing group. We know the landscape architect as teacher in an adult education center. We know the YWCA secretary as a valiant defender of civil liberties in a town where they are not always easy to defend. We know that one unpublicized role of the radio commentator has been that of helping at least two boys through college. We know the librarian also as a widow who is doing a first-rate job of bringing up three children.

Both the richness and the stability of a life are reported in the roles that are enacted and in the manner of their enactment. Both the richness and the stability of a culture are reported in roles enacted by its members—and, again, in the manner of their enactment. Once we know this much, and face its full implications, we know that it is by way of our own unchosen, half-chosen, and freely chosen roles that we stand our best chance to make some dent upon the human situation in the furtherance of the values we cherish.

ELEVEN

LIFE LINE TO CHILDHOOD

IT HAS BECOME a commonplace of psychology that many forms of "problem conduct" on the part of adults can properly be called *childish*. They express a carry-over of ego-centric, irresponsible attitudes that are normally outgrown —or at least, greatly modified—during the years of growing up.

Such analyses have helped us to understand types of adult misbehavior that might otherwise seem altogether random and inexplicable, and have emphasized the importance of sound growth. Yet we both distort our image of childhood and impoverish our conception of maturity if we fail to see that a happy child lives on in the happy and creative adult quite as truly as an insecure and demanding child lives on in the self-centered, obtuse, willful adult.

The plain fact is that no human being, no matter how full of wisdom or "full of years" he may be, ever puts his childhood completely and conclusively behind him. Nor should he. The vital contrast is not between a person's being childish or being fully mature. It is between being childishly immature or childlike in his maturity. One question, then, we can rightly ask about any adult—including ourselves: *what kind of child lives on in him?*

If the child who lives on in the grown person is chiefly a spoiled brat or a querulous, timid dependent—so that he constantly refuses to face up to the normal demands of adulthood—we can expect the individual's life to be marked by both inner and outer conflict.

But a very different sort of child may live on. This is the child who is an eager explorer of his world—full of questions about the make-up of things; interested; responsive; imaginative; close to the earth under his feet; ready to like people who are competent and friendly whether or not they are "important"; eager to try things out; playful, and yet often serious; intensely alive in the passing moment and yet given to daydreams that have the future in them; capable of being moved to laughter and tears. Where such is the nature of the residual child within the grown-up, there need be no conflict between that child and the adult self. Instead, the two, as good companions, can live and grow together, each better for the other's presence.

We remember one early spring day, several years ago, when the two of us, both convalescing from illness, were feeling particularly housebound. To our own minds, we were well enough to be out of doors in the sunshine, with the spongy growing earth under foot. But because the doctor said, "No," there we had to stay, safe—and trapped—within our wall-and-window enclosure. Toward the end of the afternoon, as we sat dawdling in front of the fire with books that we were tired of reading, a knock came at the door; and we opened to the most welcome of guests—an artist friend of ours. He stood on the doorstep, tall and windblown, wearing a plaid flannel shirt open at the neck. In one hand, he held an offering of pussywillows; in the other, a landscape he had been working on and wanted us to see. He had been out painting all day, he told us, and had decided to drop by on his way home. Welcoming him was like welcoming the out of doors that had been denied us.

He could stay only a few moments, he said. Yet afternoon had slipped into early evening before he left. For the three of us got talking, there in front of the fire, about how spring comes after winter—what the first signs are in different parts of the country; and then about form and color in painting. Setting up the canvas on which he had been at work, he showed us what he was driving at; and when we commented on the magic of a certain shade of green, he angled off to the history of oil paints and told us why this particular green, because of its metallic content, was different from other greens. Somehow, then, our talk drifted from color in painting to "color" in words; and we spent the better part of another hour savoring lines of poetry that we remembered.

How did it happen that this friend could thus bring into our living room both the immediacy of spring and the long discipline of art? We would say without hesitation that it was because he entered that room as both perennial child and mature adult. He had never put behind him the child's nearness to the earth: the joy of being right down with the grass, so to speak, almost feeling it grow. He had never let the tremendous importance of sun and shade, or of the textural difference between earth and air, be crowded out of his consciousness by "important" matters. Yet he neither painted nor talked about painting as a child would. Every word he spoke showed him to be at home within a long tradition: at home there because he had earned his place.

Where the child self and the grown-up self are thus happily fused in a personality structure, each brings to that fu-

sion unique and appropriate gifts. The child brings an awareness not yet narrowed by the blinders of habit and preoccupation. He brings, also, a certain untamed quality: an elusive power to remain free, and freely himself, in the midst
of demands and pressures that tend to put upon life the mark
of prudence and conformity. No happy child, we might say,
is ever quite taken in by adult pretensions; nor is he ever
wholly converted to the notion that order for order's sake—
or for safety's sake—is a supreme value. Thus, he adjusts
enough to enjoy the warmth of belonging and the satisfactions of meeting various standards of performance, but not
enough to let his privacy or his individuality be taken from
him. The happy child, moreover, wants to get on to the hang
of things; wants to try out his own hand and mind; is generous in his admirations; believes in the yet to be learned and
the yet to be tried.

What are the gifts that maturity brings? It brings gifts of
perspective; established purpose; a sense of responsibility
toward others; pride in good workmanship, and enough
knowledge and disciplined skill to be able to deliver the
goods. It brings, also, certain types of understanding that apparently do not become possible to a human being until
he has coped with his share of unwanted experiences—of
loss, disappointment, failure, grief—and come to terms with
these. Sandburg gives us the line, "Laughing even as an ignorant fighter laughs who has never lost a battle." [1] We do
not expect such "ignorant" laughter to be warmly inclusive;
nor do we expect that the individual whose laughter is of
this kind will, in other mood, be deeply sensitive to the
hurts that other people suffer or deeply appreciative of the
manner in which these others carry on in spite of the hurts.
One chief gift of maturity, in brief, is that of *seasoned* judg-

[1] Carl Sandburg, "Chicago," in *Complete Poems,* p. 3. Harcourt, Brace
and Company, 1950.

ment: judgment that does not confuse the tawdry with the excellent, but which recognizes that the excellent is not always easy to come by.

The fusion of child and adult that made our artist friend a welcome guest is a type of fusion we have noted and valued in many different people. We think, for example, of a certain biochemist. Is he at work or at play in his laboratory? Is he boy or man when he sets up an experiment? The only answer to either question is "Both." The intentness to find out and the eager sense of what is possible have been carried over unimpaired from childhood. But his skilled mind and fingers are not those of a child. Nor is his dedication to his job a child's dedication.

The more we think about it, the more we realize that the friends we most like to be with are invariably those in whom we can feel the fused presence of the child and the grown-up. The individual who really enjoys words and whose talk never becomes a monotonous repetition of worn phrases has kept alive in himself one vital aspect of childhood. The individual who enjoys some collection he has made—of stamps, minerals, wild flowers, or what not—is similarly enacting childhood. So is the person who has a comfortable respect for old clothes; who knows how to break out of a routine and take a holiday; who enjoys watching expertness at work; who just naturally stops to look at a bird in flight or at two puppies rolling together on a lawn; and who rarely finds any answer so conclusive that no further question stems from it. In like manner, a person is enacting childhood when he takes it for granted that the future is open, not closed; and that solutions to problems can somehow be figured out.

The more genuinely mature an individual is, the more unabashedly he lets himself remain, in certain respects, a child —and the more at home he feels with those who are still children. In contrast, the type of adult we call *childish* is not, as a rule, happy and at ease with children—nor are they at ease with him.

Such an adult may either indulge his childishness or try to repudiate it. To the extent that he indulges it, he cannot be to children what an adult properly is: someone they can rely on, who knows more than they do about the how and why of things. Instead, he is, bafflingly, a grown person who acts as they are told not to act. He grabs; sulks; loses his temper; shifts the blame to others when things go wrong; is jealous and demanding; makes promises he does not keep; gets out from under chores that are his to do. To the extent, on the other hand, that he repudiates his childishness but does not outgrow it, he is a baffling stranger to children. Holding his impulses sternly and watchfully in check, he acts more like an automaton than a human being. Even when he tries to talk or play with children, he can offer only what he has to offer: his own stiff uneasiness with life.

It is the person who has genuinely matured in the ways that make him a competent and responsible adult, without losing the flexible, creative interests of childhood, who thrives on being with children—as they thrive on being with him.

Robert Frost has pointed up for us one of life's finest reciprocities: that between youth and age. When he was young, he tells us, his teachers were the old. Sometimes, in the process of learning what they had to teach, he "suffered like a metal being cast." But he took on form. He moved into patterns of thought and conduct that had been part of human experience long before he was born. By the age of fifty, however, because he was not willing to be *only* a creature of form, he was seeking new teachers: "I go to school to youth to learn the future." [1]

[1] Robert Frost, "What Fifty Said," in *Collected Poems*, p. 344. New York: Henry Holt and Company, 1939.

We were reminded of Frost's words when we were told, recently, about a distinguished biologist—a man of international reputation—who misses no chance to go out into the fields and woods with his grandchildren.

We can be sure that he takes with him on these trips a store of knowledge so deep and well-seasoned that the youngsters, recognizing its authenticity, put to him question after eager question. This knowledge is one badge of his maturity.

There is, however, a second badge of his maturity: the fact that he is glad to "go to school to youth." His prime purpose in exploring forest and meadow with his grandchildren is not to instruct them but to be instructed by them. He reports that they—with their vital curiosities and untamed awareness—often draw his attention to what he would otherwise miss. Looking through their eyes at a world he is accustomed to see with the trained and channeled vision of a scientist, he sees a new heaven and a new earth. He becomes as a little child—and is all the better adult, and all the better biologist, for thus becoming.

In like vein, we think of the satisfaction and the constant sense of renewal that a musician friend of ours gets out of conducting a children's orchestra; or that another friend—a mailman by occupation—gets out of his work with a Boy Scout troop. Or we think of one psychologist we know who welcomes every chance to sit in where teen-agers are talking about their problems—from those of dating to those of arriving at religious convictions. He tells us that his experiences with teen-agers are for him a constant safeguard against stereotyped thinking in the area of human relations: not a session goes by without his being surprised both at the importance of some problem he has overlooked and at the honesty of the young people in facing questions that adults are cautiously inclined to avoid or authoritatively treat as disposed of once for all.

Perhaps as clarifying a story as we have of reciprocal friendship between youth and age is the one that Edwin Arlington Robinson gives us in *Isaac and Archibald:* a story of two old men, lifelong friends, who admitted the boy Robinson—then twelve years old—to their friendship.

On a certain summer day, he tells us—and this is all the plot the story needs—Isaac, having decided to walk over to Archibald's farm to see whether the oats were being cut, invited him to go along; and he

> "with a small boy's adhesiveness
> To competent old age, got up and went." [1]

Recalling the experience of that afternoon, he writes:

> "We walked together down the River Road,
> With all the warmth and wonder of the land
> Around us, and the wayside flash of leaves,—
> And Isaac said the day was glorious. . . ."

The day was glorious, but also hot; and the pace that Isaac set brought the boy Robinson to a point, long before Archibald's farm came in sight, where he felt he was sweating blood. Though he watched hopefully for some sign that Isaac too was slowing down, he found none—and had, in the end, to suggest outright that they stop and rest in the shade.

It was during this interval of rest, when the talk turned to Archibald, that the boy felt for the first time—with one of those premonitions that only childhood knows—that his familiar world was being touched by change. Isaac, talking as he would not have talked to a fellow adult, confided his lonely, growing awareness that Archibald—his closest friend —was failing in mind and body. What made Robinson, as he

[1] Edwin Arlington Robinson, "Isaac and Archibald," in *Collected Poems*, pp. 169–81. New York: The Macmillan Company, 1937.

listened, become less of a small boy than he had been even
an hour before was not so much what Isaac said as what he
himself abruptly understood: that the man at his side, who
seemed to be talking only of Archibald, was in fact trying to
fend off his own mortality.

Not until that moment had he ever really thought of Isaac
as old. Rather, this man had been one of the eternals in his
own young life; and Archibald had been another. Never until then, for that matter, had the term *old age* held much
meaning for him. But as Isaac talked to him—or thought
aloud to himself in the boy's presence—Robinson learned
what he had not known before: that life made up chiefly
of the past is a different thing from life made up chiefly of
the future.

Facing the fact of change in these durable old friends of
his, he learned another thing also: that he himself was changing. He was feeling a new kind of grown-up sympathy for
the man at his side. Moreover, as he realized that a relationship that had long been an intimate part of his life would
soon belong to the past, he found himself absorbed in a new
way with what his own future might hold.

So he listened, and thought his own thoughts; and the new
grown-up part of himself wanted to speak words of sympathy to Isaac that the shy, small-boy part of himself could
not quite bring out:

> "Therefore I watched the ground;
> And I was wondering what made the Lord
> Create a thing so nervous as an ant,
> When Isaac, with commendable unrest,
> Ordained that we should take the road again."

They took the road; and when they had reached their destina-
tion and Isaac had struck off across the fields to size up the
oats, Archibald stood looking after him—and confided to

Robinson what he would not have confided to any fellow adult: his lonely sense that Isaac was failing: he was not the man he used to be. . . .

Thus the boy added another cubit of understanding. But he was not yet grown up. He was simply growing—and enough of a composite, still, so that when the two old men sat down later to their game of seven-up he was content to lie beside them on the grass,

> "Calm and incorrigibly satisfied
> With apples and romance and ignorance,
> And the still smoke from Archibald's clay pipe."

Lying thus, looking across the fields, dreaming in part about stories he had been reading and, in other part, about what lay ahead of him in life, and half-way listening to the two old men, he found that

> "The present and the future and the past,
> Isaac and Archibald, the burning bush,
> The Trojans and the walls of Jericho,
> Were beautifully fused;"

Supper, tangible and welcome, took the place of daydreams, finally; and then, after the two old men had smoked a while, and the boy had watched them and thought his own comfortable thoughts,

> "the time came for the long walk home
> With Isaac in the twilight. . . ."

Remembering, across the years, the experiences of that afternoon and evening, Robinson recognized that they had held the makings of both humor and sympathy—the two not incompatible, because "there's a laughing that has honor in it." Perhaps, in fact, the growing that he himself did that day —as he both made his first acquaintance with the lonely self-deceptions of the old and faced his own future with new eyes—might best be defined as growth into a sense of perspective.

It would be foolish to ask who got the most out of such a friendship as we have here described between a twelve-year-old boy and two old men. In the best sense of the word, the relationship was reciprocal—as relationships between members of different age groups tend to be if they are allowed to take their right and natural form.

We recall a conversation we had, recently, with the mother of three children—the oldest of them going on ten. One problem after another, it seemed, had beset their household—until it would have been understandable if she and her husband had felt that fate was ganging up on them. "When I feel myself getting discouraged right down to the bottom layer," she told us, "I take the children on a picnic. They're so good for me when they're happy; and I'm a new person after I've been right down on the ground with them, digging, or have taken off my shoes and socks and gone wading. Besides . . . I don't want them to think I'm sunk. I'm not trying to overprotect them, mind you. They've got to know we have problems, and I'm not trying to make them think life is always easy. But I certainly don't want them ever to get the notion from me that having problems has to mean being flattened out by them."

Who gets the most out of these picnics—the mother who lets herself be a child again, or the children who are privileged to enjoy companionship with maturity? The answer again has to be that both thrive on the relationship. The mother can enter into it because she has grown up without disowning the child within herself. The children can enter into it—in more complex ways than they now realize—because even while they are occupied with wading and digging, they are also occupied with growing up: building their conception of what life is and how it is to be handled.

If we understand why these picnics are good for both mother and children, and why it is good for a distinguished biologist to explore the fields and woods with his grandchildren, and why it was good for both old Isaac and the boy Robinson to walk together down the River Road and talk as they went, we are in a position to understand why we should resolve that certain types of experiences must not be crowded out of life.

They must not be crowded out by anxiety, fatigue, sheer busyness, a too constant preoccupation with bringing the children up right, confused notions as to what "advantages" are or what has prestige value, or social pressures and expectations that tend, nowadays, to "stratify" our human activities by age-levels.

Experiences that bring different age-levels together in mutually fulfilling relationships are simply too good to lose out of life. Where they are lost, the creative child that quite properly lives on in every adult gets too little exercise, too little encouragement; and the future adult that lives in every child gets too little chance to learn the direction of sound growth.

It is a commonplace of sociology—and of ordinary observation—that certain forces within our society have been tending, for some generations now, to isolate different age-groups from one another. We know what these forces have been. We know, for example, that urbanization means, among other things, that family living-space has grown smaller and that it has therefore become less customary for grandparents to be included in the family unit. It means also that large schools have replaced small, so that few children now do their learning and reciting in the presence of those older and younger than themselves—as they did in the one-room school. We know that our present nomadism means that the child is less often surrounded than he used to be by a drove of "his cousins and his aunts." Again, we know that an economy in which the man works away from home—and often commutes to his work—is one in which children less often see their father actively engaged at the top level of his expertness; and have far less chance than they once had to be, so to speak, apprentices at his side.

While it is important for us to recognize these changes, we must not miss the fact that opposite trends are also apparent: that, in one way and another, by choice rather than socio-logical or economic compulsion, families are putting them-selves together again. The one-child family is becoming con-spicuously "dated." As the size of the family increases, each child in it automatically has the experience of associating with brothers and sisters older or younger than himself. Families, moreover, are playing together again as units, and are working together on projects that center in the home. The much discussed "do it yourself movement" becomes, in most homes, a "do it together movement." Further than this, the family *as a unit* is moving out into the community again. Increased church attendance on the part of the whole family is one sign of this. Another and different sign is that more and more adult education centers are introducing classes— from bird study to craft work—to which whole families are encouraged to come and for which special family rates are offered. The number of hotels and restaurants that now make special appeals to the family to come as a unit tells the same story.

Nor is it simply the individual family that is thus saying, in effect, that whom God has joined together, economic and social forces must not put asunder. What we might call the "community family" is also, unobtrusively, putting itself together again: as witness the number of groups in which adults voluntarily work with children and young people.

Waiting our turn at a drug store counter, one recent day, we heard someone back of us say to a companion, "I spent most of the weekend helping a bunch of small fry make radio sets." The voice sounded so quietly satisfied with the project that we turned to look, and saw that the speaker was not himself too many years beyond the stage of being "small fry." Who, we wondered, had most enjoyed the weekend: this boy who had lent his skill to a "bunch of small fry"— and who had, in the process, given himself a chance to do what he enjoyed doing—or the youngsters who were privileged to be with him, measuring themselves by the standard of his comparative maturity. We can be sure that the experience had been a happy one, and a sound one, for both. It had been a happy one because experiences built on interest, creativeness, and a will to learn can scarcely be otherwise.

We said earlier in this chapter that one role each of us must fulfill as long as he lives is that of being partly a child: if not an eager, searching, friendly child, then a timid, querulous, demanding one.

To the extent that we play fair with the child in ourselves we will know it to be right and natural to do two things: to make many occasions for being with those who are still young in years, and to enjoy the companionship of those who have, in their adulthood, happily fused the childlike and the mature.

In James Stephens' *The Crock of Gold*, we may remember, the woman chose to marry the old philosopher rather than either of two young suitors who had competed for her hand. So shocking was her choice to the young men that they put aside their differences and went to her together to ask her reason. She gave that reason: both of them, to her mind, were just tinkers going from place to place—absorbed with strictly practical concerns but with no eyes at all for the world around them. The philosopher, on the other hand, when she had met him had been walking along the road "looking for strange, high adventures"—and that was the sort of man to marry and spend a life with, no matter what his age might be.

To the unconvinced suitors, then, she put a question—a foolish-sounding question to literal minds: "When did either of you go out in the daylight looking for a god and you not caring what might happen to you or where you went?"

One suitor, answering for both, stated a plain, hardheaded view: that if you leave the gods alone, they'll leave you alone. But the woman saw through the answer: "I thought all along that you were a timid man. . . ."

We might take this incident as a kind of parable. The suitors were young. The philosopher was old. This difference between them was plain to see. But it took a discerning eye to discover what their behavior—even their way of walking along a road—told about them: that the suitors were already old men—old and rigid; but that the philosopher, ancient and scholarly, was young. He was young in the right way for a person to be young who is a grown-up member of the human species. In gaining his adult wisdom, he had not "unlearned" what a happy child knows: that there are fine, strange things to be found for the seeking; and that regardless of what is found, the search itself is fun.

The suitors, having repudiated the child within themselves, wanted only to feel assured that the gods would leave them alone. They did not want to be disturbed, confused, reminded of the rich disorderliness of life. But what the philosopher would most of all have feared was precisely that the gods might leave him alone: that he might stop being tantalized by the enigmatic make-up of things. Therefore, he had to take the initiative—going out as a child goes, with his mind on what there was to see rather than on what might happen to himself. The woman's wisdom in recognizing that he would be a good companion to walk with and think with about all sorts of things is the same wisdom that we show whenever we reach through to the perennial child in a fellow adult and let ourselves enjoy the creative, interested vitality of that child.

TWELVE

BRIDGES BETWEEN MINDS

AT A NEW YEAR'S EVE party, during the final hour of 1955, the usual prophecies were being made. Most of them were routine affairs, to be spoken and forgotten. But one was to be remembered. One man said, "I predict that the talking of both solemn and bad-tempered nonsense will reach an all-time high in 1956."

Certain of his listeners demurred—one on the ground that it would be impossible for any year to outdo the one just past so far as the output of nonsense was concerned; another on the ground that we seemed to be recovering our national sanity and that our talk would gradually reflect this fact.

But the prophet stood firm: the product that would pour out in unrestricted abundance during the year ahead would be words that made no sense at all. He ticked off his reasons for saying so. It would be an election year. It would be a year when the most talked-about domestic issue would be deseg-regation. On the world front, it would be a year when prep-arations for a shooting war, while continued in every country, would take second place to verbal maneuverings in a cold war. Here at home, it would be a year when extremists of the right would increasingly find that their haphazard charges of Communism and pro-Communism were falling on skeptical ears—or bored ears; and when they would, therefore, in frightened desperation, find even more wildly nonsensical things to say than had been their recent stock in trade. In unbroken continuity with all recent years, it would be one in which so-called "moderates," infected by extremism, would provide their share of immoderate talk.

It would be, further, a year in which a great many people would misquote a great many others, or quote them out of context, and then roundly denounce them for saying what they did not, in fact, say, or for meaning what they did not, in fact, mean.

It would be one in which a number of vital issues would be elaborately evaded; in which vital facts would be withheld from the public behind an elaborate façade of frankness; and in which nonexistent unity would, at one point and another, be elaborately declared to exist.

It would be a year when the human race would continue being human—and therefore prone to substitute positiveness of tone for accuracy of knowledge, rationalizations for reasons, and rumors for facts. It would be a year in which most people would, when they encountered disagreement, raise their voices and multiply their words, instead of quieting down and trying to find out what was on the other person's mind. It would be a year in which most people would continue, as always, to distrust both themselves and others enough that they would do a great deal of talking to cover up, rather than to express, their actual thoughts and feelings. It would be an anxious year—and therefore one in which most of us, occasionally at least, would pour out words to ease the nervous strain of keeping still.

In addition to all these reasons, this prophet singled out certain specific issues that would be coming up before Congress and specific investigations that were shaping up that seemed made to order for the talking of nonsense; and he singled out various individuals who, to his mind, could be relied upon to provide that talk.

If this man's prophecy had, in truth, applied to only one twelve-month span, we could just endure the flood of nonsense and then, when it had subsided, clean up after it and rebuild the washed-out bridges of understanding between minds. Unfortunately, however, the problem he thus dramatically posed is not bounded by the calendar. If we subtract a few incidentals—such as a presidential election—the "year" thus described is typical of the period in which we live: a period marked both by the enormous multiplication of words, spoken and written, and by a widespread irresponsibility toward the meaning of what is said and its long-range consequences.

We might take, here, just one sample of the sort of verbal nonsense our age produces: "The Kremlin has quietly recalled its top envoys in major Western capitals to discuss a new Soviet 'peace offensive' aimed at driving a wedge between the Western allies." [1] Is that word we read in this sentence really the word "peace?" The reporter acknowledges with quotation marks that the customary meaning is not to be attached to it. We would scarcely say, for example, "Blessed are the peace makers, for they will aim to drive wedges between nations friendly to one another."

Quotation marks have increasingly become, in the printed news of our day, a warning against treating familiar words as though they carried familiar meanings. But we cannot

[1] A dispatch from London in *The Washington Post and Times Herald,* February 14, 1956.

thus distinguish more than the smallest fraction of the ambiguities and misleading statements that are offered us as though they made good sense and were to be taken at face value. Few of us, moreover, are responsible enough, or free enough from self-deception, to put quotation marks around the nonsense we talk ourselves.

We have explored in earlier chapters the fact that each of us, moving around in a human environment, is a unit of mental and emotional influence. Each of us helps to establish the psychological atmosphere of every situation he enters. We do this, of course, not with our words alone or our manner of speaking them. Yet our words are important factors in determining the effect we have upon other people's thoughts, feelings, and behaviors. Because we are human, one of our constant roles is that of being "talking animals"; and the closer we can come to making this role one of "sense-talking animals," the better for ourselves and everyone around us.

"Communication . . . is a matter of interchange, of challenge and response in the human spirit." [1] *A matter of interchange.* . . . Here is one human being. There is another. They are obviously individual and separate. Yet we know something can "spark" between them. There can be "challenge and response." What we call *understanding* can be aimed for—and sometimes achieved. It will not be complete understanding. But since we never completely understand even ourselves, and yet manage to live with ourselves, the fact that our understanding of one another—or of issues, problems, and situations—is at best approximate rather than total is not a fact that need make us despair.

If we wish, in an age like ours, to encourage the talking of sense rather than nonsense, how do we go about it? What are

[1] F. Fraser Darling, "The Ecology of Man," *The American Scholar*, Winter 1955–1956, p. 39.

some of the sound and creative ways in which we can promote the human drama of *interchange?*

The new science of semantics aims to clarify questions like these from its own particular angle. It emphasizes the fact that what we call a common language is never, in truth, common to any two individuals who use it: experience always colors the meaning of words, and their emotional overtones. "What does a sentence say?—the thing the speaker had in mind or the thing the typical hearer gets?" [1]

To make even an amateur's venture into the field of semantics is, we believe, to gain a lesson in humility and patience, and is at least to be persuaded that the individual who fails to hear in our words what we think we have put into them is not automatically proved thereby to be either a fool or deliberately obtuse. Also, semantics reminds us that the first hasty interpretation we put upon another's words is not necessarily fair or accurate—and that it is, at best, our interpretation, not his.

The approach we wish to use here, however, is not that of semantics. We wish, rather, to ask what any one of us, moving around within the atmosphere of our time as a total personality, can do to increase the likelihood that sense will triumph over nonsense—or will at least hold its own.

The practices that lead to mutual understanding must, of course, stem from an honest will to have such understanding prevail. They must reflect a preference for having our human relationships proceed along lines of constructive good will rather than destructive antagonism and mutual liquidation. This fact may seem too obvious to mention. Yet we believe that it needs to be not only mentioned, but underscored. For there is no major issue today that is not being tested for its

[1] I. A. Richards, *The Republic of Plato, In a New Version Founded on Basic English*, p. 10. New York: W. W. Norton and Company, 1942.

explosive potential by those who, for personal or ideological reasons, would rather have us split up into irreconcilable camps than explore together the ways of practical give-and-take. If we permit such as these to reach with their calculated words our own latent unreasonablenesses—so that, in the name of all that is decent, we add our voices to the chorus of indecent nonsense—we are serving no good end, no matter how valiant we may like to think we are in behalf of a "good cause."

Assuming, however, that we would rather build bridges of understanding between minds than prevent their being built—or blow up those that already exist—how do we start? What can we do?

We ourselves have come to a sort of trial-and-error conclusion that at least eight practices are worth trying. Our own experience has been that where we have grossly fumbled our human relationships, or missed a chance to make them more happily sound, it has usually been because we have slipped up on one or another—or several—of these practices. And we believe that there have been many other occasions when even our imperfect and sometimes tardy practice of them has proved their value. Thus we have come to feel that, prosy as they may sound, and awkwardly as we may enact them at times, they constitute in this age of ready fears and angers, "the only wall/Between us and the dark." [1]

The first practice is simply that of moderation where powder keg problems are concerned. This means, first of all, that we must disabuse ourselves of the strangely prevalent notion that the person who takes a temperate, exploratory, middle course with regard to an issue is hedging on it. One of the oldest and most tempting errors to which we humans are

[1] Mark Van Doren, "Wit," in *Collected Poems 1922–1938*, p. 241. New York: Henry Holt and Company. Copyright by Mark Van Doren, 1939.

prone is that of identifying strength with a quick, unyielding readiness to take sides: which means, in effect, a readiness to see all issues as having two mutually exclusive sides, the right and the wrong.

We call this error a tempting one for several reasons. For one thing, it lets us cut short our hesitant, often clumsy processes of thought and move into action, which gives us a chance to see ourselves as decisive rather than indecisive. It also lets us release whatever physical and emotional tensions we may have built up. It puts the stamp of righteousness upon our hostile feelings. And further than this, the taking of sides is one of the easiest methods known of getting a firm sense of belonging.

The individual who elects the way of moderation, exploration, and, if possible, reconciliation where issues that induce ready angers and partisanships are concerned has to contend with enemies within and without—and on all sides.

The enemies within are subtle but nonetheless present: the weariness of dealing with complexity rather than simplicity; the self-doubtings that go with being told that one is evading an issue, sitting on the fence, trying to play safe, afraid to stand up and be counted; and, not least, the loneliness and often the practical disadvantage of being an outsider, caught in the cross fire between two camps and a favored target of both.

The enemies without are various. Some of them may be "friendly enemies" who make him feel that he rightly belongs on their side: that he has let them down; disappointed them; weakened the "cause." Others are enemies plain and simple—the most dangerous of them being those who thrive on conditions of blind conflict and who do not intend to let the exploring mind be described in any save derogatory terms.

Our very tradition and the structure of our society seem designed at times to discourage any effort we make to treat problems whole rather than to treat them as being made up of this side and that: our side and theirs. Politically, we make a decision between parties and vote for or against candidates and proposals. Thus, a bill that is to be voted on may contain elements we approve and other elements we disapprove; or it may have riders attached to it that are almost irrelevant to the original bill and even distasteful to its framers. Yet in the end, the only way to vote is for or against. A mixed proposition, in brief, has to be treated, here, as a two-sided proposition.

The notion that partisanship is the way of strength is encouraged by the practical fact that political bipartisanship is always a brief and unstable expedient, while the two-party system is of the very essence of our structure; and by the further fact that those we call "Independents" are independent only in the sense that they have to be wooed by both parties right up to the time of an election—at which time they will choose one to support.

When it comes to dealing with social and economic problems, we find again that our customary ways of talking are those that split the human race up into sides and that tend to ignore common ground between the sides: labor-management; North-South; rural-urban.

The individual who, when an issue comes up, wants to state as fairly as he can the truths that are on both sides and the problems that are common problems may even find that he is firmly reprimanded in phrases borrowed from our religious tradition: "He that is not with me is against me" . . . "No man can serve two masters. . . ." Thus put on the spot, he is likely to become self-defensive rather than properly amused at the assumption that the confused human issue he is trying to look at whole is, in its present and specific form, one on which God has taken sides.

Almost any situation we have to deal with is a mixed one.

It is mixed both in the causes that have brought it about and in the values it embodies. This is true in as ordinary a case as that of a child's saying "No" to a parental ruling. It is no less true, certainly, where the issue is desegregation, foreign aid, national sovereignty, States' rights, or the control of nuclear weapons.

At any given moment, and with regard to any given problem, we human beings move not in a two-dimensional reality called *here and now*, but in a three-dimensional reality, the third and deepest dimension of which is the past that lies behind the here and now. That past holds countless acts of wisdom and foolishness; countless efforts to solve immediate problems of survival and well-being; and countless mixed motives. Yet each person who lives in the present has been so related to that past through his personal experiences that certain aspects *of things as they now are* seem to him obviously right and natural and others obviously wrong.

The extremist mind always tries to exploit established habits and attitudes, vested interests, traditions, and deep loyalties of individuals and groups so that they will be defended as absolutely rather than partially right.

The far more exacting and lonely tactic of the moderating mind has to be one of *respecting* the established habits and attitudes, vested interests, traditions, and deep loyalties of individuals and groups on both sides of a given issue; and yet, at the same time, *inviting* those on both sides to think of these as able to be modified: as partly, rather than absolutely, right; as products of human history rather than of "nature."

When we say, then, that the first practice called for by the will to encourage mutual understanding and workable relationships, in an age like ours, is that of moderation, we are offering no counsel of weakness: no invitation to play safe. We are speaking of what we take to be the hardest of human enterprises—and yet one which is indispensable if an atmosphere in which problems can be solved is to be created and maintained.

A second practice is that of putting our minds at the disposal of others before we pass definitive judgment upon their words and actions. However we may phrase it to fit a specific occasion, the question we must learn to ask of one another comes down to this: "How does the situation look from where you stand?"

Pontius Pilate stands condemned in history because he asked a great question—"What is truth?"—and "waited not for an answer." In this age of many issues, involving people of many different backgrounds and many different stakes in the current scene, we may stand condemned in our turn unless we are willing to ask, before passing judgment, "What is *your* truth?"—and be patient enough to wait for an answer.

A third principle is that of trying to put our own experience and particularly our own specialized knowledge into words that can be understood—so that whatever of worth we have to offer stands a chance of being received.

Many centuries ago, Paul spoke cautionary terms to those whose religious expression took the form of "speaking in tongues":

> ". . . except ye utter by the tongue words easy to be understood, how shall it be known what is spoken? for ye shall speak into the air.
>
> Wherefore let him that speaketh in an unknown tongue pray that he may interpret." [1]

[1] I Corinthians, XIV, 9, 13.

Precisely because our civilization today is complex rather than simple, and because it has been enriched by many different kinds of specialized knowledge, each with its own technical language, we all seem to one another, at times, to be "speaking in tongues." Each of us, moreover, at the very time when he is speaking at the top level of his knowledge, is likely to have, again and again, the sudden frustrated feeling that he is speaking "into the air."

The temptation, when this occurs, is to retreat into the company of those who talk our specialized language and to give up trying to make ourselves understood by people at large. This is no true solution to the problem, however—for it simply means that the contribution we might make if our knowledge and skill could become part of the common climate of opinion remains unmade. Also, there are two specific dangers: first, that we will underestimate the intelligence and undervalue the experience of those who do not understand our particular knowledge and skill; and second, that they, put on the defensive by their inability to understand, will brand our knowledge as either impractical or dangerous.

While it is inevitable, then, that we must often speak in an "unknown tongue" if we are in any sense an expert, we need, as Paul observed, to pray that we "may interpret"— and to work hard enough at the job of interpretation to give our best knowledge and insights a fair chance to make a dent on the human situation.

A fourth principle can best be stated negatively. It is that of not using "loaded" words: words that beg the issue, by-pass the mind to reach raw emotions, or needlessly put other people on the spot, and therefore on the defensive.

We ourselves, years ago, became acutely conscious of what we called "horn and halo words." The adult education movement was, at that time, setting up all sorts of experimental groups for the exchange of ideas across lines of difference and disagreement. Forums, round tables, symposiums, panels —these were springing up all over the continent.

Taking part in many such groups, we became aware of how often potential understanding was blocked because one person or another could not resist using his favorite "label" words—bestowing a halo upon attitudes and causes he favored or attaching horns to those he opposed.

We became aware, also, of how often words were used as a kind of soothing syrup—to smooth over differences or to pretend that agreements had been reached when nothing of the sort had taken place. Thus, in situations set up to encourage the exchange of ideas, words were employed to establish a pseudo-benign atmosphere in which honest talk was smothered and all vigorous disagreements were made to seem like rowdy disturbers of the peace.

There are, we all know, a host of ways in which words can usurp the place of thought. One man of our acquaintance uses the term "semantic sabotage" to describe the dubious art of making legitimate practices seem illegitimate by applying to them odious labels that automatically alienate people. He notes, for example, that in the field of security investigations the word "informer"—long associated with the shady practices of the talebearer and stool pigeon—has been planted in the public mind with such calculated effect that it has crowded out the word "informant," which carries no such dubious connotation. Thus, a vital distinction has been wiped out: that between the responsible citizen who, because he is a citizen, puts at the command of duly constituted authorities such factual information as he believes they should rightly have for the safeguarding of the common welfare and, on the other hand, the irresponsible or self-seeking individual who makes a trade of talebearing or puts other people on the spot solely to save his own skin.

With this distinction well-nigh obliterated, all official efforts to dig out information about conspiratorial and subversive activities are made to seem shady practices; and the responsible citizen is hard put to it not to feel guilty if he helps them do their appointed job by giving them relevant facts that are at his command.

A second example of "semantic sabotage" is the use of the phrase "Fifth Amendment Communist." Here it is not the work of a specific arm of government that is sabotaged, but the Constitution itself. However much we may deplore the many instances of cynical, obstructive, or misguided resort to the Fifth Amendment, we can scarcely remain unconcerned about this verbal alienation of the public mind from one of the basic legal safeguards of our tradition.

It is not to be expected that even the most responsible among us will wholly refrain from the use of "loaded" terms. We are creatures of emotion—and would be a tepid lot if we were otherwise. Being creatures of emotion, we use words and phrases that are charged with emotion: use them for good and ill. But if we wish to build bridges of understanding between minds in a time when misunderstandings come easily and cut deep, we do well to watch our words. There seems no point in our using them to dig unbridgeable chasms where bridges are called for.

The fifth principle is that of crediting other people with the capacity to understand the best we have to offer; and therefore of putting this best at their disposal.

We ourselves learned a great deal on this score from one wise and valued friend: Father Jimmy Tompkins of Nova Scotia. This dedicated priest, living and working among poverty-stricken lobster fishermen, felt that no ideas he had in his own mind or could dig up from the human tradition were too good for the hard-working men and women of his parish. He hoped to inspire these people to build their own co-operatives: to raise themselves by their own bootstraps. To this end, he wanted them to think beyond their immediate hardships and get some dramatic sense of what it means to be a member of society and cope with its problems. Therefore —to his mind a wholly logical *therefore*—he introduced them to Plato's *Republic*.

Was this basic text of our western civilization so far beyond the grasp of these "ignorant" folk in an isolated coastal region that the offering of it was a quixotic gesture? One answer to that question came our way later: it was an eyewitness account of how a crew of these folk, working on a road building job, took turns reading Plato aloud while they sat eating lunch at the side of the road. Perhaps another answer is more tangible: the solid co-operative movement that has raised the economic level of the whole area, with its accompanying adult education movement.

Had Emerson and Father Jimmy ever crossed paths, they would, we think, have understood each other. For we recall how Emerson lent his copy of *The Republic* to a neighboring farmer who said, upon returning it, "That book has a great many of my idees."

Plato, of course, was not the only thinker whom Father Jimmy introduced to his parishioners. He had a habit, when he dropped in at some fisherman's cottage, of leaving on the kitchen table some book or magazine article or perhaps a clipping from the daily paper. "I wish you'd read this," he would say, "and let me know what you think about it next time I come."

We remember, from some years back, one prominent

author's statement that if a book of his was widely read, he would doubt that it was much good. Contempt for the average human being's capacity to understand is not often so openly stated. It is, however, we have come to believe, dangerously widespread. It even taints the thoughts and behaviors of many who urgently defend the very institutions of freedom that have no ultimate defense except our abiding faith in man's capacity for self-government.

It is, of course, always tempting to believe that when our ideas do not get across to someone the fault lies in his incapacity to grasp them. It is tempting, also, to play safe by keeping most of our back-and-forth talk with other people on the level of the flippant or the obvious. But we have learned, when we feel thus tempted, to remember Father Jimmy—and other people we have known, and other people back through history, who have dared to believe that the best they had to offer was none too good for a fellow human being. Holding to the faith implanted in us by our contact with such as these, we have found it altogether right and natural, on more occasions than we can count, to talk of poetry, philosophy, psychology—or whatever we are caring most about—with people who might be supposed to have no interest in these things. Therefore, because of these occasions, we know what we know: that *the best bridges of understanding between minds are built out of the best materials those minds possess.*

The sixth principle is that of firmly declining to accept evasion or elaborate nonsense when we have a right to know the facts.

The citizen of a democracy, after all, is or should be a thinking creature. One of his perennial tasks is to get hold of the sort of information on which sound judgments can be based.

He must refuse, therefore, to be put off with shabby half-truths or with claims that security requires the withholding of answers to his questions.

We spoke above of the intellectual arrogance of those who do not put to the test the average person's capacity to understand because this is arbitrarily assumed to be inadequate. Here, we must note a corresponding arrogance on the part of various public administrators who adopt toward the average citizen the attitude that "papa knows best" and that "children should be seen and not heard."

With all proper respect for the successful business man or industrialist, and for his famed capacity to meet a payroll and produce the goods, we are forced to wonder many times, these days, whether his characteristic way of going at problems is what we most need in government. Within the economic world, the managerial mind deals with the human majority as *labor force* or as *consuming public,* but not, for the most part, as a body of individuals who have both a duty and a right to be in on the making or evaluating of policy decisions. Unless we misread what is happening, the citizenry today is far too often being treated as *consuming public.* "Goods"—in this case, policy—are to be produced in its behalf, properly advertised, and distributed. Public opinion polls are rated as useful in determining whether or not the goods are acceptable and the advertising successful—and also to get hints for new marketable products. But when citizens ask questions proper to their role as citizens—questions that the sound political mind would know at once to be legitimate and deserving of answers—the business mind in government seems often to be moved to impatience as though workers or customers were invading the managerial domain.

If we are to bring understanding to bear upon the problems of our time, and to carry our proper responsibility for the solution of those problems, we have to recover the art of asking questions of those in public office—and making sure, before we take *No* for an answer, that there is a better reason than the administrator's convenience for that answer's being *No* and not *Yes.* For just to the extent that we let ourselves be put off with half-answers or none, or simply abdicate our citizen role and let the administrators take it over, we ourselves will talk nonsense about what is going on and will simply add to the general confusion.

In the seventh place—and this can be briefly stated—there is the principle of making practical arrangements for mutual understanding.

One of the most profound arts, we believe, in the whole field of human relations is that of making it unnecessary for people to take stands for reasons of self-defense, which they then find hard to change for reasons of pride. Further than this, we believe that one of the best ways of practicing this art is to anticipate problems that are likely to divide people into warring camps and to set up machinery for "peaceful negotiation."

In one situation, this may mean the establishing of a family council; in another, the establishing of a labor-management board to adjudicate grievances; in yet another, the establishing of the United Nations. No machinery of this sort will function perfectly—particularly if it is set up, as in the case of the United Nations, to deal with problems around which ancient fears, hostilities, and loyalties already cluster. But the principle is sound: it is, in essence, that of letting people attach their self-respect to processes of mutual understanding rather than to those of proud "stand-pattism."

Finally, there is the principle of keeping still when adding to the talk would only add to the confusion. A great many human issues are made needlessly hard to resolve by the fact that nobody seems able or willing to keep still about them.

We do not recall, now, either the name or author of a magazine story in which, years ago, we encountered a certain schoolboy whom the other youngsters called Piggy; but we do remember a one-sentence description of him: "Piggy just couldn't not talk." Piggy, we are often inclined to feel, was a fairly typical human being. In any event, most of us miss a great many perfectly good chances to keep still.

Silence—not sullen or aloof silence, but simply one which gives things time to work out—can be of prime importance where powder keg issues are concerned. Wherever a problem to which old prides and angers are attached becomes, for one or another reason, an open issue, we can be fairly sure of two things: that the first impulsive statements made about it will express hair trigger emotions rather than considered thought, and will therefore sound intemperate; and that the answering statements sparked off by these will go them one better.

There is thus started, many times, a process that no one seems able to stop. As energies are focused for fight and flight, charges and countercharges are likely to form a mounting spiral; and this spiral may become that of a destructive cyclone if those who might well remain bystanders—or better yet, go quietly on about their business—feel obligated to join in the talk. Blessed, on such occasions, is the person who knows how to stay out of the fray; and even more blessed is he who knows how to give others a self-respecting chance to drop the subject and allow time and silence to do their healing work before talk is resumed.

Most people who have "blown their top" will, after a cooling-off period, return to an issue with more restraint—and more sense of long-range consequences—than they showed in their first emotional responses to it. But if no cooling-off period is offered them—and offered in terms acceptable to their angry pride—they may well, like the duelist we met in the first chapter of this book, end up committed to killing or being killed. One of the ways in which we can extend to others, in time of crisis, a chance to cool off is by simply keeping still ourselves—or, sometimes, by moving the talk toward the silence of thinking things over by making our remarks brief and quiet rather than inflammatory.

These eight ways, then, of encouraging understanding in an age of many destructive misunderstandings—and of trying to be on the side of sense rather than nonsense—seem to us worth trying. They will not always work; but they work well enough and often enough to justify the effort they take.

THIRTEEN

OUR BASIC HUMAN ROLE

LIFE GETS confused unless we have some deep sense of what it is about. Here we differ from all other living creatures. The acorn does not get confused about what it is intended to be. Naturally and "unthinkingly" it grows into an oak—which is its proper destiny. For fifty, a hundred, a hundred and fifty years, it acts out its role of oak tree and makes no mistake about it.

This is the way of nature's unthinking creatures. It is not the way of man. Man has mysteriously been granted the ability to think as part of his equipment; and thought has played the devil with him. Eating of the tree of the knowledge of good and evil, as the Bible story reports it, he gave up his "innocence"—an innocence like that of the acorn—and took on the confused sophistication of the thinking and evaluating creature.

Nevertheless, like every other living creature, man has his own role to play—that of being, not a tree or oyster or lion or whatever, but a human being. Although he has a role to play

—a form to grow into, a function to carry out—he is unlike every other creature in the fact that he does not grow into this role naturally, by just staying alive long enough. He has to decide for himself what his own basic role is; and he can be mistaken about the nature of his own nature.

Here is where our chief troubles have arisen. We have been as confused about ourselves, often—as uncertain about what our human nature is and what it requires of us—as an acorn would be if it were not sure whether its proper destiny was to be an oak or a cabbage.

We have already spoken of what happens when we are confused about particular roles in our lives: when we mistake bad ones for good, or get our roles crossed. But we are most deeply of all at odds with ourselves and our situation when, being human, we do not know what it basically means to be human—what this demands of us and also grants us.

Our basic human role may be distinguished from all the sub-roles we play—"doctor, lawyer, merchant, chief"—by its defining, so to speak, the *supreme context* within which we act out all our other roles. It is the framework within which we operate. Held within this framework, we are precluded from doing a lot of things other creatures are able to do— manufacturing chlorophyll for example; but also we are enabled to do things that other creatures cannot possibly do— analyzing chlorophyll, for example; or being just and merciful; walking humbly in the presence of the mysteries; building cities and symphonies.

It is deeply important, then, that we find out as best we can what is true about ourselves. It is deeply tragic when we get a completely wrong slant on ourselves—and distort ourselves and our environment in the process of acting out this wrong conception.

In this respect our history has been a mixed one. All sorts of assumptions have been made about our human nature, from the vaunting one that we are only a little lower than the angels, to the disparagingly pessimistic one—grown persuasive in our day—that we are just plain low.

Our human behavior, we have come to know, reflects what we think about ourselves. The child who has learned to think of himself as stupid, acts stupidly; while the child who has been helped to think of himself as competent and able to become still more competent regards learning as a privilege. We thus become, by and large, what we conceive ourselves as able to become. If, then, we have been taught to think about our common human nature in mistaken ways, we can be fairly sure that we will also have learned to act in mistaken ways: ways that involve us in destructive inner and outer conflict.

For some four hundred years, now, we of the western world have had our minds and actions shaped by a number of views about our human nature that we now need very seriously to reappraise. Not everyone, to be sure, who has lived in these centuries has been consciously shaped by these views. Most people, in fact, have known nothing about them. Nevertheless, even these unknowing ones have lived in a world where those who have known and believed these views have been able to create institutions and relationships after their pattern. Thus, even the unknowing ones have not been unaffected. The world they have lived in has been one variously made in the image of beliefs that have, in one serious way after another, misjudged human nature and given it wrong roles to play.

We begin with Machiavelli. We may think that because he has long since departed this world, we need not trouble ourselves about what he thought and wrote. But the "evil that men do lives after them"; and the Machiavellian conception of our human nature still plays a part in our lives. It is particularly prevalent in the realm of political practice; and, exerting more force than we commonly realize, it has subtly blocked the efforts of less cynical people to establish generous and honest practices.

The Machiavellian view of human nature was a simple one: distrust it. "If men were all good," he wrote, "this precept [of not keeping faith] would not be a good one, but as they are bad and could not observe their faith with you, so you are not bound to keep your faith with them." It was as simple as that.

Although this sentence of his was written in the 16th century, it still controls the minds of many. Its aim was to direct the attention of those in positions of power "away from an ideal world of truth and justice to the 'real' world of power, aggression and untruth. . . ." [1]

The role that Machiavelli thus indicated for the human being who was to "do" things—count for something, exert authority, make himself felt, not be a human cipher—was that of wary watchfulness, clever deception, and ingenious counterattack. He found no place in our basic human nature for confidence in one another and a willing effort to work together.

In the 18th century, Barbara Ward reminds us, some limits were still placed upon the Machiavellian roles in international politics. Diplomacy was conducted "under a sort of umbrella of decency. There were degrees of lying and treachery that lay beyond the accepted limit." It was not until the coming of the totalitarian state, in our own time, that the "boundless lying and limitless bad faith" implicit in the Machiavellian view were openly practiced. "Then the moderate Machiavellians of the type of Mr. Neville Chamberlain . . . were completely bewildered and defeated by the

[1] Barbara Ward, *Faith and Freedom*, p. 114. New York: W. W. Norton and Company, 1954.

total Machiavellian Hitler, who announced the end of his territorial ambitions in one breath and his new claims in the next." Today, we witness the Machiavellian cynicism of Russian propaganda "in which to invade is to 'liberate,' to exploit is to 'reconstruct,' and to 'seek peace' is to arm to the teeth." [1]

In Machiavellianism, in short, our major human role is defined as one of *unlimited* mutual distrust and deception. The total Machiavellians of our time have rendered the perverse service of making unmistakably clear the catastrophic but hitherto half-concealed logic of such a view. If mutual good will and the keeping of faith have no basis in human nature, then the enactment of them is unnatural, while the repudiation of them is natural: the more complete the repudiation, the better.

Most of us have been horrified by *total* Machiavellianism. Nothing like this was envisioned by even our most cynical and self-seeking definitions of political "realism." Yet we dare not miss the fact that the total Machiavellians were able to consolidate their power to a point where they could venture to impose it, first upon their own people, and then upon one nation after another—with world conquest in view—precisely because countless "moderate Machiavellians" were not deeply shocked by either their philosophy or their tactics until these had found immoderate expression—and had done immoderate, irreparable harm.

Out of the 17th century came Thomas Hobbes's forthright invitation to think "realistically," not "sentimentally," about ourselves. What he had to say about us does not make pretty reading. In our natural state, he declared—that is, in our essential nature—we are incurable egoists, each unwilling to give up one iota of what he wants. In that natural state

[1] *Op. cit.*, p. 113.

there is "continual fear and danger of violent death, and the life of man solitary, poor, nasty, brutish, and short." [1] Our only hope lies in our surrendering some part of our egocentric willfulness to a strong government—*Leviathan,* he called it. Only thus, according to his view, can our living together be made tolerable. Nothing can make it happy. To make it even tolerable is an accomplishment: an accomplishment only possible for a government strong enough to force us to restrain our natural egocentricity.

According to Hobbes, in short, we are, at the core of our being, incurably unsocial. Everything we do is done for ourselves: ourselves as separate from all other selves. Even when we seem to enjoy one another, or to commiserate with one another, we are still only self-concerned. Thus, pity for others, he declared, is no disinterested emotion. Pity expresses our imagining that a similar calamity may some day befall ourselves. Laughter is a "sudden glory" caused either by some act of our own that pleases us, or by our seeing in someone else some deformity that we are glad is not ours. Most amazingly, in his quaint idiom, he disposes of "disinterested jollity": "All pleasure and jollity of mind consists in this, even to get someone with whom comparing it may find somewhat wherein to triumph and vaunt itself." [2]

Here is a theory of the complete, ineradicable self-centeredness of human nature. Hobbes could not see us as *outgrowing* our infant egoisms by *growing into* relationships. In his view, the human being is destined to remain throughout life as incapable of genuine mutuality as he is at birth. He prescribed strong government, therefore, to keep us in livable relation to one another.

If we listen carefully to his words, they have a not unfamiliar sound. Hobbes's theory of how to deal with man's

[1] *Leviathan,* Chapter 13.
[2] *De Cive,* I, 2, 51.

untamed propensity to "deviate" in his own egocentric behalf finds application, today, in totalitarian regimentation.
Millions upon millions of people are being held in line "for
their own good" by governments that place small trust in
human nature except as it is thus firmly held in line and made
to be what it would not be of its own accord.

The names multiply as we move into the 18th, 19th, and
20th centuries. Rousseau; the pseudo-Darwin (that is, the
popular misconception of Darwin's ideas); Karl Marx; the
Freud of *Civilization and Its Discontents;* Mussolini, Hitler, Lenin, Stalin: all of these were powerful voices; and
all of them, in one way or another, outraged our human nature.

It goes against the grain a little to put Rousseau into company with these others; for he seems, at first blush, to be
overgenerous rather than undergenerous toward our human
selves. It is not until we take a deeper look at what he had
to say that we note its paradoxical character. He was indeed
generous toward our infant nature and child nature; but not
toward our nature in its maturity.

For Hobbes, as we have seen, government was a necessary
evil—made necessary by the evil inherent in human nature.
For Rousseau, government was just plain evil—for human
nature was inherently good. What man must do, according
to Rousseau, was to find his way back to what we might call
a pre-governmental stage. He must rediscover his "natural,"
uncontaminated self. He must obliterate the society that had
turned the good "child of nature" into evil man distorted by
law and government. Only after the going society was over-
thrown, could the good society be built from the ground
up, in the image of man's natural self. So came the Revolution, the overthrow of the old regime—and the Reign of
Terror.

If we put Hobbes and Rousseau side by side, we see that neither thought of society as a product of man's maturing. For Hobbes it was something necessarily imposed upon man's intractable egocentricities. For Rousseau it was something arbitrarily imposed—and destructively imposed—upon a nature that would have been good without it. For neither of them was society *man himself in the slow, difficult process of growing up.*

For millions of people throughout the world, Charles Darwin, almost overnight, came to mean "struggle for existence" and "survival of the fittest." A new bloody vision of life was thus introduced to the mind of man: "nature red in tooth and claw." The world, it suddenly appeared, was not the dwelling place of God but a gigantic battlefield where life struggled frantically against life, intent not to be crowded out.

This new view came just in the nick of time to ease the consciences of those who were moving in on the new Industrial Revolution. Sympathy, compunction, justice, mercy—particularly mercy—could now be catalogued as sentimental, unscientific. Life was a grim business of fighting for survival; and the fact of survival was proof of "fitness." Darwin had established it to be so; and man in his brief day had to treat it so.

The tragedy was that Darwin himself had never meant this; and in justice to the great naturalist, many have come to call this hasty, sanguinary view *pseudo-Darwinism.* Darwin, in fact, in contrast to Hobbes, saw man as possessed innately of "social instincts": a "will from the first . . . to aid his fellows, and some feeling for sympathy." As man's "sympathies became more tender and widely diffused—so," he wrote in his *Descent of Man,* "would the standard of his morality rise higher and higher." Then he wrote this climactic passage which should make all pseudo-Darwinians rub their eyes in astonishment: "The social instincts . . . naturally lead to the Golden Rule, 'As ye would that men should do to you, do ye to them likewise'; and this lies at the foundation of morality." [1]

But to recall what Darwin actually meant does not help us to obliterate what he came to mean. What he came to mean, and what he still means to uncounted numbers of human beings, is that since Nature is "red in tooth and claw," man is also justified in being bestial. He is, to be sure, born without claws; but he is suitably ingenious in inventing substitutes.

A great evolutionary insight thus became falsified into a psychological and social untruth. There are many today who still live under the shadow of this untruth—who conceive of life as "naturally" an endless, brutal struggle to survive; and who shape in the image of this conception their own practices and such institutions as they influence.

Karl Marx was another who falsified life. He, too, saw it as endless struggle: struggle not between individuals, however, but between economic classes. Inevitably his view pointed toward and "sanctified" one social tactic: the fight of class against class until there should emerge, in the end, a classless society.

Had Lenin not taken over this bitter class struggle philosophy for his own revolutionary purposes, it might have died a natural death; or it might have lived on for the modicum of truth it contained. But Lenin turned what might otherwise have been the words of a passing book, by a passing philosopher, into a permanent directive for the Revolution. The book became the Revolution's Bible; its utterances those of a Savior. This, then, was the tragedy: that a too

[1] *Descent of Man,* pp. 99, 101–102.

limited and embittered view of our human nature and society was made into a religion for mankind.

Finally, there was the Sigmund Freud of *Civilization and Its Discontents.* Freud's influence upon our time has been immense—and rightly so. He has made us see with new eyes more clearly and deeply into our own make-up than we ever saw before. Yet there were places where Freud's eyes saw not so clearly.

He, too, underestimated man's social nature and misconceived man's social role. Like Hobbes, he saw man in essence —that is, in his instinctive life—as a creature of complete egocentricity. He saw him as born with "instinctual freedom," but coming to the point where he had to curb his instincts. He did this not of his own free will, however. Society compelled him to do it.

Civilization, in short, as Freud conceived it, "is built on renunciation of instinctual gratifications. This *cultural deprivation* dominates the whole field of social relations between human beings." And this, in effect, said Freud, is why civilization makes us "discontented." It diminishes our liberty. "The liberty of the individual is not the benefit of culture. It was greatest before that culture." [1]

"The liberty of the individual . . . was greatest before that culture." Here we find the root of the error that is common to practically all the thinkers we have mentioned: the error that makes us conceive of ourselves as at our happiest *when we are doing as we please, freed of any relationship to others of obligation or even of concern.*

In spite of the depth of his new insights, Freud was unable to pass beyond the view of the human individual as in essence a *separate* being. He could not see in each individual

[1] *Civilization and Its Discontents,* Chapter III.

the greater life struggling to release itself—the life in and with others; the life in and with the living whole of life.

We need scarcely mention here the monstrously self-deceived deceivers of the 20th century—Mussolini, Hitler, Lenin, Stalin. One and all, they were the proponents of the partial life, the bitter and embattled life, the life of mutual hate and intrigue. The role of Mankind's Savior that each created for himself has, in the deepest sense, shown itself to be the role of Mankind's Destroyer.

When we look back at these views, we can be rightly appalled at their psychological poverty and distortion. Not one of them described man in the full range of his possibilities. Not one of them conceived of him as a creature with the power to *grow up*—psychologically and socially as well as physically. Each of them saw him, and persisted in seeing him, only on the level of his most infantile psychological and social powers.

Obviously, we need something better than this as a view of ourselves if we are to play a decent human role; and there seems fair hope that we may be getting it. Long before any of these voices was heard, another voice described us as members one of another. Considering all the derogatory things that have been said about us since, must we now regard that voice as "quaint," "outdated," "naive"? We would say not —and for what seems to us a good reason: other voices have come into the world in our time—more recent than those of Machiavelli or Hobbes, Marx or even Freud; and these voices are saying, once more, that we are members one of another.

This is, in fact, the psychological news of our time. Through studies of the growth process, we have learned enough about ourselves to come to this old-new conclusion. As psychologists have studied human beings from infancy on, they have been moved by the evidence of their own researches to call one fact undeniable: namely, that from the very beginning of life, the human being seeks *to belong*—to be enfolded, accepted, made a member of. He thrives in the degree that his growing self is enmeshed with other selves. This enmeshing does not mean for him an engulfing. It does not mean a losing of the self, or a diminishing of the self. It means for the individual the chance to live *with*, *by*, and later *for* others; and to become more fully himself in the process than he ever could be as an isolated unit.

In brief, the human individual has the inner need and urgency to become more than an infantile, egocentric self. To the extent that he is forced to remain only himself—as is the rejected or completely isolated child—he does not become himself. He grows into a distorted caricature of what he might have been. He becomes not happily instinctual, but a creature of fears, distrusts, hostilities, and despairs.

Marcus Aurelius—anticipating this insight by some nineteen centuries—once wrote, "We are made for cooperation, like feet, like hands, like eyelids. . . ." In spite of Machiavelli, Hobbes, Karl Marx, the pseudo-Darwinians and the rest, there is in us, so we have now learned to believe, the basic need to *be with*, *work with*, and *enjoy with*. We are, in very essence, social.

James Oppenheim instructed us, in his poem *Brotherhood*, "If you want to find your brothers, find yourself." [1] The opposite instruction would be equally valid: if you want to find yourself, find your brothers.

Deeply and persistently, we have come to realize, the individual seeks himself in and through others—works with them; creates with them: builds houses, families, churches, schools, cities. He dreams his dreams with them and tries to

---

[1] James Oppenheim, "Brotherhood," in *Collected Poems*. New York: Alfred A. Knopf.

make their common dreams come true. When the individual thus "joins the human race," he does not, we find, lessen himself. Rather, he makes himself greater. Now he really has freedom—not the freedom of his small, insistent desires—but the freedom of moving into company with, of being part of, of having power added to his own power, of living for others and liking the immense expansiveness of it.

"There is only one passion which satisfies man's need to unite himself with the world and to acquire at the same time a sense of integrity and individuality," writes Erich Fromm, "and this is love." [1] This may sound like sentimental language to come out of a tough-minded, modern field of research. Yet this is the kind of language that competent psychiatrists more and more insist upon using. They accept love—not egoism and not hostility—as the central dynamic of life. "Love," Fromm continues, "is union with somebody, or something, *outside oneself, under the condition of retaining the separateness and integrity of oneself.* It is an experience of sharing, of communion, which permits the full unfolding of one's inner activities." [2]

Love thus turns out to be a way of giving up our separate individuality and, at the same time, getting more of it than we ever had before. Love of wife, child, friend: these, we know, make us greater, not less; for they make the frame of our life more expansive, inviting us to use our powers to take into account more of reality than our own instinctual urges. Love of our work; of exploring; of finding out; of getting to the root of a problem; of appreciating work well done: these bring new life to us—for each, again, gives us an expanded world in which to be ourselves.

[1] Erich Fromm, *The Sane Society,* p. 31. New York: Rinehart and Company, 1955.
[2] *Ibid.*

This is the paradox that the theorists of egocentricity never rightly understood: that we get more by giving more—of ourselves. If we do not give, we dry up; shrink; peter out. The giving of ourselves means not a subtracting but an adding. "Love thy neighbor" or "Love your work" or "Love the natural world around you"—or "Love thine enemy"—means, then, not a deprivation of freedom, a reluctant giving up of the desirable and desired. It means an increase of freedom; an enriching of experience.

The most revealing words, in the above passage from Fromm, are in the final sentence: the experience of union with someone or something outside oneself, he reminds us, is one "which permits the full unfolding of one's inner activity." What has this unfolding of ourselves revealed?

Primarily, it has revealed that in essence we are social, not egoistic. We start as little egoists—for the good reason that nothing outside the self has as yet become real to the infant *through the experience of relationship:* of reciprocity. But as we mature—if we do—we cease being sheer egoists and enter into mutually supportive patterns of give and take. We enter into these, moreover, with enjoyment rather than by compulsion.

True, as we noted in an earlier chapter, there is always a residual child—and to some extent, a little egoist—within the human adult. Yet where maturing has happily taken place, this "child" is creative, exploratory, and friendly—not primarily egocentric and willful.

To say, then, as did Hobbes, that this intractable, egocentric creature, man, must have a strong government imposed upon him because he would otherwise be wholly ungoverned begins to seem like nonsense. It does not agree with the observable behavior of the sound human being engaged in the business of growing up. Man is, rather, a being who astonishingly, and often magnificently, *creates government out of himself.*

Government *as he creates it* ministers to his own societal make-up: it provides the frame for both order and mutuality. To live within such a frame of government does not go against his nature—providing the rules are reasonable enough not to threaten his integrity as an individual.

We have just come across an article that makes this fact almost pathetically clear. In *My Child Lives Again,* Helen Moak writes of how she and her husband rescued their little daughter from "a dim and speechless world of emotional disorder after the doctors had given her up." [1] She tells what love did to release the small child from a "shell of loneliness and nightmare terror" into the beginnings of normal, happy life.

For our present purposes, the point of this moving story lies in the mother's description of how, in spite of the fact that virtually all discipline had to be abandoned for "many, many months," the child's feeling for self-discipline—and also for the discipline of the family's and society's rules—unfolded as she began to return to normal health.

For months it was absolutely necessary to let the child do utterly as she pleased, so shattered was her whole nervous system. It might be thought that this would have been the complete undoing of the child: that she would have become not only a child without speech but also a hopelessly spoiled brat; and that the time would surely have come when firm discipline would have had to be clamped down upon her for her own good—and to make her even tolerable to have around.

Yet here is what happened. "With the pressure off," writes the mother, *Sandy began to make discipline for herself.* "Sometimes we saw Sandy punish herself, slapping her own

[1] Helen Moak, "My Child Lives Again," *Saturday Evening Post,* January 14, 1956, p. 56.

hand. Now she has begun to demand some discipline, even to enjoy it."

This is a profoundly significant fact about our human nature. Innately—if we may use this out-of-fashion word—we choose *freedom within bounds* rather than wholly anarchic freedom. "Order is a lovely thing," wrote Anna Hempstead Branch in her poem, *The Monk in the Kitchen*. For our psychological selves, order is exactly that—providing, of course, it is order and not arbitrary compulsion. Our need for order is an inner need: it is our way of structuring our lives; giving them form; making them able to function. Contrary to all the disbelieving philosophers, we are social by nature: most ourselves when we are in and of a system of relationships. The shaping and accepting of patterns of order is part of the experience of belonging within such a system —and liking it, feeling at home within it.

We may take a second example—this time from the field of group therapy. In Slavson's treatment of deeply disturbed children,[1] the initial stages of therapy—as in the case above —called for a virtual absence of discipline from the outside. The logic of this was simple—though it took vast patience to apply. These children had become "problems"—distorted travesties upon sound childhood—precisely because they had suffered too much cruel, irrational, unloving discipline by force. *All* discipline, therefore, had become for them a threat: a threat to be resisted whether or no. There seemed no chance at all that they would ever discover the principles of social order, or their own hunger for order, so long as fear, pride, and rage dictated their opposing every rule and regulation— good or bad—that for them typified an enemy force.

So the rules and regulations were removed—in so far as their removal could be made to comport with the preservation

[1] S. R. Slavson, *Introduction to Group Therapy*. New York: Commonwealth Fund, 1943.

of life and limb. Anarchy prevailed—for a while; but only for a while. Little by little, as these emotionally lost children "found themselves," they found also their need for government "by the consent of the governed." They became exasperated with lawlessness—their own as well as that of others. They began to feel "crowded" rather than released by the absence of rules and co-operative procedures—and set about making such rules on their own: rules that turned out to be remarkably like those of what we commonly call a democratic society, or free society. Their inner lawlessness, in the end, was redeemed by their inner lawfulness—expressed in agreed-upon rules for their common behavior. As they thus voluntarily re-entered the province of law and order, moreover, they also re-entered that of happy reciprocity: of giving and receiving help, and of co-operative ventures.

We have taken these two examples from the field of therapy. But normal life and life at its exceptional best testify to the same "ordering" principle in our human selves: the same "law-abiding" and "law-making" tendency.

Take any group of boys, for example, who have just built themselves a "club house" out of packing boxes and odds and ends of lumber. What do they inevitably do next? They make rules and they initiate projects. They behave, in brief, like societal beings—because they want to do so.

Or take one of the dramatic events in the history of America: the signing of the Mayflower Compact in 1620. Here was a shipload of men and women, after perilous months at sea, preparing to land on unknown shores to create a community. They were far removed from the government to which they still acknowledged allegiance. If anarchy had been the first law of their nature—or if their basic wish had been for an uncurbed instinctual life—they had a unique chance to demonstrate that fact. What they did, however, was to make their Compact, beginning it simply, "In the name of God, Amen"; and continuing it, "We, whose names are underwritten . . . doe, by these presents, solemnly and mutually in the presence of God, and of one another, covenant and combine ourselves together into a civill body politick. . . ."

The fruits of that Compact—of the spirit that brought it into being, and of the experiences that resulted from it—comprise, we might say, the unique history of this country. Just twenty-one years later, in 1641, the Massachusetts *Body of Liberties*, the first code of laws established in New England, was compiled by Nathaniel Ward; and in the ninety-eight items of that code we read both the type of experience and the body of intentions that later made the Constitution and the Bill of Rights the supreme law, not only of our land, but of our thoughts.

To see what these colonists valued, and increasingly came to value as a result of having combined themselves together "into a civill body politick," we might quote one portion of the first item of the Massachusetts *Body of Liberties:* "No mans life shall be taken away, no mans honour or good name shall be stayned, no man's person shall be arested, restrayned, banished, dismembered, nor any ways punished, no man shall be deprived of his wife or children, no mans goods or estaite shall be taken away from him, nor any way indammaged under colour of law or Countenance of Authoritie, unlesse it be by vertue or equitie of some expresse law of the Country waranting the same, established by a generall Court and sufficiently published. . . ."

The disciplined, ordered, responsible life, in short, is what our maturing selves desire; and it is what we create out of our inner need and our experiences of reciprocity—if we are given a healthy chance to do so.

If we turn back, now, to the philosophies we considered

earlier in this chapter—those of Machiavelli, Hobbes, and Marx; of Hitler, Lenin, Stalin; even of Rousseau and Freud —we discover two significant facts about them. First, they were all conceived in anger—in acute distaste for some going order of things. And second, they all described human nature as being *in essence* what it showed itself to be after it had long been shaped by imposed laws and customs that never had represented the "consent of the governed."

These philosophers of human nature and society—and of the relationship between the two—had at their command plenty of evidence about how human beings behave *under law that is handed down from above;* and upon this evidence they based their covering generalizations. But they had never witnessed human beings in the process of *law-making.* They had never met people, we might say, in the type of situation that the New England colonists were in when they drew up the Mayflower Compact and later evolved through experience the relationships that were codified in the Massachusetts *Body of Liberties.* They had plenty of evidence about the distortion of human nature under tyrannical laws and customs; but they had never witnessed the sort of thing that took place in Slavson's therapeutic groups. They had never witnessed distorted individuals in the process of coming to themselves and staging a voluntary return to law and order, to mutual helpfulness and co-operation. They had apparently not even watched, with comprehending eyes, a group of boys who had built a club house—and who then voluntarily created both rules and projects "by consent."

We should, perhaps, be prepared by now to press for an answer to the question of this chapter: what is our basic human role? The process of our maturing as psychological beings, we might say with Erich Fromm, is a process of "unfolding" what lies potentially within us. When this unfolding takes place in healthy manner and measure, we show that we are by no means only intractable, egocentric creatures. We show ourselves to be, instead, societal creatures—not by compulsion only, and not only through a niggardly process of self-interested bargaining, but by free choice. We unfold, as we grow, into individuals for whom "union with somebody, or something outside ourselves" becomes the supreme achievement—and the supreme happiness. When we are most happily ourselves we are reciprocal selves: we talk together, and laugh together, in the back-and-forth exchange of conversation; we sit at table together, and pass the food to one another—not trying to hoard it all for ourselves; and we give durable structure to our shared involvements in life by combining ourselves "together into a civill body politick."

. If this is what life is basically about—this unfolding of its possibilities under conditions appropriate to our societal nature—then our deepest obligation, it would appear, as well as our deepest privilege, is to make this unfolding happen. When we make it happen, anywhere—even in the least degree—we put ourselves on the side of life. We give life its chance.

We can do this in countless ways. We can help a normal child to grow up happily and therefore expandingly; or we can help a handicapped or frustrated child to overcome his defeat. We can help plants and animals to grow: help them to become what they have it in them to become. We can help ideas that are tentatively taking shape in the mind of a fellow human being to come out into the open, unafraid. We can help to change a hostile relationship into a friendly one, so that energies concentrated for defense or attack can be released for understanding and for creative grappling with problems.

All of us, as we have observed earlier, have various sub-roles to play: vocational, domestic, neighborly, civic. Each sub-role requires that we be skilled in certain specific ways. But each sub-role needs to be lifted up and given its place as part of a more embracing role: that of our enacting our essential human nature. The best of plumbers may be an exasperating human being. The technically skilled physician may play his human role in miserable fashion. The efficient housewife may have no power to help her children unfold into the uniqueness of their selfhood but may, instead, treat their growing urgencies as of less importance than the cleanliness of a floor or the punctuality of a meal.

However successfully, in short, we may perform the specific actions dictated by our sub-roles, we are still failures unless we have taken on—happily, and with understanding—our basic human role of helping life to unfold.

How shall we recognize whether this role has been taken on? A kind of first answer can be given by appraising certain signs that it has not been taken on: that it has been repudiated.

One such sign is *ruthlessness*. The neighborhood bully of whom we spoke in an earlier chapter was ruthless toward the small boy with his boat and his harbor. Instead of encouraging the youngster's eager interest and creative power by supporting these with his own interest, appreciation, and companionship, the bully set down his ruthless boot and demolished what had been made. Ruthlessness, wherever it shows itself—in the treatment of human being, plant, animal, idea, or situation—makes life less likely to unfold into the fullness of its possibilities.

A second sign is *unconcern*—indifference to life's needs. Such unconcern may show itself as apathy and boredom. Or it may show itself as coldness, or as a remote exclusiveness.

In any case, whatever form it takes, it decreases the likelihood that the latent possibilities of life will be brought into the open and given their chance.

We might well say that ruthlessness is the sin of commission against the human spirit; and that unconcern is the sin of omission.

In the chapters that follow we shall be moving with our thoughts into the public domain: the world of our time. That world has witnessed more than enough of both ruthlessness and unconcern. It has been told all too often that the way of egocentricity is the law of life. It has been told, with impressive reference to philosophic chapter and verse, that man is *societal* only to the extent that he is compelled to be so: by outer force or by the sheer will to survive. It has been told that whenever we get a chance to "be ourselves" we are more inclined to mutual hostility and competition than to friendliness and reciprocity. Perhaps our prime obligation and privilege is to make a different kind of report upon our human nature and situation: to act out the old-new conviction that we are members one of another.

PART THREE

IN THE PUBLIC DOMAIN

FOURTEEN

CLEAR AND PRESENT DANGER

THE MIND cannot go forth very far, today, without going beyond purely personal concerns. The world is very definitely "with us, late and soon"; and it is not a world that we can ignore with impunity. For whether we ignore it or not, the causes operating within it are having their effects upon our lives.

Edwin Arlington Robinson has observed ironically that

> "Down to our nose's very end
> We see, and are invincible." [1]

It is fairly easy to be invincible if our world stops where our own nose stops. At least, it is easy to *feel* so until the consequences of our shortsightedness are right under our nose. It is when we try to see as far as our knowledge and concern can take us that we discover how "vincible" we are—all of us

[1] Edwin Arlington Robinson, "The Revealer," in *Collected Poems*, p. 361. New York: The Macmillan Company, 1937.

separately, and all of us together—and how imperative it is that our minds go forth to see what can be done about our predicament.

Perhaps the easiest way to characterize the dangers of our time would be simply to recite, "Something old, and something new. . . ." For these dangers are old; and they are new.

They are old, we might say, *in essence*. Dictatorship; crime; ignorance; mental illness; political corruption; violence; man's obtuse or calculated inhumanity to man; man's self-deceptions and self-excusings: these are so old that they tempt us to declare, "There's nothing new under the sun."

Even as we speak, however, something new may cross between us and the sun: say, a jet plane, radar-controlled. For the dangers of our time are new *in the means used for destructive ends*. They are new, also, in the spread and terrible conclusiveness of the effects these means can have. For perhaps it was not a jet plane, but the mushroom shape of an atomic explosion, that came between us and the sun.

Forty years ago there was published in this country a translation from the Danish of Arthur Christensen's *Politics and Crowd Morality*. When we picked up this book, recently, and looked into it again, the words seemed to come to us from a long way off and a long time ago. For what we first opened to was this: "Fatal mistakes may be committed in the social as well as the political sphere; but society has a long life, and time to make good what is wrong. . . ." [1]

As we read, we felt what might be called a twinge of homesickness for the pre-atomic age: for the time when a realistic scholar could say in confident good faith, ". . . society has a long life, and time to make good what is wrong. . . ."

Here is the dangerous "new" that makes the dangerous

[1] Arthur Christensen, *Politics and Crowd Morality*, pp. 258–59. New York: E. P. Dutton and Company, 1915.

"old" different from what it ever was before: time is closing in around us. We cannot afford too many mistakes now that call for slow correction; and one mistake we dare not make at all: that of starting, or letting anyone else start, a nuclear war.

Thirty-three years after Christensen's book appeared—the span of time defined as *one generation*—Harold Lasswell wrote, in *Power and Personality*, "Even today our physicists cannot guarantee the total destruction of mankind. It is not absolutely certain that chain reactions will reach an uncontrollable pitch of activity and end the story of the earth in a cloud of radioactive dust. Nor is it absolutely sure that biological warfare will exterminate each and every man, woman, and child." [1]

Lasswell did not write these extraordinary sentences to recommend that we take a chance on the slim margin between total and almost total destruction and plunge into war. He wrote to warn us: "So long as the expectation of total destruction is not entirely credible, the rulers of a despotic state may prefer the gamble of victorious war to the certainty of losing power at home."

This is danger; and it bids us employ for the saving of mankind every bit of political wisdom, courage, and creative imagination we can focus on the international scene.

Lasswell goes on, moreover, to point up another facet of hard reality: ". . . even certainty of annihilation cannot protect us from the paranoid psychotic. . . . All mankind might be destroyed by a single paranoid in a position of power who could imagine no grander exit than using the globe as a gigantic funeral pyre. And the paranoid need not be the leader of a great state. He can be the head of a small state or even of a small gang.

"Even a modicum of security . . . calls for the discovery,

[1] Harold D. Lasswell, *Power and Personality*, p. 177. New York: W. W. Norton and Company, 1948.

neutralization and eventual prevention of the paranoid. And this calls for the overhauling of our whole inheritance of social institutions for the purpose of disclosing and eliminating the social factors that create these destructive types." [1]

This, too, is danger. It bids us employ for the saving of mankind every insight we have into the workings of human personality and of social influences upon it. Also, it bids us enlist the best intelligence and deepest compassion of every sound human being within reach, putting them to work at the all-important task of creating conditions that will encourage the sorts of behaviors and relationships we are coming to know as those of mental health.

What we have been speaking about here might be called the gigantic danger of our time: nuclear and bacterial weapons at the disposal of power-seeking, fanatic, and even paranoid personalities—or, we might add, of frightened personalities; or those who cannot shake off the assumption that all you have to do to "win" is to "get there fustest with the mostest"; or those so impatient with the pros and cons of complicated problems and the ups and downs of delicate diplomatic relationships that they say, "Oh, the hell with it . . . let's get it over." How desolately "over" it might be when it was over these impatient minds seem not to comprehend.

This is the danger that could deprive us of one of our unalienable human rights: the right to correct errors. To have total or almost total extermination of the race the price exacted for our making, even once more, certain old repetitive mistakes is indeed "something new."

Yet to concentrate exclusively on this gigantic danger is itself a kind of folly. It is to condemn ourselves either to emotional paralysis or to a panic wish to fly from doom. It

[1] *Op. cit.*, pp. 183–84.

casts us, we might say, in the role of "the small girl who, returning from school after an air raid drill, pleaded with her mother, 'Can't we go somewhere where there isn't any sky?' " [1]

It may be, of course, that even Lasswell's book is dated. It may be that developments in the field of nuclear weapons since 1948, when it was published, have been such that *the danger inherent in war* now precludes *the danger of there being a war*. As George Sokolsky observed in the column with which he greeted 1956, no great power wants war "because radioactive strontium is such a very bad chemical. It is this substance rather than the immediate explosive powers of the various bombs that has the statesmen of the world scared into wanting peace. And no matter how much they scream and make faces at each other, they will always be thinking of radioactive strontium and forget about war. Maybe, at long last, the human race has discovered the weapon that makes war impossible." [2]

This may, happily, be true. Yet even if it is, we cannot take a deep breath and relax. We have, instead, to learn—rapidly and well—how to conduct a different kind of war: a well-nigh interminable cold war in which the weapons are ideas, patterns of human relationship, economic resources, and technical skill. For even if the physical sky over our head has ceased to be a place from which bombs are likely to fall, the risk remains that if we falter in world-wide cultural and economic competition, many generations to come may live under a "sky" of values and faiths very different from any we have ever known—or ever thought tolerable.

The danger is spelled out in every day's headlines. Soviet Russia is offering two attractive commodities—indeed, two

[1] Simon Doniger, *Religion and Human Behavior,* p. vi. New York: Association Press, 1954.
[2] George Sokolsky, *These Days.* King Features Syndicate.

well-nigh irresistible commodities—to the world's backward peoples; or to such among these as she wants to draw into her orbit and line up as enemies of the western world.

The first of these commodities is a kind of "friendship" that adopts the tone of equality toward those, particularly in Asia, whom the West has traditionally treated as inferior. Thus, the words of Khrushchev in Burma: "I address the generals, officers, and soldiers of the Union of Burma with a friendly wish for a further technical perfection. We, in the same spirit as you, are compelled to maintain armed forces. . . ."

Anyone versed in the history of Russian imperialism during the past few years can brand as counterfeit the phrase, "We, in the same spirit as you. . . ." But many of the people of Burma are less versed in history than in deprivation; and the generals, officers, and soldiers of Burma have too rarely been addressed as equals. Who, before, has said to them, "But are not the Burmese just as gifted as, say, the Russians or the British? People are not divided into capable or incapable ones. If they are given equal chances, they will achieve success in their development"? The prolonged applause that greeted these words—and that has since greeted similar words in other countries, both in Asia and the Near East—may, in the cold war of our time, be the applause heard round the world.

The second commodity is economic and technical assistance. Again, Khrushchev: ". . . if you need assistance, tell us and we will help you. We will help you with engineers, and we will share our experience with you. . . ." In Burma, Egypt—one place after another—the challenge to the West is being cast in these terms.

We have been schooled enough, by now, in the tactics of Communist infiltration within our own country, and other countries, to recognize the pattern here. It is one of seeing in every past mistake, sustained inequality, or unsatisfied need a calculated opportunity—not to set right what is wrong, but to capitalize on it. Such capitalizing has, we know, followed a threefold design. First, it has aimed to make the underprivileged see Communism as a saving force. Second, it has aimed to intensify old hatreds and stir up new ones wherever these can further the Communist cause. And third, it has aimed, in so far as possible, to "neutralize" persons of intellectual and moral concern: persons who have wanted wrongs to be set right; who feel angry and guilty because they have not been set right; and whose established habits of accepting *in good faith* other people's protestations *of good faith* incline them to listen to what the Communists say, to hope that they mean it, and to give them the benefit of the doubt.

The pattern has been made painfully familiar. Thus, we think of the testimony given by Mrs. Dorothy K. Funn, on May 4, 1953, before the House Committee on Un-American Activities. Mrs. Funn testified that she had, from 1939 to 1946, been an active member of the Communist Party and the Negro Congress because she believed they would prove a means for bettering the situation of the Negro in America: "You know the cause—I'll answer you, sir—the cause of the Negro is a very touching one and one on which a lot needs to be done yet. . . ." [1] Mrs. Funn, like many another person who had joined the Party for similar reasons, experienced a final sense of betrayal. She came to realize that the Communist cause is far removed from the Negro cause but that "it lends itself beautifully to an emotional tieup, and you can say, 'Well, if this is the organization that's going to do this, therefore, this is the organization with which I want to affiliate myself.'" [2]

The "new" Communist tactic, as we have witnessed it in

[1] *The American Negro in the Communist Party*, p. 11. Publication of the Committee on Un-American Activities, U.S. House of Representatives, December 22, 1954.

[2] *Ibid.*

Burma, India, Egypt, and elsewhere, is to offer to whole nations of backward peoples the "friendship" and "help" it has offered to depressed and minority groups within every nation where it has practiced infiltration. That the aim and tactics remain unchanged in essence, even though they are now being presented in a new tone, is underscored by Khrushchev's statement in India, in November, 1955, to the effect that Russia would not renounce the teachings of Lenin: teachings which declared the utter irreconcilability of Communism with any other system and which pointed to world conquest.

The appeal that has been surreptitiously made to individuals and groups within countries is now, however, open and headlined, for Khrushchev and his fellows want their words to be heard by dissatisfied peoples everywhere. They want them to be heard, also, by those within the western powers who would themselves like to be helping backward nations to develop, who are impatient with the policies of their own governments in this respect—policies they regard as tardy, half-hearted, and often bad mannered; and whose capacity for hope is such that they may "neutralize" themselves by coming to believe that perhaps the Communists, this time, mean what they say.

In a sense, of course, they do mean it. They are ready to pour in money and provide technical assistance where these will buy them, simultaneously: good will toward themselves; hatred of the west; neutrality on the part of certain nations not yet brought to point of actively hating the west or actively lining up with Russia; and, not least, divisiveness and uncertainty within the west. The cards are—in short-range terms, at least—stacked in their favor. The human needs to which they appeal are real needs. They can provide resources with every appearance of abundant, unhesitating generosity —for they need not concern themselves with either bipartisan support or the opinion of the people back home. They can, we might say, be unrestrained opportunists.

They enjoy, moreover, certain perverse advantages that come from their wanting to intensify old and ready conflicts of interest—as between India and Pakistan, and Israel and the Arab states—at the very time when the western powers want these conflicts eased and arbitrated. By taking sides in a manner that upsets the delicate balance between two mutually suspicious and fearful nations, they can make arbitration almost impossible. Thus, they can virtually force us into trying to re-establish the balance they have upset. For if they are permitted to shift that balance at will, they make all too convincing their power to play favorites, rescue these favorites from a position of fear-ridden stalemate, and give them advantages over old enemies. If we are to stand successfully for the ways of arbitration of old grievances, we cannot afford to let them establish such an image of themselves as successful saviors and patrons of those who accept their help. When we attempt to restore the balance, however, by strengthening the side that has, by comparison, been made weak, we run into another predicament. It is made to appear that *we* are playing favorites and are opposing, not Soviet imperialism, but the backward and needy people whom the Communists are helping. Thus, we become to these people objects of fear and hatred: protectors of their traditional enemies.

Through such maneuvering, finally, the Communists are able to make our policies seem nothing more than tardy and scared reactions to theirs. All the good will and creative initiative are made to appear as theirs—while we are cast as a wavering "me, too" nation, for whom the giving of help is no planned and generous policy but a miserly, reluctant response to pressure.

Countries, we know, have fallen from the inside as a result of Communist tactics of infiltration. It is painfully possible, now, that backward countries, one after another, may be voluntarily drawn into the Communist orbit by similar tactics openly practiced between nations. *This, too, is danger*—and, as in the case of nuclear war, gigantic danger. Our capacity to handle it will depend upon our power to recognize Communist tactics for what they are, instead of being confused by them, and upon our power to initiate bold, creative policies shaped in the image of our own deepest convictions.

Plato defined courage as wisdom concerning danger. Wisdom concerning the clear and present dangers we now face will have to be made out of a double awareness: awareness of what is taking place on the world front; and awareness of attitudes here at home that reduce the likelihood of our doing what is necessary.

We would number among the most destructive tendencies of our time, and, unfortunately, among ourselves, *factionalism* and *psychological browbeating:* the two are closely related in action; and both of them are powerful in preventing our solving problems by rational means.

"Some ages are lukewarm and complacent. . . . Other ages, of which the present is one, are unbalanced and prone to faction. . . . Any small coterie, bound together by some interest which other men dislike or ignore, tends to develop inside itself a hothouse mutual admiration, and toward the outer world, a great deal of pride and hatred which is entertained without shame because the 'Cause' is its sponsor and it is thought to be impersonal." [1]

Factionalism shows itself in its most unalloyed form in extremist groups of the right and the left, and in the various "fringe" movements. But what concerns us here is the extent to which it has run through our society like a contagious disease, attacking the higher thought centers and making

[1] C. S. Lewis, *The Screwtape Letters,* pp. 40–41. New York: The Macmillan Company, 1943.

people respond with automatic hostility or loyalty when what they should do is to respond consideringly and considerately.

There are reasons for such ready factionalism. One we have touched upon in an earlier chapter: namely, that when people feel the lack of any *supreme context* they tend to fill the void in their lives by treating one or another *sub-context*—of race, class, nation, region, political party, or even artistic or literary coterie—as "sacred."

A second reason takes us back to our discussion of the distribution of energy. An extraordinary number of people to-day are aware, at some level of consciousness, of being at the mercy of forces that are enormously unconcerned about them as individuals. This means that just below the surface of their daily activities, they are *panic-prone:* ready for fight or flight. A man we know has suggested to us that the proper slogan for today's world would be, "Love me, love my dogma." Psychologically, the reason is clear: if another person loves our dogma, whether or not he loves us personally, he is not likely to attack us when we are off guard; and he will be *for* us, adding his strength to ours, if we are attacked.

A third reason for today's rampant factionalism is that our traditional bases of mutual toleration have been badly eroded. Both urbanization and the new nomadism have discouraged among us that older sense of neighborhood that Robert Frost expressed when he wrote,

> "If one by one we counted people out
> For the least sin, it wouldn't take us long
> To get so we had no one left to live with.
> For to be social is to be forgiving." [1]

Today, urbanized and on the move, we tend to revise that last line in practice, making it read, "For to be social is to find people you like and agree with, and to be with them as

[1] Robert Frost, "The Star-Splitter," in *Collected Poems*, p. 219. New York: Henry Holt and Company, 1930.

much as possible and with others as little as possible." Our modern privilege of seeking out congenial associates is certainly to be valued. But it takes watching. It too easily slips over into the practice of counting people out "for the least sin": the practice of disparaging the uncongenial, or simply the unfamiliar; lumping them together as "they"; and then avoiding all situations in which we might have to try to understand them and work with them.

Again, our sense of common stakes has been undermined by the world civil war. The ideologies that today threaten man's freedom and integrity do not stay within clear bounds, geographical or otherwise. Their apologists and adherents take the world as their province and walk abroad in a myriad disguises. Hence, the task of knowing with whom we do share common stakes is made far from simple. In the process of trying to make it manageable, people are prone to apply stereotypes as yardsticks and to see as clues whatever their personal conditioning, likes, dislikes, and vested interests bid them see.

Closely allied to factionalism is what we have named *psychological browbeating*. On more occasions than it is pleasant to recall, we have witnessed grown Americans bearing down upon one another's minds the way a schoolyard bully might bear down upon another child; and at the same time that they have badgered, blamed, and accused, they have demanded that those whom they thus drive into self-defense should acknowledge error, answer questions with explicit care, weigh facts, hold the common welfare in mind, and take a long-range view. This is about as sensible as to coop an individual up in a box where he can only crouch and then command him to stand up.

On the street, one evening, we met a friend going home from a discussion of world affairs. "How was it?" we asked.

"Oh, you know," he answered wearily. "The sort of discussion where people say to each other, 'What do you think of our policy in Asia? Answer Yes or No.'" It is thus all too often that we pretend to a meeting of minds when we are only exchanging words that are like a jabbing, condemnatory finger or a clenched fist raised to strike.

Never in our history, perhaps, have so many of us kept so busy blaming, suspecting, condemning, and denouncing one another as now. We seem to be showing ourselves—unlike the Lord—to be unmerciful and ungracious, quick to anger, and stingy in mercy. And this brings us to the point where we must look beyond the reasons for factionalism and mutual recrimination to some of the destructive consequences.

When the community of normally decent, reasonable human beings is thus splintered, and when cumulative angers, fears, and hurt prides make it ever harder for mutual understanding and reconciliation to take place, three groups thrive; and they are not those to whom we can willingly entrust the human future.

First, there are the Communists. Communism thrives on our believing the worst about one another, expecting the worst of one another, and separating ourselves into groups each of which develops "inside itself a hothouse mutual admiration and toward the outer world a great deal of pride and hatred. . . ."

In particular, Communism thrives where *extremism* invades and corrupts the thoughts and practices of those—whether they call themselves liberals or conservatives—who normally stand for moderation; for listening before denouncing; checking rumors before circulating them; sponsoring orderly change; making room for differences; and taking it for granted that errors might better be corrected than denied or defended. Wherever liberals and conservatives let themselves be tempted, frightened, or needled into acting like extremists of the left and the right, Communism is doubly the winner: not only does it face a weakened and confused opposition, but it has at its psychological disposal an increased number of individuals who have become "acclimated" to the use of force rather than reason and to tactics of mutual exclusion rather than of creative compromise and reconciliation.

A second group that thrives in an atmosphere of faction are those whom we specify, in psychological terms, as *hostile personalities*. Some of these, of course, are also Communists. But many are not; and it is of these others that we are speaking here. They may operate as individuals or pool their rage against life in some "hate group." But no matter what outlet they choose for their hostility, what they act out are their own inner conflicts, their own personality disorders. They may seem currently enraged at an actual enemy—Communism. But in deeper fact, they are so chronically enraged at life that they must always have an enemy—if not one, then another. It is, so to speak, just their good luck if history provides them with an enemy whom they can not only hate with good conscience, but can win status by hating.

When people, by and large, are extending to others a flexible good will, destructively unsound personalities stand out enough to be recognized. Thus, in a healthy community the scandalmonger is usually discredited after a time—when it has turned out often enough that Mrs. Smith's husband went to the city on legitimate business and not to see another woman; that teen-age Lucy Jones was only putting on weight and not having an illegitimate baby; and that most of the other circulated rumors were equally groundless.

When the general level of fear and anger has been raised, however, even fairly balanced people tend to become extreme enough for hostile personalities to appear only a little more so. They may even be given standing, then, in that moral limbo where ends are said to justify means; or may be taken to be informed with some secret knowledge—as they invariably claim to be. To the extent, in brief, that we get lost in mutual suspicions and antagonisms, those whose whole make-up is strongly slanted toward suspicion and antagonism have a field day.

So do a third group: the demagogues, the opportunists. Disciplined by neither ideology nor scruple, but only by their own drive for power, they make themselves heroes of the age of hate.

Different as these groups may be on various counts, and even opposed to one another, they often exert a common influence. By persuading the rest of us to look where they point, to suspect whom they suspect, to repeat rumors and slogans that they have put into our minds, and—most of all—to look at one another with wary, critical, unforgiving eyes, they narrow the mental and emotional space in which we live, and in which we impinge upon one another's lives.

From another angle, also, factionalism threatens the soundness of our personalities and our society. It is, we might say, *voluntary segregation;* and like all segregation, it fosters psychological "inbreeding."

The process of this "inbreeding" is subtle and dangerous. To understand it we have to realize that a *faction* is distinguished from a normal, healthy association of people by its hostile exclusiveness. Its members come together chiefly *because they agree in their dislikes*—and particularly in their dislike of those who disagree with them. As they talk themselves into an ever more intense fear and dislike of whomever they have cast as "enemy," each individual member finds more and more indispensable his own good standing within the company of the "elect." Therefore, he becomes more and more "conformist" within the group; less and less inclined to express opinions that might make other members look at him with questioning eyes; and less and less inclined to be seen in the company of "publicans and sinners." The more the members of a faction cut themselves off from other associations, in brief, the more mutually dependent they become and knowing one another's intolerances only too well, the more afraid they become of one another's disapprovals.

The Princeton study of the appeals of Communism from which we have quoted earlier would serve also as a study of factionalism: of the "stringent disciplines of party life, the massive risks of dishonor and falling from grace, the sharp tension and fear affecting intra-party personal relations . . ." [1] Two statements from the ex-Communist respondents will highlight the point: "While you're supposedly a member of an organization that does things collectively, you always have to be on guard for fear your best friend may expose you for some slight deviation. . . ." (p. 143) and "One was first and foremost a party member. This meant that unless we took recreation in company with other party members and in a party atmosphere, it was frowned upon as bourgeois and escapist." (p. 151)

What we see here is the process by which a human being is rendered alien to any society outside the faction. Within the Communist Party, of course, both pressures toward conformity and penalties for deviation are extreme. But the factional pattern, with milder pressures and penalties, is found in many groups today—and even in groups that ostensibly stand for the freedom of the individual.

When we talk within our various groups—educational, medical, business, labor, or what not—about the dangers of conformity, we usually talk as though the only pressures we

---

[1] Gabriel A. Almond, *The Appeals of Communism*, p. 142. Princeton University Press, 1954.

had to resist were from the outside: pressures exerted by some group opposed to our own or by some government agency. But we may well suspect that we are vulnerable to such outside attacks and pressures, where they exist, and inclined to see them even where they do not exist, to the extent that we have, *within our own groups,* served our apprenticeship to factionalism—developing the fears, passivities, conformities, stereotyped phrasings, and "hothouse mutual admirations" that go with it.

What shall we say—to take a trivial example—about the exponent of a certain "school" of literature who is self-consciously "emancipated" but who would not dare, within the fellowship of the "emancipated," to say quite simply and honestly that he liked the works of some other "school" that most members of his group specialized in viewing with self-congratulatory contempt?

What shall we say about the industrial manager who feels uneasily obliged to explain to a fellow member of the managerial group why he had lunch with a member of the union? What shall we say about the member of a county medical association who happens strongly to disagree with most of his fellows on the subject of socialized medicine—but who keeps prudently still about his disagreement?

Even liberals, today, on one issue and another, have developed orthodoxies so rigid that those who deviate from the "line" are rendered suspect: have they gone soft-headed? have they "sold out"? Paradoxically, in short, many who stand up valiantly against outside pressures toward conformity at the same time practice conformity and exert pressure toward conformity within their own group. They have subtle ways of making it seem that the strength of the group against outside evils and stupidities depends upon reliability and agreement. This attitude is not, as a rule, stated in so many words. Often, indeed, it appears to be unconscious.

But it is conveyed, nonetheless, by the manner in which a dissenter on some favorite issue is appraised; or by the tacit, unquestioned assumption that agreement prevails.

Similarly, conservative groups have developed orthodoxies, in many cases, that obligate those who want to keep their good standing—who do not wish to be looked at with shocked astonishment, or eased out of a position of authority—to prove themselves solid and "safe" by talking more like reactionaries than conservatives.

The special "orthodoxies" change from group to group and year to year. What concerns us here is the threat to our free institutions and free minds posed by the type of voluntary segregation we call factionalism. Wherever factionalism prevails, it prevents the cross-fertilization of minds, the self-correction of exaggerated viewpoints, the pooling of widely different ideas for the solution of our common problems, the courage of social initiative, and the exploring of bases of reconciliation. On the other hand, it encourages self-approval, hostility, fear, conformity, and the ruthless or subtle tactics of liquidation: that is to say, the short-cutting of problems by simply ruling people out in one way or another.

"Monologue is insufficient in human affairs," writes John A. Mackay. "If discussion is to be fruitful, a quarrel settled, men must not merely talk *at* one another or *about* one another; they must talk *to* one another. They must meet face to face." [1] These words declare a kind of minimum program for our civilized living together. It is this program of our *civilized living together* that is threatened by the type of *monologuing in unison* that we call factionalism: the self-segregation of human beings into groups so molded by outer and inner pressures that the members find it both expedient and reas-

[1] John A. Mackay, "Christian Faith and the International Situation," *Theology Today*, 12, No. 1 (April, 1955).

suring to say the same things on the same subjects, in order to feel "right" and to present a common front against the opposition.

It is precisely this *monologuing in unison* that we recognize and deplore in Soviet Russia's Iron Curtain policy. That policy involves the keeping out—the warding off—of any sort of outside influence that might disturb the unanimity of the "inside." It involves as the complement of this warding-off activity the stereotyping of what is said within the Soviet Union itself. Thus, Justice William O. Douglas reported, after he had tried on a visit to Russia to get the facts straight about the freedom or lack of freedom in the area of religion, that wherever and to whomever he put his questions, he got identical answers—and got them almost as *rote* answers. The answers did not come out of any engagement of the other person's mind with the questions he asked. They were policy answers. The individuals with whom he talked might be a thousand miles apart. Yet they did not, in any true sense, talk with him. They monologued in unison.

If we deeply understand the tragedy of this process, and what it does to the human mind wherever it becomes the order of the day, we can see the type of threat that acute and intemperate factionalism presents to our own democratic integrity. Without our seeming to realize the fact, we have inclined more and more in recent years to hold *group attitudes* on various issues rather than *individual attitudes*. Thus, it is taken as predictable that liberals will talk in a certain manner on a given issue while conservatives will talk otherwise. There is, in short, a liberal "side" of the issue and a conservative "side." Those whose feelings of allegiance and security attach to this or that side tend to join in the appropriate chorus, monologuing in unison. They do so not only because they have—far more than they often realize—held themselves aloof from evidence that might temper their one-sided convictions, but because they would feel vaguely uncomfortable, less sure of themselves and with whom they belonged if they started qualifying their statements, disagreeing with members of their own "side," and granting that the whole issue belonged in the area of the yet to be studied, yet to be understood.

What we have said here, of course, does not imply that group agreements and efforts are always to be deplored. They are both sound and necessary—so long as they do not become so rigid and automatic that they diminish the likelihood of individual thought and decision.

A second qualification is also in order. What we have said does not imply that truth is *always* furthered by bringing opposed groups together to "talk things over." The very situation that is set up to promote the exchange of ideas and to encourage mutual understanding can, we know, be exploited by a faction that has not the slightest intention of entering into honest give-and-take.

By and large, however, a movement out of entrenched factionalism into flexibility of mind is all to the good. If we could begin to stage such a movement now, with an honest wish to make it work, we might begin also to talk sense to one another about some of the curious problems that constitute present danger to our society.

One whole set of problems, for example, is tied up with ambiguities about such terms as *freedom, dissent,* and *subversion.* Our traditional concept of freedom has called for "hands off" where people's words are concerned and an official "hands on" policy only for overt acts. Most of us have taken it for granted, most of the time, that spoken and written words are not punishable actions, no matter how unwise they may be, but are simply the form in which free, private convictions "walk abroad" in the public world, to make what dent they can upon that world and to be judged in the open market places of the mind.

Yet our attitude on this score has never been—and could never be—an absolute. We have recognized the need for laws that prohibit slander and libel, incitement to riot, and the mailing of letters that contain threats. And there is always the classic example of where our toleration leaves off: no one is free to shout "Fire!" in a crowded theater.

Our current confusion might be pointed up by varying this classic example. What about a person who said in advance that he was going to shout "Fire!" in a crowded theater? Would he thus commit an "act" that would justify his being restrained? Or would he be just talking until he had actually shouted "Fire!"? If his stated intention was reported to the authorities, and if they restrained him from entering the theater, could he, on the plea that he had been "just talking," claim damage for illegal arrest? Or what if the authorities took a different course? What if they warned the theater manager of what was likely to happen, and he, in turn, warned the audience, specifying that if this given individual shouted "Fire!" they were not to be plunged into panic by the word? Would this public exposure of his intentions constitute an invasion of his rights?

Or to come at the matter from another angle, what about the person who, hearing him declare his intention of shouting "Fire!", reported this fact to the authorities? Is this individual a public benefactor or a dubious "informer?" Perhaps he has had, in the past, fairly close association with the man whose word he now reports: close enough that he knows the actual shouting of "Fire!" would be in character, and would comport with both the individual's past actions and his reiterated philosophy. Does this knowledge from past association obligate him in a special way to let the authorities know what is going on? Or does the fact of his past association with an unreliable person render his report peculiarly suspect? Does it, further than this, prove him to be a "turncoat"—a man who goes back on a former friend and who puts himself outside the pale by reporting what he would never have learned except in the role of friend?

The whole example sounds absurd. But what if we turn our minds from it to the problem of conspiratorial Communism? There can be argument still, perhaps, about the extent of Communist infiltration, but scarcely, it would seem, at this stage of the game, about its existence or about its being a calculated Communist tactic. It has been practiced with appalling success in a number of countries that now "enjoy" a kind of death-in-life as Soviet satellites. The evidence that it has been attempted, and is still being attempted, in this country is overwhelming. Further, it has been "sanctified" by statement after statement in the Communist "classics." The *intention*, in brief, has been declared and reiterated, comports with past actions, and is known to be in character: not, in this instance, an erratic individual's intention to shout "Fire!" in a crowded theater, but the intention of an armed, implacable ideology to put an end to our type of society.

Wherever the tactic of infiltration has been employed, its first weapon has been the *word*. The *word* that has thus been relied upon to spread the doctrine through secret channels, in accord with plans mapped by a foreign power, is simply not the *word* that we have traditionally taken to be inseparable from freedom of individual conscience. It is, in effect, an act: a calculated part of an over-all, long-range plan of action. It has been used deliberately, and with insidious power, to accomplish certain ends: to spread confusion and hatred; to "prove" that wrongs cannot be made right or conditions improved by democratic evolutionary means; to persuade the discontented that their only hope lies in Communism and that it is to this doctrine that they truly owe their first allegiance;

to represent as witch-hunters and forerunners of a police state those who are legally intrusted with the task of uncovering subversion and publicizing its tactics for all to understand; to persuade dedicated defenders of free speech and free assembly that these basic freedoms are being invaded by the exposure or restraint of Communist conspiracy; and to brand as the lowest type of "turncoat" behavior the reporting of conspiratorial actions and intentions by those who know them best from having been involved in them.

"The problem, therefore, is not 'Shall free government defend itself?' but 'How can free government defend itself and still maintain the liberties of the individual?' To disregard the individual, to view him as meaningless and the security of the state as all important, is equally to betray democracy. Free government cannot be defended by dictatorial methods—in so doing the defender will devour the very thing to be defended. The protection of the individual is just as important as the safety of the state. Our task, in this mid-century decade, is to proceed along a path whereby we can achieve national security and yet maintain our freedoms." [1]

"Our task, in this mid-century decade," is vitally that of learning how to deal realistically with the changed status of the *word*—the word as employed by Communists who use freedom of speech to undermine the institutions of freedom —without curtailing our traditional freedoms. It is, also, that of learning how to deal realistically with the concept of *freedom of assembly* when this has been exploited by Communists to invade and pervert by secret means our voluntary associations, or to set up their own planned associations in our midst, concealing the nature of these and winning support for them by defining their intentions in the familiar words of our American idealism: justice, freedom, and the rest.

[1] John Edgar Hoover, "Civil Liberties and Law Enforcement: The Role of the FBI," *Iowa Law Review*, 37, No. 2 (Winter, 1952), 186.

We cannot avoid the problems set before us by the Communists—whether on the world front or the home front. They are glaringly before us, to be tackled and solved. Yet a rational approach to them often seems to be rendered wellnigh impossible by our own factionalism, our entrenchment in mutually warring camps. Within each camp, we say things that are exaggerated enough, unverified enough, unfair enough, and unrealistic enough to startle our own ears if we actually stopped and listened to them: listened to them, that is to say, as discerning, responsible individuals—not as members of a group strangely and often unwittingly committed to "monologuing in unison."

It has been remarked that there are fifteen thousand ways to be one-sided. A fair number of these ways have been demonstrated in our time; and most of us, one way or another, within one group or another, have taken part in the demonstration.

It does not, as a matter of fact, take fifteen thousand kinds of one-sidedness to hold us back from a sound, co-operative engagement with the clear and present danger of our time. A few kinds will suffice—if they relate to vital problems and if they are firmly enough cast in the pattern of factionalism.

Communism—like Fascism—is *extremism* on a gigantic scale. It talks in terms of absolute rights and wrongs, with no gradations in between. It talks, therefore, in terms of the total defeat of those who disagree—never in terms of comparing experiences and viewpoints for mutual clarification, nor in terms of trying to reconcile differences. As a further *therefore*, it describes those on its own side in terms of stereotyped praise and those on the other side in terms of stereotyped denunciation; and by every means at its command, it keeps the two sides so far apart that there is slight danger of their comparing notes, becoming acquainted with each other's problems, and discovering each other's essential humanity.

Factionalism is *extremism* on a smaller scale. To the extent that factionalism splinters our society it renders improbable the solution of problems put to us by Communism. Nothing could make these problems easy. Yet we cannot count them insoluble; and they might turn out to be surprisingly manageable, even now, if we were to devote ourselves to understanding them as zealously as we seem, at times, to devote ourselves to misunderstanding one another.

Professor Ernest Hocking, of Harvard University's Philosophy Department, once declared that the world's great need is for the "unpurchasable man." Most of us would be willing to agree. Every sort of man who walks abroad is, as we have noted in earlier chapters, a unit of psychic influence: to greater or lesser degree, he shapes every situation he enters in the image of himself. There can be no substitute, as a unit of influence, for the man of integrity. It will have to be in his image that a world of integrity is built, if it is to be built at all.

This may sound thoroughly platitudinous. The man who has "sold out" is no admirable figure. We have to realize, however, that there are ways of "selling out" so gradual and subtle that we can practice them even while we are condemning other ways. The person who sells out to the highest financial bidder is a fairly obvious figure. So is the one who sells out for the sake of some position of power and prestige. So is the "Quisling" who sells out for the sake of being briefly safe. But what about the person who—unwittingly, and by almost imperceptible stages—sells some portion of his birthright of individuality and mental integrity for the companionship in agreement, the luxury of hating with a clear conscience, the oversimplified sense of "rightness," and the resonant pleasures of "monologuing in unison" that factionalism offers?

Our need today is truly for the "unpurchasable man": the man whose mind is so much his own that he can, without a sense of uneasiness, go and talk to anyone he wants to talk with across the boundaries of factionalism; or go and ask questions where he thinks he may find answers, or at least may find out how the problem looks from where another person stands; or try to measure the portion of "rightness" that each side can properly claim; and set himself, then, to figure out ways in which a common policy for this time of danger can be shaped out of all available elements of reasonableness and realism—wherever these are to be found.

FIFTEEN

VARIETIES OF VIGILANCE

MORE THAN a hundred and fifty years have passed since John Philpot Curran declared liberty and eternal vigilance to be inseparable: "It is the common fate of the indolent to see their rights become a prey to the active. The condition upon which God hath given liberty to man is eternal vigilance; which condition if he break, servitude is at once the consequence of his crime and the punishment of his guilt."

The particular issue that moved him to speak thus in 1790 may not now seem dramatic. The issue was one of how the Lord Mayor of Dublin should acquire office. But what was at stake was the *right of election*. His words date from that intense and creative period when western man was struggling to "naturalize" the concept of government by the consent of the governed. Curran spoke from strength because he felt strongly about the matter, and what he said was said for keeps: liberty is not to be won and then taken for granted. The *conditions* of its preservation and growth have to be

watched and tended; and those who care about liberty have
to do the watching.

We, today, are living in a time when vigilance—the right
kind of vigilance—is unmistakably called for. To be "indolent," now, in our concern about liberty is to invite its loss;
for the "active" are very active among us—skillfully, concen-
tratedly, cynically active. With man's future the prize to be
won or lost, they are not going to call a truce just because
the rest of us would like to take our liberties as forever established and think about something else.

Again, vigilance is called for—now, as ever; or more than
ever—because, as Curran pointed out, indolence with regard
to liberty is followed by servitude. We know, moreover, what
20th century servitude would be like. The nightmares of
science fiction have become the actualities of life. We need
not search out those nightmares, now, in the pulp magazines,
nor even in such a serious novel as George Orwell's *1984*. We
can read the direct experiences of those who have lived to tell
the story of Nazi concentration camps; of the Nazis' occupation of Warsaw; of the Communists' "liberation" of that city
into a new horror; of Communist slave labor camps and pris-
oner of war camps.

What, then, is our position with regard to "eternal vigilance"? It is that of a people who have liberty enough to be
at liberty to be either "indolent" or "active" in liberty's behalf.
Furthermore, if our choice is to be "active," we are *at liberty*
to make the flailing motions of panic—so that, like amateur
lifeguards, we drag under what we seek to save—or to make
the purposeful, disciplined motions of the individual who
knows what he is about because he has taken the trouble to
learn.

Again, we are *at liberty* to make our exercise of vigilance
just one more hypertensed expression of factionalism. If we

do so, three results are predictable. First, since factionalism keeps energies focused for fight or flight, our very exercise of vigilance will become a reason why we do not creatively bring our minds to bear upon the problems of freedom. Second, that same exercise will tempt us to condone or employ the methods of *extremism*—as sustained fear and rage always do tempt us. Third, for reasons noted in the previous chapter, we will, within our various factions, become conformists to a degree not compatible with the liberty in behalf of which we are being vigilant.

Finally, our position is that of a people whose vigilance has to take account, not of one clearly identified enemy only, but of a whole drove of intentional and unintentional enemies —not all easy to identify; and not all, by any means, in one camp. Government "of the people, by the people, and for the people" is a complex, many-sided business; and a vigilance watchful enough to serve it well must be more than an over-simplified expression of one narrowly channeled fear or one entrenched partiality. For a free people, it would seem, vigilance ought to be a calm, steady, rational undertaking; not a sudden overflow of the spirit of crisis.

It may be worth our while, then, to take a sampling of the forces we need to be watchfully concerned about—some of them peculiar to our day; most of them "hardy perennials" in our society:

Communists; neo-fascists; neurotic hate-mongers; anti-Communists who are pro-democratic in word only, not in habit structure or in basic philosophy of human relations;

Big and little usurpers of power and practitioners of corruption; criminals; delinquents; law enforcement agents who do not enforce the law; citizens who, for one or another personal reason, persuade law enforcement agents not to enforce the law;

Opportunists, in and out of office, who know a popular "cause" when they see one and who have no scruples about raising the fear-hate level if they can do so to their own advantage;

Neutralists who blur the distinction between the calculated evils of Communism and the many specific evils that represent the "homework" yet to be done by the western democracies in behalf of their established beliefs;

Public servants who intend to support the institutions of freedom but who, trying to get their jobs done under baffling circumstances and a barrage of criticism, resign themselves to one undemocratic procedure after another, make one concession after another to "pressuring" extremists and partisans, and gradually convince themselves that such measures are a natural part of politics;

"Sidewalk superintendents" of our public life who find no behavior on the part of any office holder quite good enough to approve, and whose definition of what should ideally be done results in intolerance of even the best efforts to get *something* done about specific problems under given circumstances;

Security agents who have not been either carefully enough selected or well enough trained to insure against their making such irresponsible or exacting interpretations of ambiguous security laws that the innocent suffer with the guilty and the whole security program—even in its sound and necessary aspects—is brought into bad repute;

Congressional investigators who go to similar extremes with similar consequences—so that responsible citizens are tempted into an *anti-investigationism* that often blinds them both to the actualities of the dangers being investigated and to the fact that Congressional investigations are a traditional, legitimate part of our democratic machinery;

Unofficial groups, local or national, that arrogate to themselves a quasi-official status and undertake to censor the programs and policies of other groups that are equal with them in the company of voluntary associations—and just as patriotic as they are;

Exhibitionist "martyrs"—as distinguished from genuine victims of injustice—who, having ventured to the edge or over the edge of conspiratorial Communism, and having been officially asked about it, first make a "virtue" out of being as offensive as possible and then rush to the public with the story of their rights having been invaded;

Anti-intellectuals who find the label "Communist" the most damagingly effective one yet put at their disposal for disparaging intellectual processes and institutions;

Public administrators who extend the areas of necessary secrecy to include almost any area in which they would rather have the public accept their policies than ask questions;

Xenophobes who urge, as patriotic, forms of economic, political, and cultural isolationism that ignore all the realities of the modern world and make it almost impossible for us to establish foreign policies that will clearly point up for all peoples, and particularly for the earth's backward peoples, the difference between democracy and communism;

The special brand of "internationalist" who, by his seeming ability to tolerate and defend all countries and cultures except his own, misrepresents the nature of genuine internationalism—making it appear to be simply a form of mental and emotional expatriation;

Hotheads who will not, or cannot, conceive the grim results of atomic and bacterial warfare and who—almost as though they felt these weapons would do only "benign" damage if *we* used them—urge upon us either a "preventive war" or policies that encourage a final resort to war;

Good-willed but unrealistic wishful thinkers who bid us interpret every calculated amiability on the part of Soviet Russia as a sign that the Communists have "reformed," that everything is now going to get better and better, and that we are nothing but warmongers if we continue to look to our defenses;

Political candidates and spokesmen for candidates who twist the facts of history for public consumption or use unfounded charges of subversion and "softness" toward Communism as campaign weapons;

Individuals, in and out of office, who cannot seem to outgrow those images of "backward" peoples that date from the period of western imperialism; and who therefore urge upon us policies that can only make backward countries read more hope into Communist promises than into ours;

People who label as "Communistic" the very measures here at home—such as the desegregation ruling, for example—that rob the Communists, here and abroad, of their best talking points;

People who make the best of other people's problems —that of desegregation, for example—with such arrogant self-confidence and readiness to denounce that they help to create disastrous cleavages within our society and to postpone rational solutions of the problems in question;

Liberals who manage, somehow, in all good faith, to greet each successive proof of Communist infiltration and subversion by saying, in effect, "There's no such animal";

All who circulate unverified rumors that harm other people, who claim pipelines to sources of secret information, and who help to keep the public mind focused on catastrophe and well-nigh oblivious to what is soundly going on in our midst;

And finally—but not least—such aspects of our own personalities and life-patterns as tempt us to act after the manner of the above groups.

To put it mildly, it is quite a situation that we are in— and the only rational way out of it is that of making our "eternal vigilance" also a skillful, discriminating, just, and timely vigilance.

When we start to size up all the varieties of vigilance that are being exercised among us today, what strikes us at once is the anxious concern with which their practitioners watch one another, point with alarm at one another's conduct, twitch the sleeve of the otherwise preoccupied public, and urge, "Look what's going on!" And, in truth, plenty that calls for appraisal and judgment *is* going on.

Congressional committees, all departments of the federal government, the FBI, state legislatures, patriotic organizations, veterans organizations, groups dedicated to the defense of civil liberties, groups specifically dedicated to academic freedom, groups specifically dedicated to freedom of the press, groups representing various minorities, churches, labor unions, business and professional associations: all these groups, and others—and countless individuals—have stepped up, of late, their practice of vigilance. In the crisscrossing of their convictions and anxieties, they have all been both *watched* and *watchers;* and most of them, a fair part of the time, have felt angry and misunderstood in both roles.

The worst that can be said about our intense *mutual* vigilance is that it has heightened factionalism at a time when we have most needed to find working bases of unity; has induced us, often, to carry our suspicions and denunciations of one another far beyond the bounds of reason; has driven one group after another to a blanket defense of its policies rather than to an impartial appraisal of these as measured by consequences; has many times made us focus our most intense antagonisms on one another rather than on dangers that we share in common; and has postponed our working out of policies of vigilance that could enlist the best powers of all groups while keeping their most extravagant impulses and partialities in check.

The best that can be said, perhaps, about this same mutual vigilance is that it has prevented any one slanted and hastily contrived form of vigilance from having everything its own way. It is as though we had spontaneously resorted, under the impact of crisis, to a new application of the principle of checks and balances. If, as a result, responsible individuals and agencies have often found it hard to get necessary jobs done—and to get these jobs accurately reported and widely understood—we have, at least, fumblingly, saved ourselves from coercive, one-sided vigilance of the totalitarian brand and have preserved our chance to learn by trial and error.

Underlying the pattern of checks and balances, we note another: a pattern of specialization. Groups have tended to look at our broad problems of national security and "social housekeeping" from their own habitual standpoints—their practical and emotional standing points—and have shaped their programs of vigilance in terms of what they have seen from there.

Some, for example, have focused almost exclusively on the threat of Communism; others, on threats to civil liberties and academic freedom from non-Communist and often anti-Communist sources. In both camps there have been those for whom specialization has meant chiefly a wise channeling of energy and expertness, and those for whom it has meant a warping of vision. Thus, both those who have treated Communism as virtually the only danger we need to be concerned about and those who have treated it as merely a trumped-up danger have tended, by their own one-sidedness, to render suspect even their well-founded anxieties.

Various groups, happily, have managed to keep their minds on many kinds of danger without, so to speak, losing their heads; or losing them only occasionally.

High among such groups have been several for whom the practice of vigilance has been a long, steady preoccupation: neither a sudden passion nor a sudden chance to take the limelight. They have been trained to the skills and disciplines such practice calls for; have set their sights by the Constitution rather than by erratic public opinion or political involvement; and have operated within rules and bounds designed to minimize the anarchic play of temperament, prejudice, and personal ambition.

Among official investigative agencies that have become focal points of public interest is the Federal Bureau of Investigation. Like any other man-made organization, the FBI is distinctly human—and therefore not immune to error. Yet it appears to be so organized and administered as to keep errors at a minimum and to effect their correction when they are made, rather than to conceal or defend them.

No concerned person, it seems to us, could have lived through the tensions of the past few years without having questions about the FBI take shape in his mind. No one, certainly, could keep his ears open without hearing rumors which, if substantiated, would justify the gravest anxiety. Here, as in so many other cases, however, we have found that the best thing to do with a question, once it has lodged in our minds, is to go looking for an answer—and to go, not to those most likely to confirm us in our own judgment, but to those most able to provide objective facts; and also, wherever possible, to go to the record.

Morris L. Ernst has reported the experience that first sent him searching, through a wilderness of rumors, for whatever the truth might be about the FBI. That experience, he tells us, was one of surprise: surprise at the fact that J. Edgar Hoover had asked the Attorney General *not* to endorse a law that would legalize a free use of wire tapping; and had explained his request by saying, "I do not wish to be the head of an organization of potential blackmailers."

Mr. Ernst had not served as Counsel for the American Civil Liberties Union without hearing, from many sources, that the FBI was made up of "witch-hunters"; nor had he spent years fighting for the preservation of personal liberties without learning to view law enforcement officers with a wary eye—knowing how often they broke the law and infringed civil liberties in the performance of their duty.

Surprised, then, that Mr. Hoover was flatly opposed to a law that would have made his own work easier, and curious about what type of organization he did want to head, Mr. Ernst set about learning what he could learn—with both his skepticism and his legal knowledge on the job. He studied the records; invited information from widely varied sources; tried to trace down one report after another of the FBI's abuse of its authority—only to have each one turn from positive report to vague, unverified rumor. In the end, he felt ready and obligated to say, "The FBI is unique in the history of national police. It has a magnificent record of respect for individual freedom. It invites documented complaints against its agents. It has zealously tried to prevent itself from violating the democratic process." [1]

Our own interest in learning more about the Bureau stemmed from a different experience: from an effort to confirm or disprove a specific rumor. In a certain community sev-

[1] Morris L. Ernst, "Why I No Longer Fear the FBI," *Reader's Digest*, December, 1950.

eral years ago, a man was being charged by some of his neighbors with pro-Communist sympathies; and word was going the rounds that derogatory information about him had been leaked from the FBI files—or, in another version, had been provided by an ex-FBI agent.

What started, on our part, as an effort to check up on this rumor became, as time went on, a more broadly conceived effort. For the more we learned about the actual set-up, philosophy, practices, and personnel of the FBI, the more impressed we were by the strange discrepancy between antagonistic rumor and apparent fact.

There were, we soon discovered, rumors aplenty. At one time or another, or over and over, we were told about the Bureau's flouting of civil liberties. We were also told that its agents asked absurd and "loaded" questions—about the books an individual read; about whether he had Negro friends —and that they were highhanded and oppressive in their methods. Thus, for example, there was a "well authenticated" case of an agent's taking a scientist out of his laboratory at a midwestern university, driving him around and around the block, and browbeating him into giving derogatory information about a colleague. (The facts of the case turned out to be otherwise: the scientist had been leaving his laboratory when the agent arrived; had suggested that he could, as well as not, answer questions while they walked out together; and then, to continue the conversation, had sat with the agent in his car for some twenty minutes in front of the building.)

We were told, again, about the FBI's indiscriminate wire tapping; the deliberate mixing in its files of unverified rumor and verified fact; its "leaking" of information from the files to favored, reactionary Congressmen and columnists; its determination to set up a file on every adult American; its abuse of prisoners to get confessions. We were told that it tried to place its former agents in other government departments, there to use them as spies; that it "loaded" its files with derogatory information—or pure invention—in the case of individuals who had criticized its policies, and that it removed from these same files the most telling favorable information; that it edited its reports on individuals holding governmental positions, or applying for such positions, to guarantee its friends being hired and its enemies being fired; that it started investigations on its own; that it was surreptitiously taking over the proper work of local and state authorities, preparatory to setting up a police state.

We heard all these rumors—and others; but when we tried, as best we could, to verify them or hunt them down to their source, they had—as Morris Ernst had discovered before us —a way of vanishing into thin air: they went back to what somebody had told somebody. What did not vanish into thin air, but became constantly more solid as we studied the record, was evidence that showed the Bureau's respect for professional standards of law enforcement; its rigorous self-limiting to its own proper field of operation; its refusal to interpret or slant its own findings; its determination to protect the innocent as well as to expose the guilty; and its deep concern for the preservation of civil liberties.

We have become convinced, in brief, that the FBI has held to a remarkably steady course through the years—in spite of its having had to find means for coping with secret and completely ruthless adversaries; and of its being flagrantly misrepresented by its enemies—and also by its friends.

To see how various these sources of misrepresentations can be, we might recall that the Princeton study of the appeals of Communism showed that the FBI has been a chief target of the Party's hatred in America; and side by side with this fact, we might place the all too many instances when extremists of the right have tried to wrap up their own procedures in the Bureau's prestige. Citizens do well, we have concluded, when trying to make up their minds about this key agency in our "vigilance equipment," to look with prompt and visible skepticism both at those who declare the FBI to be the cynical, oppressive precursor of a police state and those who claim secret information leaked from the FBI, or a source of special information in the person of an ex-FBI man. Perhaps the best way for us to greet most of the random, unverified things we hear about the Bureau is to say to ourselves, in the words of the song from *Porgy and Bess,* "It ain't necessarily so. . . ."

Among those unofficial groups which have kept rational minds on their jobs in spite of praise, pressure, and denunciation, we would certainly place the national organization of the American Civil Liberties Union high on the list. Here, again, the keynote has been the *sustained* practice of vigilance; and here again we note the voluntary limiting of the field of action, the effort to get facts straight, and the reference to objective rather than subjective standards. While the organization has seemed to us on a few occasions to lean over backward, on the national level, at least, it has proved a staunch and expert defender of constitutional liberties—including, often, those of individuals and groups with whom it has profoundly disagreed. It has, moreover, demonstrated one way in which the layman and the legal expert, when they share a common concern, can render a common service to a free society.

Even groups with a far briefer history—groups born of crisis, with their undertakings defined by that crisis—have often shown a distinguished immunity to hysteria and a high-level capacity to do a specific job without losing sight of broader concerns. The American Committee for Cultural Freedom is a case in point. Intent on educating the American public how to penetrate the disguises of conspiratorial Communism *while keeping clear the all-important distinction between subversion and dissent,* this group has done its self-appointed task with intelligence, careful factuality, and integrity. Though often charged with being too far to the right and too far to the left, it has avoided squandering its energies in angry self-defense or in retaliatory denunciation.

Among the groups that have proved able to face the dangers of our time and to exercise vigilance without making it a hybrid mixture of hysteria and self-indulgence, have been many of the long established voluntary associations of our culture.

Level-headedness here seems to be correlated with long practice in handling human relations and getting problems solved within the human community. The voluntary associations, by and large, that have best kept their heads—without tucking them into the sands of obliviousness—have been those that have been creatively involved with the larger housekeeping of our democratic society. They have been long and steadily engaged in trying to satisfy people's basic needs; open up new opportunities; replace ignorance by knowledge; bridge gaps of misunderstanding; minister to the lonely and handicapped and excluded; foster better relationships between adults and children, native and foreign born, minority and majority groups, different creeds and religions; release and encourage creative abilities; and generally keep our democratic life moving along on the path of its best intentions.

In a time of crisis, such groups, we have discovered, are doubly fortified against panic and the temptations of factionalism. They have, for one thing, known human nature in its decency, nobility, frustration, inhibition, excitability and cussedness well enough not to be easily caught off guard by it. And their long experience in taking people as they come and learning to work with them as they are has not given them much chance either to indulge, within their own fellowship, in "hothouse mutual admiration," or to exaggerate the difference between themselves and others.

There have been cases, certainly, where such organizations or their local branches have yielded weakly to pressures or have been caught up in a wave of hysteria or have turned from their rightful tasks to ventures in vigilance for which they have been ill-prepared. But by and large, voluntary organizations with broad, long-range programs have proved themselves a power for sanity. In spite of all stereotypes to the contrary, they have shown that they are not so much makers of the "mass mind" as of the freely co-operating, problem-solving mind.

A special word of appreciation, we believe, should go to certain professional groups that have met the challenge of crisis by putting their expertness to work in new ways. The American Bar Association, for example, has made notable efforts to clarify issues related to civil liberties. Physical scientists have tried, through both their long-established associations and new special committees, to reveal the actualities of atomic warfare. The American Library Association and the American Book Publishers' Council have defined and redefined the stake of a free people in *freedom to read*. Psychological and psychiatric groups have explored problems that range from the make-up of the totalitarian personality and the nature of prejudice to the tactics of Communism and the impact upon employee morale of ill-conceived, ambiguous, or arbitrarily administered security measures. And these are but a small sampling of the associations that might be named.

Our best proof that many individuals and groups have both kept their heads and exercised vigilance lies, perhaps, in the fact that we seem to be finding our way out of extremism without lapsing into "indolence"—and to be doing so by democratic means.

A top administrator in a southwestern university—a man who has had his own troubles with extremism and fanaticism—wrote us recently about a "marked drop in the tension and hysteria of the past few years and the reassertion of a more equable temper in the discussion and management of public affairs." What he thus noted from his vantage point, many of us can, so to speak, feel in our bones. The tide of sanity is rising.

Our personal feeling is that we Americans ought to make a special thank offering for this return of a "more equable temper": an offering of sustained, realistic interest in the problem of democratic vigilance. Now if ever, it would seem, is the time for us to make ourselves so much at home with this "eternal" problem that we will not again be caught off guard by its 20th-century complexities and ambiguities. Here is a project that could be approached by a myriad different groups, each employing its own experience and expertness; and out of their different venturings and new collaborations might come a sounder climate of opinion and a firmer skill in democratic process than we have been living with of late.

What might such an undertaking involve—whether sponsored by a university or a government agency; by a veterans' organization or an AAUW; by a church or a mental health society; by a Rotary Club or the American Association of University Professors—or, as we would hope, by a variety of such groups working together?

As a start, we feel that it should be at least a four-fold undertaking. First of all—and regardless of the particular sponsor, this is indispensable—it would have to bring together for a comparison of problems and viewpoints certain

groups that have been standing too far apart for any fair
mutual appraisal. When groups that affect one another's freedoms know one another, in Robinson's words, "only as a motion on the landscape"; and when even this distant look is
taken through the distorting atmosphere of crisis and the fog
of rumor, each group is prone to see more stimuli to fear and
anger and fewer points of common purpose than a close-up
view might reveal.

We are not so bland in optimism as to believe that proxim-
ity alone can guarantee understanding; that all the sharp
differences that have divided us have been illusory or super-
ficial; or that joining in some enterprise of study and discussion will of itself add cubits of reasonableness to personalities stunted by fears and fanaticisms.

We do believe, however, that if moderately sound people
are invited into one another's frames of reference, they begin
to see their different and even opposed viewpoints *as attached
to reasons* and not merely as *irrational*. Also, they have a
chance to separate real disagreements from unreal and to
make them explicit. There is a large likelihood, moreover, that
they will discover both unexpected agreements and unexpected reasons for tempering their own absolutisms.

Not to believe that such results are possible would contradict our own personal experience. We have watched these
changes take place, time and again, in group after group.
Also, time and again, we ourselves have learned much from
people whom we did not, at the outset, regard as likely teachers, but only as opponents or extremists.

There is particular need in our time for the lay citizen and
the government official to know each other better in terms
of problems and purposes. Very specifically, there is need for
the liberal citizen and the government investigator or security agent to move out of their present mutual remoteness
into enough mutual understanding that they can at least dis-

tinguish fact from falsehood in their estimates of each other.

William McCleery, in his comedy, *Good Housekeeping,* observes that "men usually ignore the issues when they square off to fight over them." [1] They may not ignore them at the outset. But as the *experience* of fight hardens into the *habit-pattern* and *loyalty-pattern* of fight, their objective concern about issues becomes adulterated by a subjective mixture of fear, pride, anger, factional conformity, and a sense of being misunderstood and misjudged. It is no healthy thing, in a time of crisis, for agencies of democratic government and significant portions of our citizenry to have become well-nigh automatic in their mutual self-defensiveness.

Whether they be official agencies or voluntary groups it is of vital importance that those who have "specialized" their vigilance against Communism and those who have "specialized" it against non-Communist threats to civil liberties and academic freedom be brought within physical and psychological speaking distance of each other. For the vigilance of neither will be good enough to match our 20th century need so long as one half—*either* half—of our problem is treated as the whole; and so long as those who deal with only one half count those who deal with the other half as natural enemies.

Two results of such automatic hostility are particularly painful to witness. One is that each group, intent to "corner" the other and to avoid being "cornered," becomes more and more intemperate and intolerant in its charges and judgments. The other is that those individuals within each camp who have most resolutely tried to improve procedures and meet all reasonable demands made by their critics are left discouraged and unsupported. What they are trying to do is either not noticed at all by those who say it is the very thing that should be done; or else, perversely, it is noted and viewed with suspicion: what are they up to now?

[1] William McCleery, *Good Housekeeping,* p. 105. New York: Samuel French, 1950. Copyright by William McCleery.

If we do indeed have a fresh chance, within an atmosphere of comparative moderation, to develop proper standards and procedures for the practice of vigilance, we will do well, in brief, to make as many occasions as possible for those who have looked at our common problems from opposite sides, and *only* from opposite sides, to meet together, talk together, and walk all the way around these problems in each other's company.

A second part of our undertaking must be that of mapping our proper areas of democratic vigilance. All the dangers we catalogued earlier in this chapter call for "watchdog" vigilance. But on whose part? The government's part? And if so, through what agency? The private citizen's part? The voluntary group's? Or, co-operatively, on the part of all these? The effort of a free people to map and allocate areas of vigilance is in itself a growth-inducing effort.

Nor is "watchdog" vigilance the only kind we need to cultivate and allocate. "Preventive" vigilance is equally called for: the sort of awareness that can take stock of where conditions in our society, and in the world, need to be made better before their destructive influence makes matters worse.

In a statement entered in the Congressional Record of January 26, 1953, J. Edgar Hoover reported that the FBI had reviewed the origins of 5,395 members of the Communist Party. Of this number, "4,555 or 91½ percent were either of foreign birth or born of foreign parents." These striking figures do not signify, nor did Mr. Hoover intend them to signify, that "foreigners" are a bad lot. What Mr. Hoover's report underscored is the fact that we still have not achieved the level of cultural hospitality we need in this country: too many Americans of foreign background still feel themselves to be, in one or another hampering way, *outsiders*.

This fact, in turn, illustrates a broader insight that we are learning to bring to bear upon problems as various as those of delinquent youth and displaced old people: the insight, namely, that those who feel themselves to be unwanted *outsiders* in situations where they urgently need a sense of belonging will seek some way to balance their emotional budget. People of intelligent good will must learn with ever increasing expertness and generosity to bring their "preventive" vigilance to bear upon conditions that make other people feel like outsiders—*and that are therefore likely to make them act outside the rules and shared values of our going institutions.*

This, however, is by no means the only call upon our "preventive" vigilance. Where do undernourishment, poor sanitation, lack of medical services, or plain ignorance make likely a high incidence of disease? Where do overcrowded or inferior schools make likely the waste of human powers? Where do elements of obtuseness, complacency, or paternalism in our foreign policy threaten our good relationships with other nations and peoples?

But even "preventive" vigilance is not enough. "Supportive" vigilance is likewise called for: an appreciative alertness to what is being valiantly attempted or well done; and a generous and practical ability to approve, encourage, and cooperate. In view of all we have come to know about the ways of human growth, it is a safe guess that the wiser we become in the arts of "supportive" vigilance, the less we will be called upon to exercise "watchdog" and even "preventive" vigilance.

In the third place, as a people we deeply need to come to grips with the problem of *means* and *ends:* specifically, means suitable for the practice of democratic vigilance.

Too often, in recent years, we have seen *methods* become uncoupled from *purposes* and run wild—like freight cars that have broken loose on a steep grade: freight cars that not only cease to move upward toward their proper goal but that go careening in the opposite direction. Some of the means employed, officially and unofficially, for the defense of our liberties have seemed more likely to carry us back toward tyrannies we thought we had left far behind down at the foot of the grade, where we began our long upward pull toward constitutional government.

Yet a proper vigilance, here, will not expend itself wholly in exposing wrong means. It has also a constructive job to do: that of evolving right means. What precise means, for example, would liberal citizens recommend *as both effective and just* for locating and exposing persons who are genuine security risks? Whether actually there be many such persons or few has little to do with our need to find proper answers to questions of method.

What specific means, again, would we approve for dealing with active, conspiratorial Communists—few or many—who, at large in our society, work through various channels and media to sow seeds of dissension and to give a bad name to good causes? What means would we consider both effective and reasonable for bringing the public to an awareness of how the tactics of infiltration work, and of instances where these tactics have been successfully practiced? It would be a far from dull business, and a solid project in self-education, for us to move beyond opposition to dubious methods to the framing of methods acceptable as balanced, efficient, and fair.

Another related part of our self-education as a people would rightly have to do with our learning far more than we now know about our machinery of vigilance. What, for example, do we understand to be the proper function of Congressional investigating committees? What has determined, in various specific cases, whether they were operating within their proper domain or making irresponsible sallies outside it? In like vein, what do we understand to be the proper functions and procedures of the FBI; the attorney general; a grand jury; public hearings; various White House conferences; various citizens' committees? Under what circumstances, and for what purposes, will the Supreme Court accept cases for review? In other areas of vigilance, what do we know about the control of narcotics; about the administration of our pure food and drug laws; about the type of watchfulness that precedes the bringing of an anti-trust suit; about fact-finding processes with regard to matters as various as our national health, the needs of our public schools, depressed areas that need economic stimulus to get back on their feet, the conditions of the land, the care of our public forests, and infringements of civil rights?

These are but a few questions out of many that we need to try to answer; and seeking answers to them in the good company of our fellow Americans, in groups and communities all across the land, would be a far from dull business.

Finally, as the fourth part of our undertaking, we recommend what we call self-vigilance. If there is one thing that modern psychology has taught us, it is that we are not always, in our minds and motives, exactly what we like to think we are. And if there is one thing that our "cold civil war" has taught us—or should have taught us by now—it is that we all have a large power to fall short of the glory. Part of our nationwide "homework" might well be coming to know as much as we can about the tendencies in our individual and group selves that work to compound the darkness of fear, animosity, conformity, irresponsibility, and factionalism.

While William Pepperell Montague was Head of the Department of Philosophy at Barnard College, he told a story about himself that is not irrelevant here. On a certain day there came into his street-level office a woman who announced that she had conclusively resolved all the mysteries of the universe—and who proceeded to give him, at length, the benefit of her all-embracing insight. When she left, finally, he watched her with compassionate eyes as she walked past his window, thinking to himself, "There but for the grace of God, go I." Suddenly, then, thinking of his own constant efforts to encompass the universe in a man-made frame of thought, he said to himself, "My God, maybe there I go!" There are few of us, today, when we are so often tempted to look at others with eyes far from compassionate, who might not profitably recall Montague's startled words to himself.

We end this chapter with a bit of dialogue from the comedy from which we have already quoted: *Good Housekeeping*. It is part of a family conversation about the plain citizen's responsibilities. Since the talk is getting nowhere and yet promises to go on indefinitely, the mother announces that she is going to bed.

"A tired liberal," her teen-age daughter quips.

"Any liberal who isn't tired isn't working at it," her father assures her;[1] and the humor in his remark is grim around the edges.

Scholars and analysts aplenty have told us that modern man is becoming robotized man or mass man because he is tired of being free; of making decisions without knowing enough to make them; of being told he should take on responsibilities for which there is never time; of feeling guilty about what is left undone; of weighing the hazards of making up his own mind against the self-contempt he feels if he lets someone else make it up for him; or simply of being his lonely, separate, supposedly independent self within a system of huge impersonal forces.

The scholars and analysts may be right: some of our behaviors in recent years give weight to their words. Or they

[1] *Op. cit.*, p. 49.

may be wrong: for certain different behaviors suggest that we are getting ready to say, with a compound of humor and grimness, that any free person who isn't tired isn't working at his freedom. If we are ready thus to speak, and to convert word into action, we can be sure of one thing at least: that our tiredness will be the legitimate result of effort, not the illegitimate result of boredom or inner conflict. In no small part, if we obey the imperatives now set before us, it will be the comfortable weariness of our having undertaken a new job: not that of just being vigilant in the way that comes easiest to us, because of our own stakes and conditionings, but that of learning how to practice "eternal vigilance" wisely and patiently in our own time and place, and in the company of those who may or may not readily agree with us, but who share our stakes in a free society.

SIXTEEN

WHEN PERSONAL PROBLEMS
BECOME SOCIAL PROBLEMS

M ENTAL ILLNESS is never a private affair. Physical
illness may be—comparatively speaking. It can, in a
sense, be contained within body limits, and kept to the self.
There are, of course, contagious diseases. Also, there are by-
products of illness—loss of work, medical bills, and the rest
—that can disrupt the plans and curtail the experiences not
only of the afflicted person but of his family as well. Yet physical illness can come far closer to being a private affair than
mental illness can.

We were recently surprised and distressed, for example, to
learn that a certain man we know and profoundly respect has,
for the past five years, been unobtrusively coping with a bad
heart. We have sat with this man on committees; visited in
his home; had good sessions of talk with him and come away
the better for them; watched him reanimate an organization
that we would have said, two years ago, was dying in its

tracks. But it was not until he explained diffidently why he could not take on an additional task that would have involved extra physical strain—and a lot of standing around talking to people—that we learned that his heart had constantly to be taken into account in his plans.

Suppose, however, he had been afflicted by an equally serious mental illness. Could we then have talked and worked with him on so many different occasions and yet not have suspected that anything was wrong? It seems highly unlikely. True, we might not have been able to put our finger on the nature of his trouble, or the cause of it. But there would have been an uneasiness in our relationship to him: an undefined sense of "thus far, and no further." Instead of relaxed, confident sharing—of laughter, perplexity, remembered experience, and deep concern—there would have been a certain constraint: what we have earlier called *guardedness*.

Also, since many of the situations in which we had seen him operate had called for the delicate handling of human beings and the warm appreciation of their various ideas and efforts, it seems improbable that he could have carried them off had not he himself been basically sound in mind and emotion. Neither good resolutions nor carefully learned tactics would have served him had inner health been lacking: tensions would have shown through.

What is the vital difference, then, between organic illness and personality disorder? We might put it thus. If an individual has a headache, he knows he is the one who has it. He does not, projectively, think that someone else's head is doing the aching. But if he has a neurosis, whom does he take to be the "problem" person? Not himself, as a rule. Somebody else. Experiencing friction, anxiety, smoldering anger, resentment, he seeks a cause. He does not commonly discover this cause, however, within himself. He "discovers" it in the other person: in the wife who doesn't understand him; the boss who sets no proper value on his services; subordinates who, the whole drove of them, are lazy and unreliable; neighbors with whom no reasonable human being could get along; children who delight in crossing him.

The essential difference between physical and mental disorder is to be found in the *relational* pattern. Each represents, we might say, a breakdown of relationships. But whereas physical illness reports a disordering of relationships within the body, mental and emotional illness reports a disordering of relationships between the individual and his environment: primarily, his human environment.

Neurosis can best be described, perhaps, as a way of going at life that does not fit the case—and that therefore puts the neurotic individual at odds with reality. For practical purposes, we might define it as *a misinterpretation of life that is so habitually acted out that it gives the afflicted person no respite from conflict.* The story of how such misinterpretations are built into personality—most often in early childhood, as a result of experiences that painfully threatened the ego—is an old story now, in this psychological age. We need not repeat it here. But what concerns us is the *outwarding* of inner conflict: its effect upon other people's lives and, more broadly, upon our shared institutions and climate of opinion.

To understand what such *outwarding* of inner conflict does to our human relationships, we might take a look, first, not at deep personality disorders, but at what we might call "brief neuroses": moods that may not last long but that can, while they last, not only induce tensions but start a veritable contagion of them.

Take anger, for example. Horace, many centuries ago, defined anger as "short madness." And an old folk proverb has it that "A man in a passion rides a runaway horse." Most of us know from experience that what is thus stated is true. The person who is possessed by anger is not *self*-possessed. He says and does what he would normally know to be exaggerated, unfair, even cruel. "Blind anger" is an apt phrase; for what intense anger does, while it lasts, is to make the individual unable to see what is objectively there to be seen.

Like sustained neurosis, in brief, a passing rage induces behavior *from the inside out:* behavior directly expressive of the person's own emotions and not truly responsive to any outside situation. When a man, apologizing for words spoken in anger, says sheepishly, "I guess I lost my head," his words make sense. For he has not been doing with his head what his head normally enables him to do: with eyes to see, he has not seen; with ears to hear, he has not heard; having the power to think, he has not thought.

We all have emotional ups and downs that color our reactions. The more mature a person is, the less likely his moods are to be wildly fluctuating affairs; and the less likely, also, they are to be irresponsibly acted out—as though just having a certain feeling licensed behavior in kind, regardless of other people's feelings. But we all have moods. Sometimes we experience a mood as a result of a known stimulus—as when loneliness follows the departure of a close friend whom we will not see again for a long time. More often, perhaps, we experience a change of mood for reasons too elusive to pin down—as when loneliness invades a state of well-being, like an uninvited ghost at a party.

We all have moods; and even the best of us act them out in ways, now and then, that put us at odds with our world. We say, on such occasions, that we are *out of sorts*. More precisely, we are *out of touch*. The world is there, with all its realities calling for response; but we, for the time being, are too *in-turned* to be aware of those realities.

When we recognize that a mood of ours has made us a

problem for somebody else, we may say, "I'm sorry I was so abrupt with you. I guess I got out of the wrong side of the bed this morning." Unless we have been destructively offensive, the chances are that the other person will say, "Oh, that's all right. No harm done"—or words to similar effect; for he will know that it may be his turn next time to lean on the serviceable excuse. To some extent, in brief, we all have to live by taking in one another's moods, and dealing with them as we would want ours to be dealt with.

What shall we say, however, about the person whose anger is chronic—or so frequent that it has always to be taken into account by those who live and work with him? What about the habitually sullen person; or the one in whom even the slightest affront is enough to induce deep resentment—and daydreams of revenge? What about the man who is always involved in an argument? What about the teacher who misses no chance to hone the blade of her sarcasm? What about the boss whose office force waits in daily apprehension? By the time he has passed through the outer office in the morning, every worker present knows what kind of day it is likely to be—and all too often it is likely to be the kind when they do well to watch their step; and when, even if they all watch their step, someone is sure to be called on the carpet.

If anger is "short madness," then there are certain types of personality disorder—"madness"—that might well be called "long anger." The element of hostility—though not always obvious—is a prime characteristic of mental illness. It expresses the fact that the individual who is so out of touch that only his own feelings are real to him is bound to experience the outer world as stubborn and unreasonable. His "answering" behaviors, therefore, are not just occasionally exaggerated, unfair, unfitting, and even cruel; they are habitually so. We might say that such a person always gets out of the wrong side of the bed—because his bed has no right side.

When we are even briefly out of sorts—angry, peevish, disgruntled, fearful, hurt, dejected, sorry for ourselves—certain of our best *relational* powers practically cease to function. For the time being, they are lost to us. Among the first casualties, for example, when our own mood alienates us from our world, are such redemptive, unifying powers as tenderness, sympathy, warm humor, appreciation, a sense of how much alike we all are, the capacity to see and admit our own shortcomings, and that most inclusive of attitudes that we call reverence for life.

With these powers temporarily out of working order, we have no real equipment for "approach": for going toward a fellow human being with interest and a will to understand. Almost inevitably, therefore, we become "hard" in our relationships: intolerant, exacting, obtuse. We become, in brief, far from pleasant to have around; and we may become dangerous to have around—destructive of other people's legitimate prides and plans. With the gap between ourselves and others grossly exaggerated, we tend to treat these others less like human beings and more like impersonal objects than we normally do. Nor is such treatment confined to some particular individual who has wronged us: who is, in some true sense, responsible for our mood. Because our behavior stems *from a pervasive emotional state within ourselves,* it tends to become a covering sort of behavior. It spreads out to touch everyone with whom we come into contact until our mood changes—and since it is well calculated to turn others in upon themselves, its final range of influence is hard to measure.

If we know this much—as we should, from experience—about how we act when we are out of sorts, we are in a position to estimate the threat to human happiness and social stability posed by deep personality disorder. In the neurotic person—and more drastically, in the psychotic—the *relational* powers are underdeveloped, even atrophied. Such an individual does not simply, now and then, depart from tenderness, warm humor, a uniting awareness of his own shortcomings, reverence for life. The *in-turning* of his attention has been so constant for so long that it has rendered him well-nigh incapable of experiencing these emotions. He is, we might say, so far removed from the emotional company of his human fellows that he does not know how to start moving toward them, even when he wants to do so. Nor does he know how to receive them with warm hospitality if they venture the approach.

He may glory in his remoteness from the "herd"; or pathetically yearn to love and be loved; or be constantly bewildered by other people's lack of response to him—or their withdrawal from him. Or he may try to establish himself by one or another rigid contrivance. Intense factionalism may be his resort. By dividing the human race into friends and enemies, and lining himself up with one side against the other, he achieves a spurious sense of belonging: spurious because it does not actually require him to understand any individual, and also because it forbids his seeing any aspect of reality that does not comport with his division of people into good and evil. More drastically still, he may try to remake society—in whole or in part—and give it a form that would guarantee his having status and power. Or he may simply try to dominate every situation he enters; or, where he cannot dominate it, prevent anyone else from getting anything accomplished.

John Donne said of Goodness that it "dares appear and spread and glister in the World." We might say with regard to the type of evil that stems from mental illness that it dares appear and spread and make darkness in the world. The trouble-making propensity of mental and emotional disorder is enormous: how enormous we are just beginning to realize —as we learn to look past irresponsible, callous, and destructive behaviors to their causes. In case after case, it is all too apparent that the cause does not truly lie in the objective situation. It lies within the person's own make-up; and no matter what situation the disordered person enters, he will act out, in one or another fashion, to the world's hurt, his own inner conflict, his own resident hostility.

The behavior of such a person has to be singled out as different from normal behavior. The disordered individual has to be restrained from having his own way with other people's lives. The words he speaks about others must be largely discounted; for as a rule those words tell less about the people in question than about how the world looks to him from his strange emotional "standing place." Again, his driving ambition has to be recognized, in its urgent ruthlessness, as different from normal and healthy ambition—the latter always being marked by the fact that there are firm limits to what the individual will do to others to further his own ends. Or, if his need to make himself secure takes an opposite direction, his leech-like dependence has to be recognized as outside the healthy human pattern of give-and-take—and as exploitative in its consequences even when it appears to be a veritable study in meekness and submissiveness.

Not to recognize the sort of individual who is "hard" in his dealings with others—because they are scarcely more than puppets to him, to be manipulated by the strings of his need —is to leave these others at his mercy. Also, it is to leave at the mercy of his trouble-making tendencies whatever situation or institution comes within his reach. Yet it is not enough to recognize and restrain him—or, where actual restraint is not called for, to diminish his influence by learning to discount his version of what is going on in the home or place of work, the neighborhood or the world. He, too, is a human being—and a far from happy one. He, too, has rights—though he may seem chiefly engaged in flouting those of others; and not least among his rights is that of having his sort of problem understood and reasonably dealt with.

Mental illness, then, we repeat, is never a private affair—not even when it is fairly mild. It acts itself out in small situations and large—to the world's hurt. Toward it, moreover, we are beginning to acknowledge a new responsibility beyond that of curtailing its influence in this or that specific case. Our larger responsibility is to learn enough about its causes to diminish its incidence. This is our preventive undertaking. Beyond this, there is the task of healing—which means the task of building into our own minds new attitudes toward mental and emotional disorder; and building into our society such agencies of healing as can put to work, for the saving of individuals and the securing of our common welfare, every bit of hard-won knowledge we now possess about our human make-up.

To recognize the signs and patterns of personality disorder; to curtail the influence of the disordered personality upon other people's lives and our social atmosphere and institutions; to look through and beyond unhealthy behaviors to their causes, and thus to learn the arts of prevention; and to set the task of healing high on the agenda of our social concerns: this is the program through which we can act out our understanding that mental illness is not a private affair.

Mental illness, like physical, can run the full scale from mild to severe. It is not always easy, therefore, to single out in the human community the person who can rightly be called "disturbed." As a starting point, however, we can say that the "disturbed" individual is one who habitually imports into the situations he enters an emotional problem of his own that is acute enough to make him see more reasons for fear and anger than are objectively present.

In one individual this slant toward hostility may show itself only as a constant habit of carping: of never finding anything that anybody does quite good enough to approve. In another, it may show itself as a fear of taking on normal responsibilities. In yet another, the state of tension may be revealed in proneness to accident. In extreme case, as we have noted earlier, it may express itself as an urge to destroy. The delinquent youth who breaks the windows of a church or school or who beats up a helpless old man; the rumormonger who tears down the reputation of one person after another; the warmonger who can scarcely wait to have his nation beat up some other nation; the "reformer" who has far less interest in the process of *re-forming* than in that of tearing down the *status quo* as a preliminary to making things better; the devotee of an ideology that gives him a specified enemy to hate and promises him the pleasure of destroying that enemy: all these, we might say, are cut from the same emotional fabric—and it is not the fabric out of which a sound society can be made.

We are still far from expert in recognizing personality disorder. Even our courts, with the services of the psychiatrist at their command, do not always find it easy to distinguish the legally responsible person from the legally irresponsible one who belongs in a mental hospital rather than a prison; and those versed in the subtleties of the human make-up know only too well that the line drawn by law is at best a practical expedient, and that the term "responsible" is highly ambiguous.

One day's newspaper, for example, recently reported two wholly separate cases of extreme parental cruelty: cruelty that in one case resulted in the death of a child. One parent was eventually sent to a mental institution; the other, fined and given a jail sentence. Perhaps, under present circumstances, each decision was "just." That is to say, each reflected the judge's honest effort, on the basis of evidence at his command, to draw a line that has to be drawn somewhere because we do not yet know how to handle the problem of brutality and destructiveness without drawing it. Yet from all we know of the patterns of personality disorder, it seems clear that both parents were out of touch with reality, blinded by inner rage and obeying the dictates of that rage.

If it is often hard for a judge, with the resources and evidence at his command, to make a decision, it is far harder for the rest of us to be sure that the random judgments we pass upon human misbehaviors are accurate and fair. Thus we see a man suddenly lose his temper—and his sense of proportion—"over nothing." Is he acting out a "brief madness" brought on, perhaps, by fatigue and anxiety so great that even a minor irritation proved the last straw; or is it the "long madness" of personality disorder?

Some persons, we ourselves feel, are too brisk in deciding: too ready to announce the hidden cause of each type of overt misconduct. It is almost as though they had found in the vocabulary of the psychological sciences one more language in which to express their own inner problems. It is almost as though they had found a way—highly conducive to ego-satisfaction—of verbally "liquidating" people they do not like; or, more broadly, of verbally dominating the "wildness" of human nature.

To be wary of hasty labels is not to conclude, however, that there are no signs at all by which we can distinguish sound conduct from unsound. There are signs; and we are learning more about them every day.

In the preceding chapter, we ventured a list of persons with regard to whom, we said, "eternal vigilance" is in order; for if their attitudes are converted into action, and if their actions go unchecked, the confusions of our time are made more confused and our problems become harder to resolve.

Let us return here, briefly, to that list of persons who bear watching. Are their behaviors symptomatic of personality disorder, mild or severe? Or are they simply mistaken behaviors? By what signs can we judge? As we try to answer such questions, we discover how much solid psychological knowledge has actually moved out of textbook and clinic into our climate of opinion. In significant measure, we have become citizens of the psychological age; and one proof of this is our emergent capacity to make certain distinctions between types of behavior.

Some "problem" types—gangsters, delinquents, practitioners of corruption—show themselves so morally obtuse with regard to the effects of their conduct upon other people's lives that we feel safe in designating them as "disordered." It seems clear that they are blocked off from reality by ever present acute inner problems which repeatedly make their behaviors callous, irresponsible, and destructive. Both the extent of deviation from normal and the sustained pattern of that deviation suggest deep unsoundness.

Certain other types, however, achieve a "protective coloration" that makes their disordered behavior dangerously able to pass as normal; and even, sometimes, as unusually idealistic or realistic.

Thus, one type we mentioned was the exhibitionist "martyr"—as distinguished, *but not always easy to distinguish,* from the genuine victim of injustice. One sign that the "martyr's" ego is at the center of his universe is the dramatic haste with which he puts himself at the center of the public stage. His not to explore possible paths to mutual understanding.

His not to take on the workaday role of presenting, as best he can, the facts of the case. His not to grant for a moment that those who oppose him may be honestly mistaken—or may, even, be justified in some measure. What the self-appointed "martyr" typically does is to convert every adversary into an agent of the Evil One: a figure with whom it is clearly impossible for him, as an Agent of Good, to have any traffic. Thus, he translates an objective issue into highly subjective terms —and into a black and white pattern of right and wrong. It is then presented to the public, we might say, as a dramatic allegory: a significant scene in man's long struggle with evil.

It might not be out of place, here, to recall a few sentences from the first chapter of this book: "Life is not more dramatic in noise than in silence, in conflict than in peace. . . . Unless we are deeply disturbed in our emotional make-up, we know that destructive conflict is a poor substitute for the adventures of searching things out together. There may be a crescendo of noise and action when two men get going in angry argument and pass from angry words to angry blows. Yet far more is actually happening—more human powers are at work— when two men, finding themselves on the edge of angry argument, veer away from that edge and sit down to talk things over. . . ."

A thoroughly sound person may be a victim of injustice. He will, because he is sound—and therefore puts a proper value upon his own life and life-plans—defend himself as factually and firmly as he can. He will stand up for his rights —because they *are* rights. He will do all within his power to clarify the situation; for he will recognize that until it is clarified not only he himself, but others like him are in danger. If, in the end, he is still cast as victim, he calls upon all his resources to meet the situation without falling apart. If outside help is offered in a form he can self-respectingly accept, he accepts it gratefully. But he does not *enjoy* being a victim; nor seek the limelight in order to adopt the stance of hero; nor set the pattern of conflict in such black and white terms that its resolution becomes virtually impossible. The sound person, in brief, as an individual of integrity, *deals as best he can with a problem in which he has a vital stake.* The "martyr," in contrast, *makes the most of a problem.*

We have lingered over this type for three reasons. In the first place, the "martyr," to our common confusion, often wears the protective coloration of the idealist. If we simply take his word for what is going on, and do not look through and beyond that word to his *taste for conflict* and his *insistent self-dramatizing,* we can easily commit the mistake of lining up on his side against an "enemy" he has described to us, in order to support a "cause" that he is emotionally exploiting or to solve a problem that he does not actually want solved.

In the second place, the person who thus takes on the role of "martyr" because he is deeply disturbed in his emotional make-up—deeply at odds with life—has a peculiar counterpart today: the "ideological martyr" of the extreme right and extreme left. This character plays the same sort of role for a different reason. He, too, sets the pattern of conflict in terms that prohibit its resolution. He, too, makes a public display of being victimized, and unjustly treated. He, too, rallies to his "cause" a great many who would not be there if they looked through his words to his deeper motives. But he is not so much a self-appointed "martyr" as a person whose appointment to "martyrdom" is part of the calculated stratagem of the group he serves: which may be a Communist group or a right-wing "hate group." The more able we are to recognize the "martyr"—whether emotionally compelled or ideologically assigned—the less likely we are to add to the confusion that he creates.

In the third place, we discover in the "martyr," highlighted for our recognition, certain characteristics that appear in other types also—and in which, also, they are marks of unsoundness. A rigid, uncompromising distinction drawn between good and evil, with all the good on one's own side; a matching tendency to divide the human race into beleaguered supporters of the good and powerful supporters of evil; the casting of problems in subjective rather than objective terms, with an eye to the ego-role that can be claimed; the rejection of methods of reconciliation even before they are tried; quickness to see all disagreement as *enemy* disagreement; the use of the word to confuse rather than clarify; and a general inability to experience drama in a state of peace: these, played out in one manner and another, are conspicuous characteristics of many different sorts of people who bear watching in our democratic society. They bear watching because their trademark upon any situation they influence will be a mark of ill health.

We are often puzzled, today, by striking similarities of attitude and behavior on the part of individuals who profess widely different—and even opposite—convictions: the Communist and Fascist, for example; and between these extremes, a smattering of those who speak of themselves as liberals or conservatives. What we need to realize, perhaps, is that personality type goes deeper than political label. While Communism and Fascism seem ready-made for the unsound, they do not, by any means, snare all of them. The accidents of life-conditioning may locate the egocentric with a taste for conflict anywhere on the ideological scale. If he happens to land in the liberal or conservative camp, he enacts "liberalism" or "conservatism," not in the honest tradition of either, but after the manner of his own hostile make-up.

Not all the individuals, however, who invite our vigilant appraisal are of the type we have been describing. There are some who distort the situations they touch, not by imposing upon them a rigid black and white pattern, but by reducing all their elements to a flat grey. Here we find, for example, the opportunist; the cynic; the neutralist; those who feel that ethical standards are irrelevant in the political area or, as the case may be, in the economic area; those who adjust the law to their own personal convenience and that of their friends; those who make it seem not quite smart to care very much about anything—except, perhaps, about being smart.

If we visualize the "martyr" and the totalitarian type as posturing in the limelight, we can visualize these social invertebrates as simply sprawling in the most comfortable spot they can find. In their amorphous state, differences are not seen as making any difference that really matters. Such persons are, we might say, pre-social: the structured relationships by which we live together, and in terms of which we distinguish right from wrong, have slight meaning for them. The mark of unsoundness that such as these leave upon our society is that of tawdry practice and deteriorated standard. And again we must note that seemingly opposite types can have a strikingly similar effect. The shabby politician, the go-getter, and the pseudo-sophisticate may be more alike than any one of them would choose to think; for all of them base both their personal decisions and their judgments of other people on factors that have little to do with either individual integrity or the common welfare.

In our effort to understand the many ways in which personality problems become social problems we begin to have at our command, now, not only general psychological insights but many specific studies.

Studies of juvenile delinquency are a case in point. Here, recognition, prevention, and treatment begin to form a cohesive unit, and certain pre-delinquent patterns of behavior begin to emerge clearly. While our studies of age-levels enable us to take in stride many forms of conduct that we recognize in our children as part of a passing phase, and also sudden changes in their behavior as they go from one phase to another, we are also learning what rightly to be concerned about. Habitual destructiveness—even though minor in each instance; petty stealing; abnormal secrecy about plans and resentment at being asked about them; an abrupt drop in standards of accomplishment at school to a level far below capacity: in these behaviors and others we are learning to read, as it were, a warning sign—*Danger: Inner Conflict at Work.*

Studies of prejudice are another case in point.[1] Here, perhaps, the most important development of the past ten years lies in a shift of emphasis from *an individual with a specific prejudice to the personality type that is prone to be prejudiced.* On the basis of far more kinds of evidence, far more tests and studies, than we can possibly describe here, we are learning some startling facts about other traits that tend to form a "constellation" with prejudice.

At first glance, there may seem no logic at all in such a "constellation"—no reason why this or that "irrelevant" characteristic should team up with, say, racial or religious prejudice; or with prejudice, often, on many different fronts. Yet there is overwhelming evidence for such "teaming up."

In hasty summary, we might note, for example, that highly prejudiced students tend to have an ambivalent attitude toward their own parents: what they say about their parents in a verbal interview is almost too favorable, too all-approving—and they seem to feel guilty and uneasy if they make the smallest criticism; yet when they take projective tests that bring out their attitude toward these same parents *without*

[1] Gordon W. Allport's *The Nature of Prejudice* (Beacon Press, 1954) brings together in clarifying and highly readable detail the essentials of many different studies that have been made in this area, and, on the basis of these studies, suggests conclusions of major importance for the recognition, prevention, and treatment of prejudice.

*their realizing the significance of the test enough to "edit"
their responses,* they show a marked hostility and anxiety.
Students, in contrast, who have few prejudices—who, on the
whole, are *for* the human race and ready to let many different
sorts of people be themselves—are far more able, without
signs of guilt, to make specific open criticisms of their parents; but show on the projective tests a basic affection for
them and relatively little resentment, fear, or anger with
regard to parental authority.

Again, highly prejudiced students are more anxiously conformist than those who are less prejudiced—and far more
harsh in their judgments upon other individuals and upon human weaknesses in general. Thus, when "asked the question,
'What is the most embarrassing experience?' anti-Semitic girls
responded in terms of violations of mores and conventions in
public. Whereas non-prejudiced girls spoke more often of
inadequacy in personal relations, such as failing to live up to
a friend's expectations." [1]

Or to take a third characteristic: prejudiced children, far
more often than non-prejudiced, agree to the proposition that
"there are only two kinds of people: the weak and the strong";
and male students with strong ethnic prejudices are far more
likely than the unprejudiced to agree that "there are only two
kinds of women: the pure and the bad." Here, in brief, we
recognize another outcropping of the black and white tendency: the same tendency that shows itself in the extreme
factionalist.

Once more, the prejudiced person is far more uneasy than
the unprejudiced in the presence of any ambiguous or indecisive situation; and far more prone, therefore, to jump to a
hasty, definite, "simplifying" conclusion—and stick to it in
the face of all evidence. The unprejudiced person is, as a
rule, far more able to postpone a decision until the evidence

[1] *Op. cit.,* p. 398.

is in; and also far more able to modify it after it is made—or to give it up, if need be, in the face of new evidence.

Again, prejudiced students show themselves more prone than the less prejudiced to base their sense of security, status, and personal significance on their membership in, and their intense allegiance to, institutions. They appear to have a particular attachment to *exclusive* institutions—so much so, in fact, that they often manage to impose an exclusive pattern, as it were, upon their church or their nation by exaggerating the differences between it and all others and then belittling the others. The relatively unprejudiced seem to get more satisfaction than the prejudiced do out of human relationships that they have built on their own, in terms of personal liking and shared interest.

Finally, the prejudiced individual tends to believe in the strong hand of authority as the only means of keeping human nature in line. "Living in a democracy is a higgledy-piggledy affair." This goes against the grain where highly prejudiced people are concerned. "The consequences of personal freedom they find unpredictable. Individuality makes for indefiniteness, disorderliness, and change. It is easier to live in a defined hierarchy where people are types, and where groups are not constantly shifting and dissolving.

"To avoid such slipperiness the prejudiced person looks for hierarchy in society. Power arrangements are definite—something he can understand and count on. . . . When students were asked to give the names of great people they most admired, prejudiced students usually gave names of leaders who had exercised power and control over others. . . ." [1] Napoleon and Bismarck were favorites, for example.

It is no small matter for us to be learning the many ways— the many surprising and subtle ways—in which the deep

[1] *Op. cit.*, pp. 406–407.

emotional problems and conflicts that obsess people move out into the open to become social problems.

Such learning, we would say, cannot be a mere intellectual exercise. It has to become a preface to policy. The more we understand in these areas, the more we realize that a new firmness and a new constructive tenderness are called for in the handling of "problem" behaviors.

It is not enough, where such behaviors are concerned, to act as though *understanding* meant *condoning;* for it takes more than understanding to check their consequences—their destructive influence upon individual lives and our shared society.

Neither is it enough just to dismiss such behaviors—so long as they stop short of criminality—as expected manifestations of human cussedness: unfortunate, perhaps, but to be lived with as part of the nature of things. They do too much harm for such easy dismissal. Also, *minor* problems which are rooted in personality disorder have a way, we now realize, of becoming *major* by neglect. Criminal conduct has its antecedents in pre-criminal conduct. Destructive prejudice, authoritarian practices, and blind factionalism also have their antecedents.

Finally, it is not enough just to clamp down on the offender; for his offense consists in doing what he, with his distorted vision, sees to do—and every person, sound or unsound, does what he sees to do and not something else. Not exhortation nor ridicule nor punishment can make the fear-ridden person discover in his environment reasons for confidence. Neither can they make the rigid person—repressed, inhibited, afraid of every honest emotion and every spontaneous action—into one who is flexible and adaptive. Fear of punishment may, to a limited extent, deter an individual from acts of destruction and cruelty. But only to a limited extent. And only so long as the fear lasts. We are beginning to realize that many individuals who do not act out their consuming hostility directly do so indirectly; and not the least of our dangers is that they will encourage our society's becoming, and the world's becoming, a place where hatreds can be vented with impunity.

It seems to us that, as newly "naturalized" citizens of the psychological age, we are going to have to put two contrasted types of error behind us. One is the error of indiscriminate "softness" toward those who hurt others: the type of sentimentality, for example, that becomes so concerned about the delinquent as "poor boy" that it forgets all about the victim of delinquency—and all about the probable future victims of the "poor boy" turned loose in society to act in the only way he can act: *as himself*. It is not enough, in short, to understand that misbehavior has a cause and that it has to be rated, often, as compulsive rather than voluntary. Our understanding has to include this fact, but must go beyond it. It has to include our awareness of what uncorrected disorder does as a force in society; and therefore our determination to restrain its influence while getting at its cause and trying to effect its correction.

The opposite error—all too common—is that of indiscriminate "hardness" toward the offender: that of sheer retaliatory anger. This attitude, treating all misbehaviors as voluntary, ignores all that we have learned about mental illness and its inevitable ways of externalizing itself.

The answers, in this area of our perplexity, are certainly not all in. We are as yet, we can guess, at the primer stage of our self-understanding and mutual understanding. We are barely beginning to spell out the lessons of personality disorder converted into public behavior. We stumble even more when we try to spell out our obligation toward the emotionally disturbed individual, his specific victim, and our democratic society.

But we will learn. The proof that we can learn is already

accumulating—and with dramatic rapidity. We find such proof in the swift growth of the mental health movement and the movement for parent education. We find it in new programs of industrial relations, in the development of pastoral counseling, in new methods of treatment for the delinquent and the criminal.

There are also, we would say, more subtle types of proof. In our personal lives we are developing a new sense of psychological cause and effect—and therefore a new readiness and skill in making psychic space for one another: giving one another both room to grow and companionship in growth. In our larger society, moreover, we are showing signs of a new maturity: almost, we might say, a sudden maturity, under the impact of crisis. More and more of us are becoming ready to say that, from here on in, we are going to attach a new importance to making word and action, belief and policy fit together. The drama of understanding is merging into the drama of social creativity as we set ourselves to extend opportunities, safeguard rights, build up our therapeutic resources, and, most of all, support our democratic institutions with democratic behaviors in the small, intimate places of life—in the home, classroom, place of work—where habits and attitudes are built into personality structures.

SEVENTEEN

SPACE-MAKING INSTITUTIONS

IN THE EARLY chapters of this book, we explored the ways in which we "corner" one another or, in contrast, make psychological room for one another: room to move ahead, turn around, and, if need be, back up and start over.

Upon this mutual granting of space, we ventured to say, depends the very texture of our individual and common life. When we make generous room for one another, ego-defense becomes a secondary matter. We can afford to be absent-minded about it most of the time. Our primary occupation becomes that of using our powers constructively—and therefore happily—in our environment.

When, on the other hand, room is denied, ego-defense has to remain a primary concern. It is as though, instead of being able to take out life and fire insurance and then go on about our business, we had to spend most of our waking hours studying our insurance policies and checking and rechecking the safety devices by which we had surrounded ourselves.

Under such circumstances, our life might indeed be "insured" —but scarcely worth living.

If psychic space is thus important, the person who can spontaneously and consistently grant it to others is, we have noted, the type of human being our world most needs. Where he lives and moves, things happen within people and between people that can be called *good,* because they are on the side of life.

In his poem *The Creation,* James Weldon Johnson gives us the image of God walking upon his new-made planet and ventures a superbly intimate picture of what takes place when a great creative force moves through an environment:

> "Then the green grass sprouted,
> And the little red flowers blossomed,
> The pine tree pointed his finger to the sky,
> And the oak spread out his arms. . . ." [1]

What he thus describes is scarcely more mysterious than what happens in the way of "creation" when we feel ourselves suddenly made real, or remade, in the presence of a fellow human being.

We ourselves gratefully acknowledge that within our own minds, many times, we have experienced renewal and growth because some person whom we have been with—in some cases, even a stranger whom we have just met—has mysteriously made it seem right and natural to be ourselves: to be as characteristically ourselves as the pine tree is itself when it points a "finger to the sky," in contrast to the oak tree that spreads out its arms.

Or we can turn from the insight of the poet to that of the psychological scientist. On the basis of his varied training and his long experience at the Counseling Center at the University of Chicago, Carl R. Rogers has recently given us what he

[1] James Weldon Johnson, "The Creation," in *God's Trombones,* pp. 18–19. New York: The Viking Press, 1927.

takes to be the essence of sound counseling. He seems to
have discovered, he tells us, that success or failure with his
patients depends upon his being able to create a relationship
that is characterized *on his part* by "genuineness and trans-
parency" with regard to his own feelings; by "a warm acceptance of and liking for the other person as a separate individual"; and by a "sensitive ability" to see the other person's
world as he sees it.

He testifies that if he can create this sort of relationship,
then the other individual—the patient—

"will experience and understand aspects of himself which
previously he has repressed;

will find himself becoming better integrated, more able
to function effectively;

will become more similar to the person he would like to
be;

will be more self-directing and self-confident;

will become more of a person, more unique and self-
expressive;

will be able to cope with the problems of life more ade-
quately and comfortably."

Rogers makes it plain, further, that he is not talking only
about the therapeutic relationship: "To me, the exciting thing
about these research findings is not simply the fact that they
prove the efficacy of one form of psychotherapy, though that
is by no means unimportant. The excitement comes from the
fact that these findings justify an even broader hypothesis re-
garding all human relationships. There seems every reason to
suppose that the therapeutic relationship is only one instance
of interpersonal relations, and that the same lawfulness gov-
erns all such relationships. Thus it seems reasonable to hy-
pothesize that if the parent creates with his child a psychological climate such as we have described, then the child will
become more self-directing, socialized, and mature. To the ex-

tent that the teacher creates such a relationship with his class, the student will become a self-initiated learner, more original, more self-disciplined, less anxious and other-directed. If the administrator, or military or industrial leader, creates such a climate within his organization, then his staff will become more self-responsible, more creative, better able to adapt to new problems, more basically cooperative." [1]

We have harked back to the matter of the space-making personality and the space-making relationship because we wish to move ahead to a broader but closely allied concept: namely, the space-making institution—and beyond it, the space-making society.

The institutions of any given society are, we might say, the durable frame of action within which the members of that society either feel crowded, pushed around, on guard, robotized, or, on the other hand, free to become their unique and contributive selves.

What Carl Rogers says of the counseling relationship can, we believe, be said in general about the relationship between any given institution—home, school, church, governmental structure—and the many different individuals who come and go within its atmosphere. A sound institution is not a static force in the human scene. Neither is it a dictatorial force— one that arbitrarily bends and twists human personality to match its purposes. It is more like the God of James Weldon Johnson's poem: a creative force exerting a creative influence. No matter how much more powerful it may be than any one individual, and no matter how much more lasting than any one life span, its effect is that of inviting the human "pine tree" to be a pine, and the human "oak tree" to be an oak; and of inviting all the different entities to form a world.

[1] Carl R. Rogers, "Becoming a Person," *Pastoral Psychology* (February, 1956), pp. 7–13.

If this can be said about a sound institution, then certain closely related things can be said about a sound society:

First, it is one in which most of the institutions, most of the time, have this sort of creative effect upon individuals—of giving them room to grow, be themselves, and make a contribution that is an honest "outwarding" of themselves;

Second, it is one in which no members are arbitrarily excluded from the experiences and advantages provided by its basic institutions;

Third, it has achieved such stability and clarity of intent that all its basic institutions support rather than contradict one another's influence—so that the individual is not subjected to constant pulling and hauling, with resultant inner conflict and loss of integrity, as he moves, say, from home to school, place of work to polling booth, or playground to place of worship;

Fourth, it has insured itself against rigidity by providing, in all its major institutions, for processes of orderly change—so that it manages to combine stability with flexibility, and itself grows through the insights and efforts of those in whom it has encouraged growth.

When we think of a society in these terms—of the creative influence it exerts and the room it provides for growth and individuality—we begin to see what the major issues of our age are all about. They are, in essence, issues that have to do with making institutions, societies, and more broadly still, a world in which psychic space is wide and sure: in which human beings are far more often engaged in using their powers constructively than in simply defending themselves; and in which they are not crowded, pushed into corners, trapped, distorted, and stunted.

Perhaps the most important question we can ask about any institution or any form of society is about the individual who finds himself within it: where can he go from where he is;

how freely can he move, and in what company? We said in an earlier chapter that one of the most important things we can know about ourselves is how other people act not only when we are around but *because* we are around. A parallel judgment can be made about institutions and societies: their soundness or unsoundness is constantly evident in the way that people act within them—and because they exist.

We are exceedingly lucky in our western civilization, and specifically in this country, in the fact that so many of our bedrock institutions are space-making. This is so basically true that when individuals are denied room to stretch their minds, develop their powers, participate in government "by the consent of the governed," or move into associations of their own choosing to enjoy the company of others as free as themselves, the basic intention of our society is somehow being flouted. Either someone is exerting more power over other people's lives than he has a right to exert; or else our basic intention, at this particular point, has not yet equipped itself with the secondary institutions through which it can rightly be enacted.

In its essence, our constitutional government is as well designed to grant "living space" and "growing space" as any institution on earth has ever been. This is not merely a political fact. It is a psychological fact. To state it as such is not to be guilty of chauvinism or boasting. It is simply to acknowledge an opportunity and a responsibility; and to learn how vital both of these are, we have only to look at the world as it now is.

There are today, we know, vast areas of the earth where psychological space has been made so tight and confined that no one has room to speak a free word without looking to see who is listening; where there is no room at all for a dissenting idea; where no one can decide to pick up his traps and go from one job to another; where no one can explore, on his own, the vast perplexities of life.

During the first world war, Carl Sandburg wrote, in tribute to the aviators and scientists of that time,

> "They have taken the ball of earth
> and made it a little thing . . .
>
> There are no bars across the way. . . ."[1]

When these confident words were first published, we did not yet know what the totalitarian dictators have since taught us: that there is a different sense in which the ball of earth can be made "a little thing"—too small for anyone on it to escape the watchful eyes of those who may report him for the slightest deviation. We did not then know what we have since learned about ideological bars "across the way."

But we know now; and are in a position, therefore, to appreciate certain space-making factors in our own culture. First among these we would name the Constitution itself—with its provision for checks and balances and for orderly change—and those "roomy" amendments we name the Bill of Rights.

"Congress shall make no law respecting an establishment of religion, or prohibiting the free exercise thereof. . . ." To feel the breadth of space guaranteed by these words we have only to think of the long centuries of religious coercion, persecution, and war that the human race had struggled through before the words could be written. The Constitutional Congress did not, obviously, conjure up this first provision of the Bill of Rights out of nothing—or out of sudden revelation. Rather, it reported what the colonists had learned the hard way: that when any one religion makes itself the only one,

[1] Carl Sandburg, "Leather Leggings," in *Complete Poems*, pp. 108–109. New York: Harcourt, Brace and Company, 1950.

insisting upon its right to define for all men the proper relationship of man to the universe, it becomes so small that even
its own willing adherents are "crowded" within it. They begin
to move in prescribed, ritualized circles; and their minds become so preoccupied with distinctions between saved and
damned that they no longer venture toward sublimity. Most
of what is tantalizingly unknown about the universe is thus
crowded out of consciousness.

Sixteen words against centuries of man's bleak determination to compel the religious convictions of his fellow
man. . . .

These words made room for people to find their way into
the faith of their own choosing; or to acknowledge that, so far
as the universe was concerned, they did not know the answers
—and had their doubts, even, about most of the answers so
far codified.

Also, they surrounded those whose faiths were established
and sure by constant reminders that these faiths were not the
only ones—and that, even within the fold of confident assurance, the search for truth and meaning had best go on.

These Constitutional words guaranteed another sort of
"roominess," moreover, that we often overlook in talking
about religious freedom. They made it not only lawful but
culturally acceptable for persons of different faiths to talk
together without trying to argue each other down or brow-
beat each other into conformity. In brief, they gave us a
right to be generous and civil rather than coercive and cruel
in the face of the mystery that is life.

We see the fruits of this Constitutional provision, today,
not only in the presence of many different creeds and religions, each operative within its own institutions, but also in
such organizations as the National Council of Churches, the
World Council of Churches, the National Conference of
Christians and Jews, local ministerial associations, and more

and more efforts, on the world front, to bridge gaps of misunderstanding and hostility between the various major religions of the earth.

A human being can, of course, be granted room to move and yet not move. In a mental hospital, for example, we may witness the rigid immobility of the catatonic: the type of insane person who stays precisely in the same position for hours on end. It makes no difference to this victim of catatonia whether the room he is in is large or small; for he is not going anywhere.

It would be extreme, perhaps, to say that sometimes, in the very areas where the most generous room to move has been granted them, our minds practice a sort of voluntary catatonia: they go nowhere, simply stay put.

So far as religious freedom is concerned, it seems to us that three directions of movement are constantly called for if the human mind, as well as the institution, is to remain free. One involves searching for a frame of belief able to hold otherwise disparate scraps of experience together and give them meaning. A second, within the frame of this belief, is that of trying to move toward ever new vistas of insight: in brief, of keeping ourselves in touch with the elusively unknown. The third is a movement—in behalf of mutual illumination and shared effort—toward those of different denominational and religious faiths.

We would note, in passing, that to our minds this third movement should include not only those who have found their faiths, but those who have not. Many persons, today, frightened by Communist atheism—by the phenomenon, that is, of a coercive "state religion" made out of a denial of religion—seem ready to start among ourselves a new enterprise of "crowding." While they grant that the individual should indeed be free to choose among established creeds and religions, they take the attitude that he had better make his choice *among these* and not dare to remain outside of them all. On the other hand, many who elect to remain outside all established creeds and religions exhibit their own sin of pride. The catatonic atheism of the person who never talks to a religious believer except to argue with him, or about any religion except in tones of contempt—and with absolutistic sureness about what is not true—is at no far remove from catatonic orthodoxy. Neither the catatonic believer nor the catatonic disbeliever is using the room guaranteed him by the Constitution to make the religious area of life one of continual search and wide generosity.

"Congress shall make no law . . . abridging the freedom of speech, or of the press; or the right of the people peaceably to assemble. . . ." It is good to read these words and feel how broad and open the space is that they provide for our human minds and consciences. And the same holds true for all the other provisions in the Bill of Rights: provisions that make us variously secure in our persons and property—and thereby enable us to take our minds off problems of self-defense and occupy them with the constructive enterprises of living.

We need scarcely repeat, here, what we have said earlier about our having to exercise "eternal vigilance" with regard to our basic freedoms. But we need to recognize that such vigilance alone cannot keep these freedoms alive. Watch can be kept over a corpse. What is profoundly called for is the "eternal practice" of our freedoms—the day in and day out employment of them, wherever we are. And not only the constant practice of them but the *spacious* practice. Again, the Constitution can give us room to stretch and grow; but it cannot force us to grow.

Thus, freedom of speech cannot be protected by our merely keeping an anxious eye on those who would shut us up—though such watchfulness is necessary. It is best protected by our saying things that make accurate, responsible, and generous good sense; and by our being willing, when we have said our say, to listen to others—or even to listen *before* we say our say. It is best protected, in brief, where minds behave like minds—and not like mere appendages to vacuity, prejudice, or blind factionalism.

One reason, we ourselves feel certain, why the extremists among us have had more influence than their numbers would justify is that the rest of us have largely failed to use the psychic space open to us for exchanging ideas across lines of difference. We have too often been satisfied simply to express our own ideas, read newspapers we agree with, assemble with our own kind—and call this the practice of freedom. We have thus tended to become self-repetitive rather than self-corrective; self-defensive and self-congratulatory rather than open and generous.

This has been true even among groups dedicated to the defense of freedom. In the teaching profession we have seen this sort of thing at work. As a professional group, we teachers have to be firm and clear in stating issues we take to be basic to the mind's freedom and in holding the line against invasion of that freedom. Yet we can scarcely afford to retreat into an exclusive, high-tensioned companionship with those who share our fears: those with whom we insistently talk about them in a language of ready agreement; and from whom we borrow, if not a sense of security, at least the comfort of having someone to shiver with.

The very temptation we face, in a time of fear and anger, to "huddle" with our mental, emotional, and professional kind can lead us into a far from healthy state. It involves the risk that, exercising freedom of speech and assembly, we will talk ourselves into adding phantom threats to real ones—hitting out as furiously, or as nervously, at the one as at the other.

It involves the risk, also, that we will tacitly agree to play down certain dangers that are both real and important. To our minds one of the strangest phenomena of our time is the extent to which those of us whose very profession depends upon the mind's freedom have "agreed" that the issue of Communism in our midst is to be deprecated rather than wrestled with. It is almost as though, having come late to a recognition of what Communism really is in aim and method, and having found anti-Communism already the stock in trade of certain groups we have committed ourselves to calling reactionary, we have not been able to find a way consonant with our professional self-respect of taking hold of the problem and making it one that concerns all free men. Thus, while we have opposed excesses of anti-Communism, we have not carried through on our knowledge that Communism, for a long time to come, and by whatever tactics it can devise, is going to oppose the way of life on which our very profession depends.

Further than this, the temptation to "huddle" with our kind involves the risk that we will, as a "fear-sharing" group, talk ourselves into a strange "apartness" from our society—an "apartness" that can all too easily turn into a sense of being *excluded, discriminated against,* and *undervalued.*

As a matter of fact, working as we ourselves do and have done over the years, with many different types of groups—racial, economic, religious, professional, political—we have been struck by the number and variety of groups that seem increasingly to feel themselves excluded, discriminated against, and undervalued. More than once, we have found that when two groups—liberal and reactionary, or labor and management—are opposing each other over some issue, *each sees itself as a beleaguered minority.*

When a *sense of minority status* is thus simultaneously experienced by both parties to a conflict, it means, we believe, that each party has been talking too exclusively and too anxiously to itself. To recall a phrase used in an earlier chapter, the members of each side have been *monologuing in unison*—and have monologued themselves into a state where they feel that their one consuming task is that of self-defense. Or to put the matter another way, they have exercised their Constitutional freedom of speech and assembly to trap themselves: to induce in themselves the distribution of energy that goes with fear and anger rather than with constructiveness and clarity of thought. Above, we ventured the term "voluntary catatonia" to describe the immobility of a mind that has been given room to move. Here—even though we recognize that the term is an exaggeration—we are tempted to speak of "voluntary paranoia" to describe this use of freedom to talk ourselves and assemble ourselves into a conviction of being persecuted.

The psychological space our society grants us is not, of course, experienced only in relation to our basic governmental structure or our Bill of Rights. It is experienced more intimately within the many smaller institutions—the secondary institutions, we might call them—that represent our will to enact, and not merely pronounce, our basic principles.

From our beginnings as a nation we have been constantly engaged, we might say, in furnishing the large house of our social intentions. Within it, we have located the public school system, courts of law, churches, libraries, playgrounds, universities, parks, businesses, factories, hospitals, museums, welfare agencies, a host of voluntary associations, and, needless to say, homes.

We are reminded often of the faults and shortcomings of our society. Also, we are encouraged often to feel that any dub can praise the virtues of his own society, but that it takes a peculiarly penetrating and valiant mind to discover and point up its faults. Finally, we are exasperated often by the double talk and slippery tactics of various individuals who make themselves conspicuous within the large, hard-working company of those to whom the common welfare is entrusted.

The net effect of this is that we often lose sight of how much there is to which we can honestly point with pride. We ourselves find endless encouragement and incentive in one fact about our society: namely, that in almost every one of our secondary institutions the line of evolution, through the years, has been toward the providing of more and more space for the human spirit to grow in. Almost any institution we can name is more spacious—less given to hemming people in or crowding them out—than it was even fifty years ago.

Take our public school system, for example. It was designed in the first place to give people room: to set them free from the trap of illiteracy and ignorance. But at first the school was able to open up only a few fields of knowledge—and to open these to only a scant portion of the population, for a few weeks of each year and a few years of life. The space thus granted to the learning mind turned out, in all sorts of ways, to be too small. Therefore, gradually, the broadened curriculum; the lengthened school term; the stretching out of the system to embrace high schools, junior colleges, and adult evening schools, at one end of the scale, and nursery schools and kindergartens, at the other; the provision of special classes for retarded children and migratory children; home teachers for the ill and the handicapped.

Or take our colleges and universities. In the beginning—made in the image of European institutions—these gave a very few people room to move into professional life: into the ministry and the law. But again their evolution has been to-ward making space for people: for more individuals, and for most aspects of each individual. The enriched curriculum; free public colleges and universities; extension divisions; fellowships and scholarships in ever increasing numbers; the GI bill of rights—all these, and many other developments, are part of the story.

Or take our courts of law. To make the story brief, we might mention only such developments as the court of domestic relations, the juvenile court, and the use that the court makes of the psychiatrist. Each of these has meant in its own way that some troubled human being would have more room to state his case, more room to move without being pushed around or cornered, than he had before.

The library affords yet other evidence of how we have, within our institutions, learned to make room for people, for what they have in them as individuals, and for more of them. When an urban library, for example, adds a Reader's Adviser to its staff, it opens the way for a host of readers to move toward books they need which they would never have discovered for themselves. When it equips itself to lend not only books but records and museum prints, it again becomes more roomy; more types of experience can be enjoyed within its frame. When a rural library acquires a bookmobile, it becomes large enough to open its doors to people at country crossroads to whom those doors would otherwise be closed.

One afternoon, some years ago, we arrived early in a certain small town where we were to talk to a church group. With time on our hands, we decided to find the public library and browse a while. Walking along the street, looking for it, we met a small boy. "Can you tell us where the library is?" we asked. "Oh, gee!" he exclaimed, pointing down the street. "It just went around that corner." We did not race after it. But we stood where we were a moment and enjoyed feeling that, even as we stood there, the "walls" of the public library were being pushed back to take in a whole countryside.

Parks, playgrounds, summer camps, settlement houses: these provide room, we know, not for the body alone but for the mind and spirit. We were told, last summer, by a man who worked in a New York settlement, about one small boy's summing up of the difference between the camp he had been privileged to enjoy for two weeks and the city apartment, in a depressed area, where he normally lived. In the latter, he said, there wasn't any "hollering place." Children, we realize, need their "hollering places"—and their places to run, skip, and jump; their places to throw a ball and have it thrown back to them; their places to make things and to enjoy what others make. And not only children—teen-agers and adults need room, also, to "outward" themselves in recreational and creative action. In a host of different institutions, the trend has been toward giving them such room.

The polling booth has become, in psychological terms, a far larger place than it used to be. With the institution of the secret ballot, it became, overnight, large enough to grant privacy—and therefore a new freedom from pressure—to the person casting his vote. With the passing of the Fifteenth Amendment to the Constitution, and later the Nineteenth Amendment, it became large enough to accommodate whole segments of the population that had previously been excluded from it: "The right of citizens of the United States to vote shall not be denied or abridged by the United States or by any State on account of race, color, or previous condition of servitude"; and "The right of citizens of the United States to vote shall not be denied or abridged by the United States or by any State on account of sex."

It goes without saying that there are still many "bars across the way." Facilities are still far from adequate—in schools, libraries, clinics, playgrounds. Also, there are bars of custom, prejudice, and ignorance. The important thing in a society like ours, however, is to know what we are about. We are a space-making and space-seeking people. During the early stages of our history, there was always room on the geographical frontier. When our economy was burgeoning into its unique form, we characteristically said, "There is always room at the top"—thus expressing the fact that the old pattern of rigid class levels had been broken. Oddly enough, we have not made for ourselves a matching phrase to express what we have, since the beginning, been doing in almost countless ways: making more room for more people, and for more aspects of our human nature, within one educational, cultural, economic, and political institution after another.

To think and feel our way through this drama of space-wanting and space-making is to achieve, it seems to us, a certain clarity in the midst of confusion. It is to achieve a standard of measurement that can be applied to a host of different situations, and to a host of different problems.

This standard of measurement, for one thing, suggests an answer to the citizen's perennial question, "What can I do?" That question, we know, can be asked despairingly or self-excusingly, eagerly or consideringly. Or it may not be put into words at all. But it lies at the heart of the democratic process and of the individual's relationship to it. Here, we begin to glimpse one kind of answer: in any institution to which we belong—as parent, worker, administrator, parishioner, learner, community member, citizen—we can look for the points where people are being "crowded," "trapped," "cornered," and can try to make more room for them.

Who, for example, is needlessly shut up in himself, without a chance to speak out his mind or share his experiences? In whom are latent powers held back from development and expression by lack of opportunity? Who is excluded from full participation in the activities of his group or country? Where do groups stand apart from each other in fear or misunderstanding because no common ground has been provided for their meeting? Who is standing pat in error because he does not know how to move out of it and still keep his self-respect? Who, because of age or disability, has been pushed out of the main stream of life into some stagnant and lonely pool? When we start looking around us with such questions as these in mind, the space-making adventure of our society becomes an intimately personal one.

After expressing his warm admiration for what other people had finely brought into being, Robert Bridges declared simply,

> "I too will something make
> And joy in the making . . ." [1]

It is with equal simplicity and directness of intent that we can turn from our appreciative survey of what has characteristically been brought to pass in our democratic institutions to say, "I too will make room for human beings to move, grow, meet one another, become more themselves— and will joy in the making."

What can I do? is not, however, the only question that the space-making concept, applied to our institutions, invites us to ask. A second question comes readily to mind. *What is now being done that deserves appreciation and support?* Here the answers are so many and varied that no sampling can properly suggest their range.

Into the offices of the New York Adult Education Council, day after day, come men and women, young and old, all of them tacitly asking, "Where is the right place for me—with my background, interests, resources, and limitations—to go on growing?" One woman spoke for many when she explained that "four walls and empty rooms can break your spirit" and that "classes mean people and ideas." For others, the problem is that of moving beyond work they do not enjoy

[1] Robert Bridges, *I Love All Beauteous Things.*

and preparing themselves for what they have always wanted to be; and for others it is that of growing on their present job. Still others want to learn more about themselves as human beings, about their children, and about their world. But all of them, in one way or another, feel crowded and are seeking more room in which to stretch their minds. With the help of the Council's Consultation Service, they are finding that room.

Or the mental health movement comes to mind: this newest development from the grassroots of the American community. To help people understand themselves and one another; to build a climate of opinion in which people can, without being catalogued as pariahs in the minds of their neighbors and employers, seek psychiatric help when they need it; to acquaint the public with the services and needs of their state hospitals; to equip communities with clinics and child guidance centers; to bring the layman and the psychological scientist together for mutual understanding and shared effort: these are space-making ventures of the new mental health movement. When we ourselves think of that movement, we find ourselves thinking not only in these general terms, however, but in terms of actual community groups, pioneering in the field, with whom we have been privileged to work: in Phoenix, Arizona; Tucson, Arizona; Huron, South Dakota; Rock Island, Illinois; Jacksonville, Florida; Peterborough, New Hampshire. In these communities, and many others, we have heard America talking and planning its way into the psychological age.

At Hillsborough High School, in Tampa, Florida, in the spring of 1955, the students in *family living* classes met as a group with their parents once a week for six weeks, to think their way through to better mutual understanding and to arrive at family policies that would be accepted and respected by teen-agers and adults alike. What the teacher of these classes, Dale Womble, was effectively doing was to give the two generations room to move toward each other and, in the words of one historic American document, "to sitt down here close togither." [1]

Under the auspices of the University Religious Conference of the University of California at Los Angeles, four different project teams of twelve students each have gone to India during recent years—there to make America convincing by the simple process of enacting American democracy and good will. "We're here to make friends": that was all the purpose these students found it necessary to verbalize. The rest lay in the area of behavior. The members of the fourth and most recent of these project teams "spoke to more than 50,000 Indian college students in nine weeks" and "they left behind them a clear impression of America at its best. . . . On campuses, in the streets and over countless cups of coffee, the U.C.L.A. students met young India." [2] As these young people of two nations thus talked, played, ate, and worked together, the distance that had hitherto lain between them became a meeting place for minds.

Who, then, are the space-makers among us? Their name, happily, is legion. They are in organizations that work for the rehabilitation of the handicapped. They are counselors and educators in penal institutions, helping prisoners to become more truly themselves, and more ready for the business of living than they have ever been before. As play therapists, they are making room for small frightened children who have been crowded into emotional corners to find their way back to a world of reality, creativeness, and affection. As supporters of the Urban League and the United Negro College Fund, or the Association on American Indian Affairs, they

[1] The original charter of Watertown, Connecticut.
[2] See "America at its Best in India," by Thomas B. Morgan, with photographs by Bob Lerner. *Look* (February 7, 1956), pp. 56–64.

are opening up new opportunities for growth where these have been denied. As supporters of such groups as the Iron Curtain Refugee Committee they are opening a way back toward freedom for those trapped within totalitarian regimes. Through such organizations as CARE, Save the Children Federation, and Foster Parents Plan for War Orphans, they are giving substance to the term "human family." As members of a host of voluntary associations—from Rotary International to Association for Childhood Education International —they are quietly enacting "one world" by bringing peoples of different lands together in terms of basic common interests.

After we have looked long enough, and in enough different directions, at those who are actively engaged in space-making, we have one kind of answer to those who say that the pioneering spirit in America is dead, that our society is old and tired, and that it has never matured, but merely settled down.

After we have looked at them long enough, moreover, we are ready to look at some altogether different kinds of things that are happening and to ask, "What's wrong here?" For the standard set for us by the concept of space-making tells us not only what to approve and support, but also what to oppose and reject. Where, in short, are people being needlessly trapped and crowded into corners—and by whom; and by what attitudes and policies?

Here again the briefest sampling must serve. But it is clarifying to note that constrictive influences within our society tend to fall chiefly into six categories.

First, there are the forces of *sheer inertia*. What we have to cope with here is not so much deliberate ill will as a simple human tendency to translate the familiar into the "natural." Slums have "always" existed; certain types of people have "always" done menial work; nations have "always" been separate and competitive and we cannot expect that an "unnatural" set-up like that of the United Nations will really work.

Second, there is the force of *limited imagination*. Those, for example, who cannot imagine what it feels like to be "retired" after a long life of usefulness into loneliness, futility, and dependence are not likely to contribute much to the releasing of our older people into new experiences, occupations, and companionships. Similarly, those who cannot put themselves into the position of a displaced person are not likely to bestir themselves to make room for that person.

Again, there are forces of *entrenched prejudice*. Prejudice may be fairly mild and harmless, or deep and destructive; but invariably it is marked by two tendencies: the tendency to bring all members of the disparaged group under one covering judgment and to lose sight of their individual differences; and the further tendency to exaggerate the difference between this group as a whole and the favored group with which it is contrasted. A person may be quiet in his exercise of prejudices: may simply not go near certain groups if he can help it. Or he may be violent. But two things he does not do: make room for the individual qualities of those in the disparaged group; or make room for that group and his own to know each other better.

Next we note the force of *vested interest*. We normally think of vested interests as accumulations of economic power. But there are many other kinds. Within a certain national organization, for example, policy has become the vested interest of a handful of people who live within one area. These individuals see one another often between meetings; call one another by their first names even in convention sessions where most people are strangers; and quietly "run things"—so that the organization has become, in effect, a tight local unit with a large national membership as a dues-paying appendage. Or we might take other examples: the good will organization where there are never hands enough to do the work, but where the volunteer has been crowded out; or the labor union in which the number of apprentice-ships is kept so limited that, we might say, there is never room at the bottom.

The fifth force that makes for crowding is *fear*, particularly when it is widespread or intense enough to be called panic. We see the physical demonstrations of this when, for ex-ample, fire in a public gathering place sends people into a destructive frenzy of mutual shoving and pushing. We see the cultural demonstration of it in many places today: people are fired, for instance, with no chance to state their case, because a rumor has reached their employer or department head that they once belonged to certain front organizations.

This type of "crowding" is, in psychological terms, *over-reaction*. Intent on safeguarding himself, and looking at the danger through the magnifying lens of his own anxiety, the employer or department head resorts to more immediate and drastic action than is called for.

Another and final type of crowding and cornering is the *deliberate exploitation of fear*. One of the favorite panic-rousing warnings of today is against social security. "Beware the government when it brings gifts," cry the modern Cas-sandras. "Social security is an invitation to laziness," they scream. "It will weaken our moral fiber; make us a people who live by handouts." Meanwhile the deep and often tragic issues of illness, accident, and aging in a society in which the individual is increasingly at the mercy of forces he cannot control are completely overlooked.

Before we bring this chapter to an end, we would like to pose a further question. Beyond our many-sided enterprise of making space and preventing entrapment within our various institutions, is there, perhaps, a still larger adventure in the making?

We say often that we are living in an age of change; and to specify what we mean we point to such factors as urbanization, automation, our new nomadism, and the rest. As we contemplate these, we often seem appalled. It is as though everything that nobody knows how to do had to be done at once to prevent our being turned into futile creatures of the forces we have created. At such times, when anxiety dominates, we show ourselves overready either to hit out at somebody or to scuttle for cover. Thus preoccupied, we do not ask ourselves whether it may not be that our "age of change" is, in effect, an age of transition to an order of life more mentally and emotionally spacious than any we have ever known. May it not be that we are almost ready to go in for space-making on a grand scale—and that our confusions are a prologue to this enterprise rather than merely an epilogue to the world we have known?

We ourselves readily admit that we do not have the answer to this question; nor, we suspect, will the answer be forthcoming for a long time. Yet we cannot miss the fact that more and more first-rate minds are weighing the possibility that this is what is taking place: that a new age may be in the shaping, and that man's spirit may be stretching itself to match the proportions of this new age. Neither can we miss the fact that more and more of us are hungry for adventures of mind and spirit that have some scope to them.

There are intimations of this, we would say, in the number of people—particularly young people—who are quietly *for* the human race: who are thinking of it whole, and wishing it well. It is fairly easy, where middle-aged and older people are talking together, to induce a certain amount of doleful head shaking about the young. Those whose own young adventures were in the go-getter tradition are inclined to say that the current crop of young folks have no ambition: all they want is security. Those, on the other hand, whose own young adventures were in the intellectual tradition of "debunking" and the political tradition of reform and radicalism are prone to call today's young people conservative and conformist.

We ourselves feel, on the basis of our contacts with student groups and groups of young parents, that both these criticisms miss the point of what is taking place. Young people may lack ambition in the old go-getter terms, not because they are soft, but because they are tired of conflict and would rather establish warm, sound human relations than either outdo or dominate other people. And they may seem conservative to the "debunker" and the radical of the old school, not because they do not want to make the world better, but because they are more interested in building up than in tearing down. The old-line tradition of "debunking" required that somebody be cast as dolt and fool. The old-line tradition of radicalism required that somebody be cast as villain: as enemy of the people; as an object to be hated and destroyed.

What impresses us most about young people, today—not the delinquent minority, but the overwhelming majority—is that they are singularly free of hatred. As personalities, they are, by and large, slanted toward friendliness. They are not, it would appear to us, in the old traditions of "debunking" or of turning society upside down in "righteous" anger, because they are quietly forging for themselves a new inclusive tradition that does not require them to enjoy belittling and hating: namely, a tradition of nurturing.

Countless American service men who, within one or another theater of war, have done what they could to make life tolerable for the children are in this tradition. So are students such as those who made up the project team in India. Today there are increasing numbers of such students, in one group or another, moving across old barriers in a spirit of new neighboring. The fact that every public opinion poll shows young people to be more free of prejudice than older people is another sign. And most conclusive of all, to our minds, is the extent to which young couples today are enjoying their homes and children—with both husband and wife interested in the nurturing processes; and beyond this, the extent to which they are taking on community responsibilities as a kind of larger housekeeping.

In every professional, scientific, and industrial field, today, efforts are being made to enlist the interest and energy of young people. Thus—to take a case in point—the Atomic Energy Commission is trying earnestly to induce more students to go into physical science as a life work. Yet as we read the appeals that are being made, we cannot help wondering whether the members of the Commission have really achieved an understanding of today's young minds. If they had, it seems to us, they would stress the very thing they now seem curiously reluctant to talk about, namely, peacetime uses of atomic energy; for the generation they are trying to reach is, in a profoundly new sense, a peace-minded generation. What is true in this instance would, we believe, be true in many others as well: those who want to enlist the creative energies of this new human crop we have raised must recognize the extent to which today's young are on the side of life.

A woman in whose home we were visiting made a remark that might sound as though it came from an older day: "My husband likes a woman to stay in her place." But then she added, "I don't mind, though—because he's always in it with me when he can be." In these words, affectionately spoken, we heard a new age speaking: a nurturing age; and therefore a space-making one.

There is, in brief, something new in the air—quietly but

impressively new. Young people are by no means the only ones who reveal this fact. There are well-nigh countless signs. It may seem on the surface that this is chiefly an age of new barriers raised between man and man: an age of the cramping of the human spirit. But more deeply it is an age of new searchings. To borrow a phrase from Bernard E. Meland, of the University of Chicago School of Theology, we are making a "transition to a higher form of commitment."

Rufus Jones has noted, "Strange stirrings of hope and expectation are moving across the world. It is possible that we may be on the fringe of a new and marvelous epoch. . . . It is one of the evidences of man's intrinsic greatness that it is just then, when he seems to be at the end of his human resources, that he rises above himself, and does what he could not do." [1] We would be willing to guess that the many small space-making adventures to which we lend ourselves, day by day, within the various institutions to which we belong, are part of something very much larger than themselves: part of a movement that, as it unfolds and matures, will provide more spacious room for the human spirit than it has ever known before.

[1] *Interdependence Reader,* p. 30. Interdependence Council, Philadelphia.

EIGHTEEN

THE LIBERATING MIND

WE BELONG to a race the highest glory of which is its long line of liberators. Socrates, Plato, Aristotle, Euripides, Zeno the Stoic, Euclid, Thucydides: the names run on and on. Abraham, Moses, Isaiah, Hosea, Micah, David of the Psalms; Jesus; Matthew, Mark, Luke, and John of the Gospels; Paul of the Acts and the Epistles; and the other named but mostly unknown writers of valiant letters to small groups precariously holding their own.

Confucius, Lao-tse, Gautama, Zoroaster, Mohammed: all of them liberators from one or another slavery of mind and spirit; St. Francis, St. Teresa, Thomas Aquinas; Copernicus, Galileo, Newton; Erasmus, Darwin, John Stuart Mill, Jefferson, Franklin, Washington, Lincoln—the names keep running on. And in the midst of them, the great illuminator, Shakespeare. And Goethe and Kant. Even to the birdmen of Kitty Hawk and our modern St. George, slayer of the polio dragon.

To be a member of the human race is a standing invitation

to go and be like these. We thought of this as we watched a young assistant in a play therapy clinic slowly transform a fear-ridden child into someone eager to explore the toys around him. The child had come to the clinic, at first, with arm involuntarily raised for defense or attack. When we last saw him, he was deep in the world of his happy contriving. He was not yet, to be sure, a child fully set free: this would take a long time. But he was on his way.

This clinical assistant would scarcely place herself in the same category as the great liberators we have mentioned. But if she did not have their stature, she at least had their intention. Her intention, like theirs, was to release life into its freedoms.

We can find this liberating intention in all sorts of places. We think of a radio studio in a private apartment in New York City. Helen Parkhurst is standing as one of a circle around a microphone. All except herself are children. "For many years," she wrote in her book, *Exploring the Child's World,* ". . . my constant thought was: 'Can the child be prevailed upon to reveal himself?'" In her small apartment studio, linked up to a major network, with the children around her, she is trying to find out. We think she has amazingly succeeded.

Children do not easily reveal themselves to grown-ups. Every parent knows this: tries, with wonder or bafflement, to look into a small life that is inarticulate. "I have shared the hope," wrote Miss Parkhurst in her book, "that parents and children might understand each other." But in countless cases they do not. Neither, in countless cases, do teachers and children. Nor officers of the law and children. Nor makers of the law and children.

This "apartness" of children can be unfortunate. The child who is not understood by the adults around him, and the adults who try to understand him but cannot "connect up" are both, we might say, underprivileged. Both are trapped within a too limited frame of experience. The child does not have room to move freely. The adult does not have room to act wisely.

In her small radio studio, Helen Parkhurst stands with her circle of children, skillfully and affectionately asking them questions—about punishment, stealing, lying: what they think and feel about these; about worry, prayer, winning or losing—all that goes into the drama of a child's life. "These questions are so simple," writes Aldous Huxley in an introduction to her book, "that one would think any fool could ask them. But in fact, of course, any fool would ask them at the wrong time, and in conjunction with other questions which should never have been asked. To ask them as Miss Parkhurst asks them—in such a way that the children are never intimidated into self-consciousness or silence, never made to doubt the questioner's affectionate disinterestedness —is given only to those with a vocation for teaching and the skill born of long experience."

Here, again, is the *liberating intention*—the will to set free. To the extent that the intention succeeds, everyone concerned moves in a more spacious and less guarded world.[1]

This same intention, of course, today, has a myriad "homes" in our society. It is operative in hundreds and thousands of places—clinics, laboratories, libraries, classrooms, counseling rooms—where men and women are at work trying to understand the human being and to help him to grow toward his world in interest and understanding. When we speak of this as a psychological age, we mean very simply that it is an age which has consciously taken on the problem of releasing life into the wide areas of its possibilities.

[1] For an illuminating analysis of Miss Parkhurst's methods and suggestions for their use, see *A Window to the Child's Mind*, by Dorothy R. Luke. New York: Starbridge Publications, 1955.

We think of another place. In his *Shirt-Sleeve Diplomacy,*
Jonathan Bingham describes it:

"A mud village lies baking in the punishing sun of a middle
eastern summer day. Up to its walls over the stony, treeless
wasteland crawls an American-made jeep . . .

"Driving the jeep is a lanky, middle-aged American named
Smith, a former county agent half a world away from his
native Arkansas. On the seat next to him is a staff worker
from the local Ministry of Agriculture, a thin-faced man with
dark skin and fine hands, his black hair whitened by the
dust."

As the jeep drives carefully along a narrow lane between
high mud walls, scores of ragged children appear as if from
nowhere, and tag along. Several are carrying babies on their
backs, their faces speckled with flies. The children follow
the jeep until it stops before a windowless adobe house
slightly larger than the rest.

"The two men sit down on the dirt floor with the local
elders. First, there is hospitality: a tray is passed with glasses
of water, tinted slightly pink with a kind of syrup, and sweet
cakes. Smith would like to refuse, but he does not wish to
offend his hosts. As unobtrusively as possible he slips a hali-
zone tablet into the water glass. Brushing off a few flies, he
nibbles at the sticky cake and pronounces it delicious.

"Then the talk starts. Smith and his companion ask what
the village needs most. Malaria is bad, they are told . . . the
village well is foul, and unreliable most of the year; the sheep
are dying off; there is no school for the children . . . the
wheat crop has been poor."

Smith listens. There are ways of getting these things attended to, he tells them, if the villagers will co-operate. They
talk over what can be done. By the time he leaves, Smith can
take it for granted that together they will go at the job.

"Twenty years ago," the author continues, "or even ten,

there might have been a missionary out where Smith was, or an agent of an oil company, but there would have been no official representative of the United States Government. To-day Smith is one of a small peaceful army. In military terms, it is a tiny army—about the size of a regiment—and it is deployed all the way from Mexico City around the world to Manila. But it is fighting a . . . war that has been going on since man first rose on his hind legs." [1]

The arresting thing about this story is that what religion, in its lonely heroism, long ago set out to do, government, within its secular limits, now attempts. It is taking on the liberating function of bringing life more abundant—and beyond its own borders.

This fact is perhaps the most significant news of our generation. Nor should it be wholly surprising news, for these men of today—the "man named Smith" and the small regiment of his fellow workers, as well as the initiators of the program—have found their stimulus and dedication within a governmental form that the great liberators, Jefferson, Washington, Lincoln, and the rest, helped to create.

Nor should this kind of dedication surprise us after the many liberating things that have taken place within the past hundred years—and one in particular that is too little thought about, now, because it is taken for granted: the emancipation of women. This—one of the greatest psychological and moral events in history—has meant far more than that women can now vote. Far more profoundly and broadly, it has meant bringing a *life-affirming view* into the forefront of our social consciousness.

The woman is the nurturer—has always been. She has had long practice not only in bringing life to birth but in helping

[1] Jonathan B. Bingham, *Shirt-Sleeve Diplomacy: Point Four in Action,* pp. 3–4. New York: John Day, 1954.

it to go on living. Today, as we noted in the preceding chapter, this nurturing point of view has begun to prevail among us: the view that life is precious; must be cared for; given its chance to grow; loved and encouraged into the release of its powers. It is the view that where there is helplessness, there must be caretaking; where there is ignorance, there must be provision for learning; where there is awkwardness of learning, there must be patience—patience with love and laughter in it.

The nurturing point of view has begun in our day to color all our life situations. The first question we ask now, whether it be in the building of a city or a nation or a world, is how the things we propose to do *affect people's lives:* their health, happiness, creative productiveness; their capacity to work together; their chance to be on friendly terms with one another, and to have a sense of rights respected and dignity enhanced.

The emancipation of women, in short—which, surprisingly, was accomplished only a few short years ago—has meant the emancipation *of our age*, and of men no less than women, into a more human regard for people. This is why today's stirrings of anger and rebellion among those whom we have called the "backward" peoples of the world are met, not with instant and retaliatory anger on our part, or a determination to force them to "keep their place," but with a growing measure of understanding and compassion. It is, also, the reason why the "race problem" in our own country has become of such intense concern to us: why it is taken as a problem that has to be worked through to some conclusion that will do justice to all involved. Also, we might say, it is why the concept of a wider and more friendly neighborliness of the world begins to capture our imagination.

We miss the point if we think of the "One World" movement as purely or even primarily political. Far more fundamentally, it is a movement of wider caring about life. Why, we begin to ask, should we lock ourselves up within our tight walls of national suspicion—glaring at one another, preparing to destroy one another—when we might have a far better time of it by talking things over together; getting the hang of one another's problems; lending a hand?

It is our nurturing, liberating mind that now talks in this way. War begins to wear a guise of sickening stupidity. It offends every life-affirming fiber of our make-up. The nurturing, liberating mind wants something better than killing and overcoming. In Robert Frost's phrase, it wants "life to go on living."

One of the enervating—and irritating—factors in the world today is a kind of leftover from the pre-nurturing age. We might call it the cult of the higher gloom. It is the habit of despair that looks at every human situation in terms of what is wrong with it, or of how difficult it is to handle, or of how stupid the people involved in it are, rather than in terms of how *alive* it is.

We recently opened a remarkable report put out by the Research Department of the Welfare Planning Council of the Los Angeles Region. One thing immediately struck us— with surprise, we must admit, for when it comes to city planning in these days of crowding and shifting populations, and particularly when it comes to statistical researches on city planning, we ourselves are often tempted into the higher gloom. The second and third sentence of this Los Angeles report, however, caught us completely off guard: "The population has increased beyond all enthusiastic predications. . . . Never before in the County's history has there been such a wealth of babies."

We rubbed our unbelieving eyes. Shades of solemn sociol-

ogy and of almost frantic reports on population trends!
Could it be that these people out in Lost Angeles frankly and
unabashedly loved their rash of babies and *wanted* them?
As we read on, there was no mistaking the tone of that report. The one hundred and five pages of tight-packed research—designed to be used as a basis for planning in the
fields of health, welfare, and recreation services—were indeed full of anticipated headaches. But these seemed almost
welcome as part of the business of planning a community—
a county-wide community—that would be a home for all
those babies to grow up in. For they would grow up. They
would eventually clutter up the roads and parking areas with
their jalopies, crowd schoolrooms to the bursting point, and
help to make more smog; but they were *all right*, these
youngsters. Obviously, in the minds of the Welfare Planning
Council, they were worth all the trouble they might make.
There could be no mistake about it: those who had compiled
this report wanted "life to go on living."

The liberating mind, we would say, cannot be the habitually or pridefully doleful mind. It can and must have the
power to face problems, with all the hard realities they present. But the liberating mind has to believe in life and be
able to feel the drama of giving life its full chance.

Throughout this book, we have been talking about our
need to give life a chance: room to grow; to experiment; to
make mistakes and try over again; to move about with confidence and affection. Our central human job, and one to be
gratefully welcomed, is to make living space for others—and
for ourselves.

We do this as individuals, we have suggested, by being
the kind of persons in whose presence others are less shy,
less driven back into themselves, less often inclined to resort

to fight and flight. We do it as a society by creating the conditions that give people the chance to be what they have it in them to be.

We do all this best, we would say, when we keep in mind the *organic* nature of ourselves. We are not machines—although we are often told we are. In spite of the triumphs of cybernetics, automation, and the rest, we human beings remain creatures who cannot be taken apart and made over promptly and efficiently. We have to be given the chance to grow—and to grow at the pace our life-patterns prescribe.

Every time we try to make people over abruptly—by command or arbitrary design—we fail. Every time we try to make a culture over in this same way, we fail. Individuals and cultures have *life* in them, not merely functioning parts that can be reordered or replaced.

The liberating mind thinks in organic terms. It does its liberating of life in accordance with the ways of living beings; and the way of the living being is *to grow*.

We return here to the words of Rufus Jones which we quoted in the preceding chapter: "Strange stirrings of hope and expectation are moving across the world. It is possible that we may be at the fringe and frontier of a new and marvelous epoch." To this, we would say, "Why not? for the liberating mind of man is now, as never before, at work in the world."

Pitirim Sorokin, the sociologist, asserts that western society is in crisis—"and not one of the ordinary crises which happen almost every decade, but one of the greatest transitions in history." [1] And again we would say, "Why not? for the liberating mind that has moved into the forefront of our time

[1] Pitirim Sorokin, *Crisis of Our Age: The Social and Cultural Outlook,* p. 322. New York: E. P. Dutton & Co., Inc.

does not, as of old, belong merely to the few moral and intellectual geniuses of the race, but increasingly to all of us."

It is easy to make mild fun of earnest mothers and fathers who come together to study the psychology of the child—and also of themselves as parents and as husband and wife. *But this is something utterly new in the world.* Because these parents have creative honesty and a willingness to try to learn what life deeply needs for its maturing, they are actually making a new world.

In one area after another, today, the pattern of thought is *forthgoing.* Even the area of economics—where, for so long, life seemed secondary to things and profits—has increasingly become one in which the liberating mind is at work. By the inherent logic of our human interdependence, free enterprise grows gradually into mutual enterprise.

The liberating mind, above all, is at work in religion. "I suggest," writes Arnold Toynbee, "that we recognize all higher religions as revelations of what is good and right." [1] These are sober, even prosaic words, but they carry within them the intensity of a mind that wills to go forth beyond its culture-bound devotions to practice reverence for what others reverently care about. Here, perhaps, is the most deeply uniting bond that can be established among men on earth. For if we can unite on what we reverently care about, then we can take our lesser differences in stride.

In this book we have written about what might well be called the pilgrim journey of the mind. The journey starts, as we know, with an egocentric, immature preoccupation with ourselves; but as our years grow generous, we move beyond ourselves.

This, perhaps, is the best present version of the profound insight that "he that loseth his life shall find it." He who goes

[1] *Time Magazine,* October 18, 1954, p. 108.

forth beyond his own limited points of view, his own half-truths and well-loved prejudices, and tries to see life from points of view unfamiliar and even forbidding, will in the end find himself at home with life. For he has made life his home.

INDEX

Abraham, 364
academic freedom, 77–80
adolescence, learning experience in, 94–95
Adorno, Theodore W., 175
adrenalin, 33
Adult Education Council, New York, 354–355
Aiken, Conrad, 67
Alice in Wonderland, Carroll, 71
Almond, Gabriel A., 171
Allport, Gordon, 29, 83–84, 139–140, 166–167, 331n, 332, 333
American Bar Association, 305
American Book Publishers Council, 305
American Civil Liberties Union, 300, 303
American Committee for Cultural Freedom, 303–304
American Library Association, 305
American Psychological Association, 77
anger:
  incitements to, 34–37, 49–52, 109
  as personality disorder, 317–320
anti-Communists, 179–180, 293

anti-intellectuals, 295
Aristotle, 364
assembly, freedom of, 287
Atomic Energy Commission, 362
Authoritarian Personality, The, Adorno and associates, 175

bacterial weapons, 268
Barnard College, 312
behavior:
  child-training in, 126
  neurotic, *see* neuroses
  as reflection of self-portrayal, 242
  wrongness in, 45–48
belittling, 68
  results of, in relationships, 72–74
Bible, the, 192–193, 195
Big Brother movement, 200
Bill of Rights, 257
  space-making character of, 343–350
Bingham, Jonathan, 367–368
biology, 162
Boasberg, Leonard, 175
body, fear reactions in, 33–34
Body of Liberties, Massachusetts, 257, 258

375

Branch, Anna Hempstead, 255
Bridges, Robert, 354
Brotherhood, Oppenheim, 251
browbeating, psychological, 274,
  276–277
Burma, 270
business, understanding and love in,
  26–27

Cattell, Elizabeth, 163
Chamberlain, Neville, 243
Chicago, University of:
  Counseling Center, 338
  School of Theology, 363
"childfulness," 93–94
children:
  "apartness" of, 365–366
  characteristic attitudes, 206–208
  exceptional, 47
  gratitude in, 124–126
  learning experiences, 93–95, 365–
    366
  of migrants, 62
  misbehavior in, reaction to, 121
  value of adult relationships to,
    215–219
childhood, in maturity, as life role,
  205–220
childishness, in adults, 209–210
Christensen, Arthur, 266
citizen, responsibility of the, 235–
  237
civility, as a pattern in relationships,
  122–123
Civilization and Its Discontents,
  Freud, 246, 249
class struggle, 248
cold war, 269
communication:
  ambiguities in terms, 284
  as interchange, 224–225
  monologuing, 282–284, 349
Communism, 98–99, 222, 348
  "affiliation" impasse, 55–59
  appeals of, study, 171–175, 280,
    302
  extremism in, 288–289
  factionalism and, 277–278
  fears of, 179

Federal Bureau of Investigation
    and, 302
  hate-mongering in, 108
  infiltration tactics, 270–274, 286–
    289
  as label, 105–106
  "liberation" of Warsaw and, 292
  power of the "elite" in, 107
  vigilance over, by society, 293–
    298, 304–311
  wrongness of, 45–46
Communist Party, 271, 280
conflict:
  limited utility of, 17–20
  personality reactions to, 22–24
  understanding versus, 14–16
  unlimited, 17–20
conformity, 293
  dangers of, 280–282
Confucius, 364
Congressional investigating commit-
    tees, 196–197, 294, 311–312
conservatives, orthodoxies of, 282
Constitution, United States, 257
  space-making characteristics, 343–
    350
Copernicus, 364
corruption, practitioners of, 293
Coulter, Ernest, 199–200
courage, 274
courts, law, as space-makers, 351
Creation, The, Johnson, 338
creativity:
  fear and, 31–33
  in life role, 197–202
Crock of Gold, The, Stephens, 218
Cummings, E. E., 25
Curran, John Philpot, 291, 292
cynicism, 68

Darling, F. Fraser, 224*n*
Darwin, Charles, 246, 247–248, 364
David, 364
Day, Clarence, 154, 156
"day vision," 38
demagogues, 45, 56, 59, 75, 112, 279
democracy:
  as an assignment in human rela-
    tions, 84

factionalism in, 283–284
importance of psychic space to, 59, 62
"limiting" attitudes toward, 80–84
responsible role of the citizen in, 235–237
Descent of Man, Darwin, 247
desegregation, 296
despair, habit of, 370–371
diplomacy, liberating intention in, 367–368
discipline, man's need for, 254–256
disease:
   differences between physical and mental, 315–317
   see also mental illness
displaced persons, 62
dogmatism, of the liberal, 76–84
Donne, John, 321
Douglas, William O., Justice, 283
Duke University, 77

economics, liberating mind in, 373
egoism, 253
ego-preserving mechanism, meaning of term, 24
Emerson, Ralph Waldo, 234
emotionally disturbed persons:
   gratitude and, 136–137
   relationships of, 163
   see also mental illness
emotions:
   gratitude and maturity of, 124–138
   knowledge and, 90–93
   see also personality
energy patterns, of human beings, 31–48
Envelope, The, Plant, 24n
environment:
   interpersonal relationships as, *see* relationships
   personality disorders and, 317
   personality influences in, 39–43
   see also psychic space
Erasmus, 364
Ernst, Morris L., 300, 302
Euclid, 364
exclusion, emotional results of, 62–64

Exploring the Child's World, Parkhurst, 365
extrasensory perception (ESP) research, 77–79
extremism, 277, 288–289, 293

faction, meaning of term, 279
factionalism, 274–276
   as cause of voluntary segregation, 279–282
   extremism as, 289
   groups that thrive on, 277–279
   monologuing in unison as, 282–284
   vigilance and, 292–293, 297–298
failure, life-role aspects, 168–170
family:
   divisive forces in modern, 216–217
   unifying tendencies, 217–218
family-living classes, 355–356
fanaticism, 59
Fascism, 45
   extremism in, 288–289
   hate-mongering and, 108
fear:
   creativity and, 31–33
   in extremists of the right, 178–179
   as force for crowding, 359
   ignorance and, 91–92
   incitements to, 34–37, 49–52, 109
   mistakes as feeders of, 105–108
   physical reactions to, 33–34
Federal Bureau of Investigation, 299–303
Ferber, Edna, 60–61
field theory, of personality, 163–164
"Fifth Amendment Communist," use of term, 233
fight and flight, 36–40, 41, 120
Fisher, Dorothy Canfield, 68–69
"foreigners," 309
forgetting, forgiving and, 117–118
forgiveness, 103
   attitudes toward, 113–118
   melodramatic, 119
   wisdom in, 117–121
Fosdick, Harry Emerson, 167
Francis, St., 364
Franklin, Benjamin, 364

freedom:
  liberating mind and, 364–374
  life roles and, 186, 194–195
  meaning of term, 284–287
  preserving, *see* vigilance
  range of reactions to, 291–293
  as the way of trial and error, 83
Freud, Sigmund, 246, 249–250, 258
friends, attitudes toward, 73
"friendship," Soviet, 270–274
Fromm, Erich, 252, 253, 258
Frost, Robert, 132, 183, 210–211, 275, 370
Funn, Dorothy K., 271

Galileo, 78, 364
gangs, life-role aspects, 170
Gautama, 364
giving, as opportunity, 136–140
Goethe, von, Johann Wolfgang, 364
Golden Rule, 248
Good Housekeeping, McCleery, 308, 313
gossip, 105
government:
  attitudes toward, 246–247
  liberating intention of, in foreign policy, 367–368
  reasons for, 253–254
  vigilance in defense of a free, 291–314
gratitude:
  broad aspects of, 128–131
  for the chance to give, 136–140
  for common decencies, 131–132
  emotionally disturbed persons and, 136–137
  emotional maturity and, 124–138
  for experiences of growth, 135–136
  for human insight and wisdom, 134
  for mutual understanding, 132–133
groups:
  factional, *see* factionalism
  quasi-official, 295
  in therapy, 255
  value of intercommunication, 307–309

grudge-holding, 68
  group, 108
Guareschi, Giovanni, 50–53
guilt by association, 81

half-truths, 99
hate-mongering, 45, 171, 293
  group, 107–108, 110
Heard, Gerald, 92
Hebb, D. O., 79n
Hillsborough High School, 355–356
Hitler, Adolf, 244, 246, 250, 258
Hobbes, Thomas, 244–247, 253, 258
Hocking, Ernest, 289
Hofstadter, Richard, 175
Hoover, J. Edgar, 300, 309
Hosea, 364
Hospitalized Veterans Service, 200
hostile personalities, 278–279
hostility:
  expressing of, 324
  in mental illness, 319–320
  mistakes as breeders of, 105–109
  neurotic, 68
House Committee on Un-American Activities, 271
"House of Dust," Conrad Aiken, 67
Housman, A. E., 110
human nature, 258
  Darwin's view of, 247–248
  Freud's view of, 249–250
  historic view of, 241–242
  Hobbes's view of, 244–247
  love as a basic need, 29, 252–253
  Machiavellian view of, 243–244
  mutual responsiveness, 39–42
  need for order, 255
  "social" need, 250–252
  unfolding and maturing in, 259–261
  see also man
hypercriticalness, 68

ignorance, 97
  fear and, 91–92
  misuse of knowledge as, 97–101
  self-imposed, 88
imagination, limited, 358

immaturity, emotional, signs of, 43–44

India, United States college students in, 356

industry, psychic-space principle in, 65

inertia, 357–358

infiltration, Communist tactics of, 286–289

"informer," use of term, 232–233

"in group," 112–113

innocence, man's, 240

insiders, 62

institutions, relationships of, 340–342, 353–357

intellectuals, spurious superiority, 97–99

interchange, human, 224–225

internationalism, 295, 369–370

"intuition," dangers of, 100–101

Iron Curtain policy, Soviet Union's, 283

Isaac and Archibald, Robinson, 212–215

Isaiah, 364

James, 193

Jefferson, Thomas, 364, 368

Jesus, 193, 195, 364

John, 364

Johnson, James Weldon, 338, 340

Jones, Rufus, 363, 372

judgment:
  mature, 208–209
  point of view in, 230

juvenile delinquency:
  methods of dealing with, 335
  patterns of behavior, 330–331

Kansas, mental hospitals in, 89–90

Kant, Immanuel, 364

King Jasper, Robinson, 169

Kitty Hawk, 364

knowledge, 86–88
  directions of modern, 102
  misuses of, 97–101
  security and, 91–93
  as a space-maker, 87–93

Kreisler, Fritz, 200–201

Krushchev, Nikita, 270, 272

labor, grievances of, 47

Lao-tse, 364

Lasswell, Harold, 267–268

Lenin, 246, 248, 250, 258, 272

Leviathan, Hobbes, 245

Lewin, Kurt, 163

Lewis, C. S., 155, 274

liberals:
  orthodoxies of, 281
  self-trapping of, 76–84, 99–100

liberating mind, the, 364–374

liberty, *see* Freedom

libraries, as space-makers, 351

life role:
  agelessness of childhood and, 205–220
  changes in basic, 191–192
  Communist appeal and, 171–175
  creativity in, 197–202
  discipline and restraint imposed by, 166–167
  extensions of, 198–199
  "fated," 185–195
  function of, 165–184
  importance of satisfaction in, 183–184
  interpersonal relationships and, 161–165
  labeling by, 201–204
  as location within "fields of force," 167–168
  pseudo-conservatives and, 175–182
  rejection of, 186–188
  of scientists, dangers to, 181–182
  self-chosen, 194, 197–198
  see also role

Lincoln, Abraham, 364, 368

Little World of Don Camillo, The, Guareschi, 50, 65

love:
  expanding self and, 40
  man's need for, 252–253
  understanding and, 24–25

Luke, 364

McCleery, William, 308, 313
Machiavelli, 242, 258
Machiavellianism, 242–244
Mackay, John A., 282
MacLeish, Archibald, 131
man:
    area of influence of the individual,
        39–43
    ego-defense by, 54–55
    as mistake-maker, 54–55
    neurotic areas in, 111–113
    see also human nature
Marcus Aurelius, 251
Mark, 364
Marquand, John P., 74–75
"martyrs," 326–329
Marx, Karl, 246, 248, 258
Matthew, 364
maturity:
    an evolving state, 102
    gifts of, 208–209
    gratitude and, 124–138
    human responsiveness and, 43–44
    learning experience and, 95–96
    role of the childlike in, 205–220
    self-limiting practices, 73–74
May, Rollo, 169
Mayflower Compact, 256–257, 258
Meland, Bernard E., 363
Melville, Herman, 161
Menninger, William C., 89
Menninger Foundation, 89–90
mental health, 268, 355
mental hospitals, 89–90
mental illness:
    recognizing of personality prob-
        lems in, 323–330
    social nature of, 315–336
    see also emotionally disturbed
        persons
Micah, 364
Mill, John Stuart, 364
Miller of the Dee, the, 183
mind:
    bridges of understanding, 221–239
    the learning, 96–97
    the liberating, 364–374
    the scientific, 79
minority status, sense of, 347–349

mistakes:
    civility in correcting, 122–123
    forgiveness and, 113–118
    man's embarrassment and glory,
        54–55
    reactions to, 101, 109–110, 113–
        115
    sins distinguished from, 113–114
    as trouble-maker's stock-in-trade,
        105–109
Moak, Helen, 254
Moby Dick, Melville, 161
moderation, understanding promoted
    by, 226–230
Mohammed, 364
Monk in the Kitchen, The, Branch,
    255
monologuing in unison, 282–284, 349
Montague, William Pepperell, 312–
    313
moods, 317–321
Morton, David, 174
Moses, 364
Murphy, Gardner, 163
Mussolini, Benito, 246, 250
My Child Lives Again, Moak, 254

nagging, 68
narrow-mindedness, self-trapping of
    liberals into, 76–84
Nature of Prejudice, Allport, 331n,
    332, 333
Nazism, 107, 292
Negro Congress, 271
negroes, situation of, in America, 271
neo-fascists, 293
neuroses:
    areas of, in every individual, 111–
        113
    brief, 317–321
    defined, 317
    personality patterns in, 66–69
    reaction to mistakes in, 109–113
    rejection of life role in, 187–188,
        194
    self-pity in, 168–170
Newton, Isaac, 364
"night vision," 38–39
1984, Orwell, 292

nomadism, new, 275
nonsense, factors stimulating belief in, 221–224
nuclear warfare, dangers of, 267–269
nurturing point of view, 368–370

offense-taking, 68
old age, 47, 63
"One World" movement, 369–370
Oppenheim, James, 85, 144, 251
opportunism, 294
Oriental peoples, 73–74
Orwell, George, 292
"out group," 112–113
outsiders, 62–64, 309–310
overreaction, 359

Parkhurst, Helen, 365–366
partisanship, 45, 80, 83, 228
past, tyranny of the, 105, 110, 229
patriotism, 68
    challenging of, by trouble-makers, 105–106
Paul, 230, 231, 364
personality:
    areas of influence, 39–43, 289
    child-adult fusion, 207–208, 209
    conflict-limiting, 148–151
    considerateness in, 148–149
    disorders of, in social context, 267–268, 315–336
    effects of exclusion on, 63
    factionalism and, 278–279
    gratitude an aspect of, 127–128
    hostile, 68
    life-role inadequacy and, 180–181
    neurotic, see neuroses
    personal responses as reality, 141–142
    reactions of others a key to, 42
    resources under stress, 152
    self-awareness, 154–155
    self-cornering in, 69–72
    space-making, 139–157, 337–340
personality disorders:
    methods of dealing with, 334–336
    neuroses, see neuroses
    recognizing of, 323–330
physical-science associations, 305

physics, field theory, 162
Plant, James, 24
Plato, 274, 364
politics:
    conflict in area of, 19
    Machiavellian view in, 243–244
    personality types and, 329
    realism in, 244
    trouble-makers in, 105–106
    vigilance needful over, 294, 296
    see also government
Politics and Crowd Morality, Christensen, 266
polling booth, as space-maker, 352
Pontius Pilate, 230
poppy incident, 70–72
Power and Personality, Lasswell, 267
prejudices, 68
    entrenched, 358
    personality types prone to, 331–333
Princeton study of the appeals of Communism, 171–174, 280, 302
pseudo-conservatives:
    anti-Communist, 179–180
    life-role aspects, 175–182
pseudo-Darwinism, 247
psychic space, 38, 337–340
    for others, 49–65
    for ourselves, 66–86
    self-limiting practices and, 72–84
    see also space-makers
psychological browbeating, 274, 276–277
psychological sciences:
    "interpersonal field" theory, 163–164
    limitations of, in personality studies, 139–140
    maturing of, 28–29
    psychic space the core concept of, 64
psychology:
    human nature as viewed by, 250–252
    modern developments in, 162–163
    personality patterns illuminated by, 330
    self-limiting of scientists in, 77–79

psychosis, role aspects, 170
public school system, as space-maker, 350

race problem, 296, 369
reactionaries, 81
  radical, *see* pseudo-conservatives
  regression, 131–132, 187–188
relationships:
  institutional, 340–342, 353–357
  interpersonal, and life roles, 161–165
  mutual responsiveness in, 39–42
  personality disorders and, 317–336
  space-making, 337–340
religion:
  freedom of, 343–344
  liberating mind and, 373
research, freedom of, 78–80
Rhine, J. B., 77–79
Richards, I. A., 225*n*
right, defining of, 45
rightists, 222
  life-role aspects, 175–182
Robinson, Edwin Arlington, 41, 91–92, 136, 169, 265, 307
  Isaac and Archibald story quoted, 212–215
Rogers, Carl R., 338–340
role:
  basic human, 240–261
  framework of life and, 241
  Machiavellian, 243–244
  man as "talking animal," 224
  signs of recognized, 260–261
  "social" character of, 258–260
  sub-, 260
  see also life role
Rousseau, Jean Jacques, 246, 247, 258
rumormongering, 82, 106, 112, 296
ruthlessness, 260–261

Salk, Jonas, 364
Sandburg, Carl, 21, 183, 208, 343
scandalmonger, 278
Schweitzer, Albert, 198
security, knowledge and, 91–93

security agents, 294
self, *see* personality
self-awareness, 155–156
self-confrontation, 155–156
self-defensiveness:
  in agencies of democratic government, 308
  in correcting mistakes, 120
  expressions of, 53, 54–55, 58
  incitements to, 34–37, 404
self-discipline, 254
self-pity, neurotic, 67–68, 168–170
semantic sabotage, 233
Shakespeare, William, 20, 364
Shirt-Sleeve Diplomacy, Bingham, 367
silence, as a problem-solver, 238–239
sin, mistakes distinguished from, 113–114
Sincerely, Willis Wayde, Marquand, 74, 75*n*
Slave, The, Oppenheim, 144
Slavson, S. R., 255, 258
Smith, Isabel, 144–146
So Big, Ferber, 60–61
society:
  areas of constrictive influence, 357–359
  areas of expanding and enriching life in, 46–48
  dangers in modern, 265–290
  forces in, needful of vigilance, 293–299
  future vistas, 360–363
  generation-isolating forces, 216–218
  growing spaciousness of, 350
  importance of psychic space in, 55–59
  the individual in, 37–43
  institutions of, 340–363
  liberating intention in, 364–374
  nature of a sound, 341–342
  need for love and understanding in, 37–38
  role-finding and, 171–175, 181
  voluntary associations in, 304–305

Socrates, 152, 153, 364
Sokolsky, George, 269
Sorokin, Pitirim, 372
sound person, 37, 70, 327–328
Soviet Union, 283
  world's backward peoples wooed
    by, 269–274
space-makers:
  areas of constrictive influence and,
    357–359
  areas of use, 356–357
  hostility opposed to, 68
  individuals as, 139–157, 371–372
  institutions as, 337–363
  knowledge as, 87–93
speech, freedom of, 346–349
Stalin, 246, 250, 258
status, hunger for, by pseudo-conservatives, 177–178
status-preserving mechanism, 24n
Stephens, James, 218–219
stereotype, 59, 61, 82, 283
success:
  egocentric approach, 74–76
  human values and, 27–28
  neurotic attitudes towards, 68
Sullivan, Harry Stack, 164, 170
suspicion, 68

teaching:
  freedom of, 77–80
  personality qualities in, 146–147
teen-ager, the "different," 62
Teresa, St., 364
Thomas Aquinas, 364
threat:
  incitements and responses, 31–34
  sense of, in neurosis, 67
Thucydides, 364
Tompkins, Jimmy, Father, 233–234
totalitarianism, 81, 112, 170
  hate-mongering in, 107–108
  Hobbesian, 246
  personality types in, 330
Toynbee, Arnold, 373
trouble-makers, mistakes capitalized
  by, 105–109
Trudeau, Francis, 144–146

unconcern, 260–261
understanding:
  approximateness of, 224
  assumption of, in relationships,
    233–235
  common restrictions on, 221–224
  expanding self and, 40–42
  knowledge essential to, 87–93, 96–
    102
  mature, 208–209
  mutual, gratitude for, 132–133,
    224–239
  in personal love, 24–25
  practice of, 13–30, 237–238
  pseudo-, 75–76
  self-, 28
United Nations, 237
universities:
  freedom of mind in, 77–80
  as space-makers, 350–351
University Religious Conference,
  UCLA, 356
unpurchasable man, need for, 289–
  290
urbanization, 275

Van Doren, Mark, 226n
Vermont Tradition, Fisher, 68
vested interest, 358
Veterans' Hospital, Kansas, 90
"viewing with alarm," 68
vigilance:
  in concern for liberty, 291–293
  forces requiring contemporary,
    293–299, 326–330
  groups exercising, 297, 299–309
  mapping out of areas of, 309–310
  means and ends of, 310–312
  mutual, and factionalism, 297–298
  preventive, 310
  procedures for undertaking, 306–
    309
  self-, 312–313
  specialization in, 298–299
  supportive, 310
voluntary associations, vigilance as
  exercised by, 304–305
voluntary segregation, 279–282

war, 267–269, 295, 370
Ward, Barbara, 243
Ward, Nathaniel, 257
Warner, Lucien, 78
Warsaw, 292
Washington, George, 364, 368
Welfare Planning Council, Los Angeles Region, 370–371
western societies:
  Communist infiltration tactics and, 273–274
  Oriental relationships, 73–74
  wrongs and rights of, 46
wisdom, 274
Wish I Might, Smith, 144, 146
Womble, Dale, 356
women, meaning of emancipation of, 368–369

words:
  importance of understanding of, 230–231
  misleading use of, 223–225, 231–233
wrong, defining of, 45–48
Wylie, Elinor, 188

xenophobia, 68, 295

youth, characteristics of modern, 360–363

Zeno the Stoic, 364
Zoroaster, 364